P9-DWA-319

PS
1713
C75
1991

137160

N.L. TERTELING LIBRARY
THE COLLEGE OF IDAHO
CALDWELL, IDAHO

PURCHASED WITH NEH
ENDOWMENT FUNDS

Critical Essays on

MARY WILKINS FREEMAN

CRITICAL ESSAYS
ON
AMERICAN LITERATURE

James Nagel, General Editor
Northeastern University

Critical Essays on

MARY WILKINS FREEMAN

edited by

SHIRLEY MARCHALONIS

G. K. Hall & Co.
BOSTON, MASSACHUSETTS

PS 1713
C 75
1991

Copyright 1991 by Shirley Marchalonis
All rights reserved.

10 9 8 7 6 5 4 3 2 1

Library of Congress Cataloging-in-Publication Data

Critical essays on Mary Wilkins Freeman / edited by Shirley
     Marchalonis.
          p.   cm. —(Critical essays on American literature)
     Includes bibliographical references and index.
     ISBN 0-8161-7306-0 (alk. paper)
     1. Freeman, Mary Eleanor Wilkins, 1852–1930—Criticism and
interpretation.   I. Marchalonis, Shirley.   II. Series.
PS1713.C75   1991
813'.4—dc20   91-14275

The paper used in this publication meets the minimum requirements
of American National Standard for Information Sciences—Permanence
of Paper for Printed Library Materials, ANSI Z39.48-1984. ⊗™

Printed and bound in the United States of America

137160

Contents

♦

N. L. TERTELING LIBRARY
THE COLLEGE OF IDAHO
CALDWELL, IDAHO

TWO ESSAYS BY MARY WILKINS FREEMAN

ESSAYS

General Editor's Note

◆

This series seeks to anthologize the most important criticism on a wide variety of topics and writers in American literature. Our readers will find in various volumes not only a generous selection of reprinted articles and reviews but original essays, bibliographies, manuscript sections, and other materials brought to public attention for the first time. This volume, *Critical Essays on Mary Wilkins Freeman*, is the first collection of essays ever published on this neglected but important American writer. It contains both a sizable gathering of early reviews and a broad selection of more modern scholarship as well. Among the authors of reprinted articles and reviews are William Dean Howells, Octave Thanet, F. O. Matthiessen, Susan Allen Toth, David H. Hirsch, Joseph R. McElrath, Jr., Marjorie Pryse, and Josephine Donovan. In addition to a substantial introduction by Shirley Marchalonis are five original essays commissioned specifically for publication in this volume—new studies by John Getz, Martha Satz, Deborah G. Lambert, Melissa McFarland Pennell, and Shirley Marchalonis. We are confident that this book will make a permanent and significant contribution to the study of American literature.

JAMES NAGEL

Northeastern University

Publisher's Note

◆

Producing a volume that contains both newly commissioned and reprinted material presents the publisher with the challenge of balancing the desire to achieve stylistic consistency with the need to preserve the integrity of works first published elsewhere. In the Critical Essays series, essays commissioned especially for a particular volume are edited to be consistent with G. K. Hall's house style; reprinted essays appear in the style in which they were first published, with only typographical errors corrected. Consequently, shifts in style from one essay to another are the result of our efforts to be faithful to each text as it was originally published.

Introduction

◆

SHIRLEY MARCHALONIS

Response to the work of Mary E. Wilkins Freeman falls into three roughly defined categories: the reactions of the reviewers who were her contemporaries, the subsequent pronouncements by early twentieth-century scholars who for a long period influenced the way she has been read, and finally the recent criticism inspired by new scholarly approaches to and interest in women's writing.

Her contemporary readers recognized Freeman as the writer of brilliant, spare short stories of New England village life; to the reviewers she was or should have been so many different things that she advised "The Girl Who Wants to Write" to be cautious, even hesitant, about paying attention to critics.[1] She spoke from experience, for during her long writing career— short stories, novels, a play, poems, children's stories—her relationship with the critical establishment must have been at best confusing. Her short stories were praised, but when they were collected, reviewers pointed to a "sameness," even monotony; when she tried novels, she was scolded for leaving what she did best. Wholly dependent on the income from her writing, she tried to balance what the critics and the public seemed to want with what she wanted to write. "I do know, and have always known," she wrote Fred Lewis Pattee in 1919, "my accomplished work is not the best work of which I am capable, but it is too late now."[2]

When critical tastes and expectations changed in the early twentieth century, it was the value of Freeman's work that was questioned. In 1926 she was awarded the Howells Medal by the American Academy of Letters and was one of the first four women elected to the National Institute of Letters, yet by then her books were reviewed perfunctorily if at all, she had virtually stopped writing, and in spite of her honors and the publication of *The Best Short Stories of Mary E. Wilkins* in 1927, on her death three years later her obituary in *Publishers Weekly* could state erroneously that she had been secretary to Oliver Wendell Holmes and, more tellingly, describe her first book, *A Humble Romance and Other Stories,* as a novel.[3] Even a long essay by John Macy, "The Passing of the Yankee," was really an obituary for the New England character rather than for Mary Wilkins Freeman.[4]

1

Mary E. Wilkins, born in Randolph, Massachusetts, in 1852, and brought up there and in Brattleboro, Vermont, began her writing career with poems and stories for children, published in such magazines as *Wide-Awake* and *St. Nicholas*. In 1883 a short story written for an adult audience won a prize, and in the next year "Two Old Lovers" was accepted by *Harper's Bazar*.[5] After the deaths of her parents she returned to Randolph, and, neither financially nor emotionally able to live alone (something socially unacceptable for young women of marriageable age), shared a house with her childhood friend Mary Wales and her family; Wales gave her the support and convenience she needed to continue with her writing. In 1902, after hesitating for nearly 10 years, she married Dr. Charles Freeman and moved to Metuchen, New Jersey. The marriage, happy at first, ended disastrously: Charles Freeman became an alcoholic, was committed to an institution in 1922, and died in 1923. She died in 1930.

Starting with the first adult story and during what Frank Luther Mott has called "[p]erhaps the most brilliant decade in the long history of *Harper's Magazine* . . . the 1890's," Freeman was a steady contributor.[6] The Harper's magazines became the most consistent outlets for her work; according to one account, she was paid $500 to $700 for "a dozen printed pages."[7]

Freeman's first important critic was William Dean Howells. From the "Editor's Study" of *Harper's* the Dean of American letters defended the local-color story from attacks that it was not broad enough; for him the tales in *A Humble Romance, and Other Stories* (1887) were unified because they gave a sense of life in a community, sharing "unity of spirit, of point of view, of sympathy," though not connected by narrative.[8] He saw in the stories humor, pathos, respect for the life they showed, and freshness, "simplicity and originality." He found them "peculiarly American" and somewhat like "Miss Jewett's more delicate work, but the fun is opener and less demure, the literature is less refined, the poetry is a little cruder." He warned that occasionally a sentimental or romantic motive contradicted the realism, a complaint he repeated in his discussion of *A New England Nun, and Other Stories* (1891), in which he noted her "never-erring eye, the sometimes mistaken fancy" that might create a "conflict of purposes—an undecided effect." This romantic tendency, he felt, was overcome by her "love of truth." He stressed the American nature of her work: "What our artist has done is to catch the American look of life, so that if her miniatures remain to other ages they shall know just the expression of that vast average of Americans who do the hard work of the country." For all his praise, Howells firmly atttached the labels—New England, America, local color—that would limit the way Freeman was read in the future by all but a very few critics.

Freeman's reception in England was even more immediate. Besides the edition of *A Humble Romance* published by Harper's subsidiary, an Edinburgh publisher divided the 28 stories in half and presented them as two volumes,

A Humble Romance and *A Far-Away Melody.*[9] By 1890, a year before her second volume, the *Critic* told its American readers,

> There is said to be "something like a craze" over Mary E. Wilkins's stories among her admirers in England.
> Our neighbors across the ocean—who are nine minutes nearer us since the latest ocean racer's record—do not, possibly, care much for us in a literary way; they often say that they do not when they come to us here. But when one of our writers, from Hawthorne and Longfellow down to this humble romancer who speaks to them of New England life in an unhackneyed way, lets them have the pleasure of hearing a new voice, they appreciate it. Our prophet, who lives half an hour out [from Boston] on the Old Colony road, is not without honor in her own country also.[10]

The *Saturday Review of Politics, Literature, Science, and Art* praised the tales, making what would be the only consistent negative criticism, that the stories published together created a "sameness" that could become monotonous.[11] The *Spectator* liked Freeman's ability to make small things important—"It needs no common artist to impart an interest to the chronicling of small beer"—and the London *Bookman* saw "variety in sameness" and made the first of many comparisons with Hawthorne.[12] Although British critics often disliked her dialect and never hesitated to scold when she fell below what they considered her standards, they and their readers remained admirers through her long career, often using her work to define the American character. Even after she was virtually forgotten, English author Sylvia Townsend Warner was haunted by her stories and wondered in an impressionistic piece for the *New Yorker* why Americans did not read Mary Wilkins anymore.[13]

Freeman's second collection, *A New England Nun, and Other Stories* (1891), includes among its 24 stories the two best known: "A New England Nun" and "The Revolt of Mother." The first two collections, in fact, contain most of what is considered the main body of her work: stories that present the New England character, stories with a bite to them. Certainly the two volumes, along with the steady publication in magazines, established if not institutionalized her as an important American writer. The *Critic* liked her ability to show the "marvellous repression of passion and feeling"; the *Athenaeum* felt it would take a "tough appetite" to get through the volume.[14] No one ignored her.

In 1892 she published *Young Lucretia, and Other Stories,* stories about children but written for an adult audience—a kind of subgenre that was common at the time but is misunderstood today, when any story about children is classified as a children's story. The *Athenaeum* reviewer was happier with this collection, praising the "artful simplicity of the style" and the "dramatic boldness of the narrative."[15] In the same year D. Lothrop issued *The Pot of Gold,* an unauthorized collection of Freeman's true children's stories, originally published in *Wide-Awake.*

By 1893 Freeman was ready to try new forms: a play and her first novel. Whether her creativity led her to experiment, whether she was responding to the complaint of "sameness," or whether she thought a novel would be more profitable, she temporarily left the genre that had made her name. The play, *Giles Corey, Yeoman,* which she intended as a closet drama, was well received when it came out in *Harper's,* but it had such a disastrous production by the Theatre of Arts and Letters that it was years before she tried a play again, and did so then only to dramatize one of her own short stories. The *Critic,* which had praised the play, viciously attacked the production. [16]

Jane Field, Freeman's first novel, brought mixed responses. Reviewers found it like her short stories, as indeed it is; its heroine is an elderly woman in a small New England village who breaks her own and the village codes and then must come to terms with her guilt. As in the stories, there is a single main character and a single plot on which all attention is focused. The *Nation* wondered, as many critics would, whether so gifted a teller of short stories should try to write novels even though in this case "the miniature-painting expands so well into scene-painting." [17] *Bookman* found it "melancholy," while *Godey's* described it as "serious and humorous." [18]

Pembroke (1894), probably Freeman's best novel, is a complex study that encompasses both a wider range and a larger cast of characters than usual and represents a real break from the short story form. Another New England author, Edwin Arlington Robinson, wrote of it in a letter to a friend,

> The book is strange in its very simplicity. Everything is drawn against a tragic background of subdued passion and some of the scenes are almost magnificent in their treatment. To the careless modern reader the plot—or rather the plots—will seem impossible and contrary to human nature; but to one who knows anything about Puritanism the book will be interesting and impressive. Narrow minded and unsympathetic readers had better keep away from it. It is a rather significant fact that it finds more appreciation in England than America, which is perhaps due to the fact of England's undeniable ability to tell a good thing and not be deceived by outward show, which I cannot help thinking that Time will prove to be a certain percentage of *Trilby.*
>
> I was surprised to find some things treated so openly in *Pembroke,* and I rather admire Miss Wilkins' frankness and nerve, if the word is required. There are a few animal touches that are hardly like anything else that I have ever seen in novels. . . . It never drags for a page, and is always either bright or gloomy. Although it "ends well" in a way, *Pembroke* is not a summer vacation. It is pretty much like any other life—that is, relatively. [19]

Writing his "Literary Notes" in *Harper's* supplement, Laurence Hutton called the novel three stories in one; he had earlier declared that *Jane Field* was an extended short story. [20] For him the novel "more than fulfilled" the "great promise" of the first novel, and he commented on its mixture of humor and pathos. *Godey's* disliked not the story but Freeman's view of the New England character.[21] Horace E. Scudder in the *Atlantic Monthly* compared the book to Mrs. Humphrey Ward's *Marcella*, finding that although Freeman's characters were "abnormal," "it is not through exaggeration that Miss Wilkins makes them vivid: it is through an imagination quick, firm, and extraordinarily sententious," and deciding that *Marcella* was a tour de force while *Pembroke* was a "genuine artistic achievement, in spite of the crumbling materials out of which it was built."[22] The *Edinburgh Review* compared Freeman with Harold Frederic, feeling that each depicted a stage of the American character.[23] The *Spectator* called *Pembroke* the "gem of Miss Wilkins's many remarkable productions," praised the "incomparable force" with which the lives are depicted, and compared her with Rembrandt; noted the *Critic,* "Wonderful in concentrated intensity, tremendous in power, this record of the heart tragedies of a dozen men and women of the village of Pembroke is not surpassed in our literature for its beauty of style, the delicacy of its character-delineation and the enthralling interest of its narration."[24]

After *Pembroke* came a small book, *The People of Our Neighborhood* (1895), which analyzes types within the village world, and then the novel *Madelon* (1896), with its exotic heroine, who not only is French-Canadian but has Indian blood and who startled reviewers by her passionate nature. The veteran critic and reviewer of the *Atlantic,* Horace E. Scudder, noted the difference from former work in "her tragedy" but was favorable.[25] Laurence Hutton found *Madelon* a "powerful story" that "will disappoint no one," the London *Bookman* was pleased Freeman had entered the "warm country of romance," but the usually friendly *Saturday Review* could not see how the author of *Jane Field* could have written this novel and hoped, as did Mary E. Wardwell in the *Citizen,* that she would never do such a thing again.[26] Even the most favorable reviews have an air of caution about them.

Jerome: A Poor Man (1897) analyzes goodness pushed to an extreme; Charles Miner Thompson in a serious essay for the *Atlantic* regretfully proved that the structure of the novel was flawed and that the unlikely premise on which it rested could be suitable only for comedy.[27] The *Dial* praised the "photographic realism," but its review was less than enthusiastic, and Laurence Hutton, though generally favorable, avoided direct comment on the novel by talking about individual characters and episodes.[28]

There is a kind of relief underlying *Bookman's* comment on the next book, *Silence, and Other Stories* (1898), which "recalls some of her earliest and most excellent work."[29] For the *Saturday Review* it was "a volume quite worthy of her reputation," and *Outlook* felt it showed not only "her original force, which is very great, but also the delicacy of touch and refinement of insight which she possesses."[30]

The Jamesons (1899) apparently startled the critics as much as *Madelon* had, but for different reasons. It is a humorous novel that the public enjoyed but many reviewers ignored; the *Spectator* ended its review by saying, "Altogether this is a delightful little book, abounding by turns in humorous, tender, and shrewd sayings," but the *Critic* disliked Freeman's presentation of people in this "hard, unshaded fashion."[31] *The Heart's Highway* (1900) was an experiment with popular colonial romance; Cornelia Atwood Pratt in the *Critic* liked the romantic story and its "study of character in pastel-shades," and the *Bookman* felt it was a good story but one anyone could have written for it lacked the unique Wilkins flavor.[32] The novel infuriated Frank Norris; in *The Responsibilities of the Novelist* he wrote:

> A writer who occupies so eminent a place as Miss Wilkins, who has become so important, who has exerted and still can exert so strong an influence, cannot escape the responsibilities of her position. She cannot belong wholly to herself, cannot be wholly independent. She owes a duty to the literature of her native country.
>
> Yet in spite of all this, and in spite of the fact that those who believe in the future of our nation's letters look to such established reputations as hers to keep the faith, to protest, though it is only by their attitude, silently and with dignity, against corruptions, degradations; in spite of all this, and in the heyday of her power, Miss Wilkins chooses to succumb to the momentary, transitory set of the tide, and forsaking her own particular work, puts forth, one of a hundred others, a "colonial romance." It is a discrowning. It can be considered no less. . . . She was one of the leaders. It is as if a captain, during action, had deserted to the enemy.[33]

If nothing else, Norris's reaction indicates Freeman's status in the literary world.

Again the reception of a collection of short stories, *The Love of Parson Lord, and Other Stories,* was warm, but by now her novels were receiving the most attention from reviewers. *The Portion of Labor* (1901) sets its heroine in the midst of labor unrest. Octave Thanet in *Book Buyer* called the novel "her finest and strongest work."[34] It evoked retrospective essays from Henry Mills Alden and Laurence Hutton, both reviewing her career and seeing her gaining in maturity while keeping the qualities that were uniquely hers.[35] The *Independent's* reviewer felt that her "sordid" material (shoe-factory workers) was redeemed by her "vast womanly sympathy"; Miriam Reese Edmonson, writing for the New York *Bookman,* found the novel poorly constructed and not up to the writer's usual work, though strong in its dealing with people.[36]

In a letter to Fred Lewis Pattee, Freeman wrote, "Most of my own work, is not really the kind I myself like. I want more symbolism, more mysticism. I left that out, because it struck me people did not want it, and I was forced to consider selling qualities. Of course I tried to make my work good along its own lines.[37] Certainly in *Pembroke* Barney's crooked back is symbolic of the distortion of his mind, but not until now was Freeman apparently secure enough to work with the "symbolism" and "mysticism" she liked. *Understudies* (1901) and *Six Trees* (1903) both reflect that interest, as do *The Wind in the Rose-Bush and other Stories of the Supernatural* (1903) and her critique of

Wuthering Heights.[38] Reviewers agreed on the sensitivity of these collected stories; although *Book Buyer* thought *Six Trees* "contrived," the *Saturday Review* called it a book "to read and read again" and the *Times Literary Supplement* found her supernatural tales "the most terrific ghost stories ever written," noting, as did the *Dial,* that much of the force came from the commonplaceness of the people who experienced strange events.[39]

The *Givers* (1904) was received happily as a return to Freeman's New England stories. James MacArthur in *Harper's Weekly* confessed to "liking Mrs. Wilkins Freeman best in her short stories. There has never been her match in this country, and few in another."[40] The London *Bookman* analyzed her "quality of allurement," pointing out that her short story collections were books to read over and over, with a "renewed pleasure on every fresh occasion."[41]

Her next novel, *The Debtor* (1905), was called by the reviewer for *Public Opinion* "an unpleasant masterpiece."[42] Isolating the quality of detachment, he felt Freeman displayed "unapproachable mastery" but no sympathy for her unpleasant characters. The *Independent,* however, declared, "No better book of the honest, old-fashioned kind has appeared this year," and *Harper's Weekly* called Freeman the "feminine realist of her day."[43]

By the Light of the Soul (1906) upset reviewers; for the first time they were almost uniformly negative. Walter de la Mare attacked its overcontrived and "absurd" main episode, from which the plot derives, and the abundance of careless discrepancies but admitted that Freeman's "vivacity, the clever and tender character sketches, the scattered and isolated glimpses of beauty" were present in the book.[44] The *Atlantic* spoke of its "gratuitously painful plot," while Herbert W. Horwill summed it up as "disappointing mediocrity" and remarked on the carelessness; the *Dublin Review* saw "high intentions unfulfilled."[45] The *Nation* softened its disapproval by holding out hope that Freeman, "seeking an enlarged horizon, will after some errors find it."[46]

If reviewers spoke harshly of that novel, they all but ignored *"Doc" Gordon* (1906), a melodramatic study of euthanasia and murder that may be Freeman's worst novel. The *Saturday Review* flatly disliked it, finishing a brief critique by saying, "[W]e look back regretfully to the middle-aged lovers and the engaging pet cats of the author's earlier stories."[47] The *Independent* focused on the peculiar publication arrangements and the morality of euthanasia, dismissing the story itself as "a rather poor affair."[48]

Another collection, *The Fair Lavinia and Others* (1907), made the *Nation* ponder Freeman's departure from New England tales, finding some of her stories too "pretty" but others "simple and faithful realism" and praising as "most striking" the Hawthornesque "The Gold" and the narrative skill she displayed.[49]

In *The Shoulders of Atlas* (1908) Freeman returned to New England. Response was mixed here; the *Nation* liked her "rustic comedy," and the *New York Times* approved her elderly New Englanders but not much else.[50] The *Athenaeum* found "a new and deeper note of sin and mystery" that was in conflict with her usual New England atmosphere.[51] A few cautiously acknowledged her creation of what they saw as a "man-hungry" young woman, and the *Literary Digest* wondered, "Has the genius of our Mary E. Wilkins of former days run dry, that she should forsake her well-beaten path and attempt to lighten up her narrative by evil things, not to say the morbid pathology of nymphomania? The book is disappointing, because it is disjointed and repellant."[52]

The *New York Times* review of *The Whole Family,* the composite novel done by 12 well-known authors, mildly praises the book and mentions Freeman's part, but the novel was treated primarily as a curiosity.[53] *The Butterfly House* (1912) was reviewed perfunctorily by the *New York Times,* as was *The Alabaster Box* (1917), which she wrote with Florence Morse Kingsley; clearly, both were dismissed as trivial. But Freeman's collections of short stories over the same period, *The Winning Lady and Others* (1908), *The Copy-Cat and Other Stories* (1914), and *Edgewater People* (1918), although not drawing the kind of response these collections would have called forth in earlier years, received better treatment. *The Winning Lady* was called by the *Nation* "the best collection of short stories Mrs. Freeman has published. It marks a definite return to her original theme and manner, with such development of both as time should naturally have brought. Her experiments in other fields, if they have seemed in themselves of comparatively little value, have no doubt served their disciplinary purpose."[54] The *Literary Digest* was reminded that "in her chosen field—the delineation of New England rural types—Mary Wilkins Freeman has no equal"; the *New York Times* compared her character studies in *The Copy-Cat* with those of Dickens, and the *Dial* found her New Englanders growing more mellow.[55]

Except for the review in the *Boston Evening Transcript* by Edwin Francis Edgett, most of the comments on *The Best Stories of Mary E. Wilkins* (1927), edited by Sidney Lanier, were so retrospective in tone that one imagines a new generation of reviewers had suddenly appeared.[56] Perhaps most ironic was the *Times Literary Supplement* review, describing Freeman as a mistress of sentiment.[57]

Freeman's contemporaries found immense variety in her work. Some saw strength and passion; others used words like "exquisite," "delicate," and "dainty." She was credited with a form uniquely her own but compared with Jane Austen, Guy De Maupassant, and Hawthorne, as well as any number of painters. Critics and readers praised the "humor and tenderness" or "humor and pathos" combined in her stories; they regretted the "sameness" of her collected tales, but when she tried novels, the same voices hoped that she would soon return to her own kind of writing or felt that the novels were too like her stories. After her marriage and move to New Jersey, she set some stories there, causing disappointment that she was abandoning her own New England setting. Through the productive years of her career, critical response read her fiction variously and, until the later novels, remained consistent only in affirming the value of her work.

If contemporary reviewers read Freeman's work in a variety of ways, the scholarly critics did not. Fred Lewis Pattee, an influential and frequently wrong scholar who is credited as one of those responsible for making American literature a subject respectable enough to be taught in colleges, first praised Freeman for her contributions to the American short story but later consigned her to the past. In his *History of American Literature* (1915), a book designed for college teaching, he sums up her writing as follows: "As a novelist and a depicter of life outside her narrow domain, she has small equipment. She stands for but one thing: short stories of the grim and bare New England social system; sketches austere and artless which limn the very soul of a passing old regime; photographs which are more than photographs: which are threnodies."[58]

This view of Freeman as the chronicler of a dying society, with its emphasis on recording rather than creating, was shared by her most prolific recent critic, Perry D. Westbrook, who saw in her work "a deep sense of the tragic dimension of life" and whose study of New England women local-color writers went even further: "More often than not Freeman found a hopeless spiritual bankruptcy. Sometimes . . . the conscience and will were diseased beyond expectation of recovery. At other times the New England soul was too feeble to be stimulated even by disease into any activity whatsoever. It simply lay in the stress of life like a rotted log, refusing to stir till disintegrated by complete decay."[59]

Much of the early scholarly criticism followed this nearly annihilating approach.[60] Even Van Wyck Brooks, who found more in Freeman's writing than others did, saw her as "fierce and primitive" but as picturing the "powers of last resistance in the Yankee soul," thus fitting nicely into his Indian summer of New England.[61] And though he recognized more complexity than what was becoming the accepted reading of Freeman would admit, he suggested that the reality beyond realism in her "plain, stark, factual tales" was there by accident.[62]

There are points in these passages that deserve examination. Brooks says that Freeman did not know what she was doing (with the implication that since she was only a carpenter's daughter rather than a Brahmin she could not have known), and Pattee calls her "artless." Both these comments suggest the nineteenth-century view that women writers were "singers," moved by inspiration rather than creative power; "artless" suggests not so much lack of artifice as lack of artistry. And the words used to describe her work are "limn," "photograph", and "picture." Local-color realism had become, in these minds, photography, though photography as representation rather than art. Freeman was no longer a creative artist using familiar material to say something about the human condition; she was a sociohistorical recorder of a time and place. The identification with the New England character had reduced her, in the minds of these scholars, to the role of chronicler—she saw something and wrote it down accurately.[63] As the recorder of a dead society, she became a curiosity of the past, not worthy of serious attention once the final words had been written. These critics missed her interest in individuality and autonomy, her vision of the individual working out a place in and in relation to a society and its codes, and they certainly missed her wry and subtle humor. The view of Freeman as reporter reaches its height (or depth) in the single existing biography, Edward Foster's *Mary E. Wilkins Freeman*.[64] Foster spends his time identifying people Freeman knew who might have been the originals of the characters in her stories, thus reinforcing her role as a mere likeness-catcher and denying her an artist's creative powers. His insistence on what Freeman must have thought and must have felt, based as it is on insufficient evidence, suggests Foster was creating a fiction of his own.

It was a long time before scholars attempted to redefine Freeman's work, and it is still true that little attention is paid to her novels. With the weight of scholarly consensus having pronounced the verdict, with the implication that this recorder of the past was no longer worth reading, who would dare to claim or take time to find out that *Pembroke*—which one scholar recently described as "the best kept secret in American literature"—is a complex novel that well rewards reading, that she gives a fascinating analysis of a confidence man and his effect on family and community in *The Debtor*, or that she presents a sensitive study of guilt in her first novel, *Jane Field*, and later in *The Shoulders of Atlas*?[65] Uneven in quality as her novels are—and they are—the good ones, although they may lack the impact intensified by brevity of the early short stories, are worth examination and serious study.

Freeman's work never wholly disappeared. Two of her stories, "A New England Nun" and "The Revolt of 'Mother' " continued to be anthologized; they are her most examined works and have evoked a variety of interpretations. When the *Independent* reprinted the latter story in 1917, Frederick Houk Law summed up its appeal, emphasizing literary quality: "The plot is simple but powerful; the atmospheric effects are given with the least possible amounts of description; the characters stand out sharply, vividly, presented without sentimentality or over-emphasis; the conversation is quick and pointed; the appeal is universal—felt wherever selfishness and inconsiderateness exist."[66] Freeman's "retraction"—her claim that Mother is not a true New England woman—is occasionally referred to, though readers seem to miss the reason Freeman declares the portrayal false, just as they miss the possibility that her tongue was firmly in her cheek as she wrote.

But if her work never completely disappeared, it was certainly marginalized, and while the occasional critic wrote about her, it was the recent interest in women's writing that led to the rediscovery of works other than her two best-known stories. Overall, reaction to Freeman has moved from her contemporaries' awareness of the wide possibilities in her fiction to the narrow view of her as a recorder of a dying culture, a view that remains influential. But pervasive as the Pattee-Westbrook doctrine was and is, more recent scholarship can break away from it and see Freeman through fresh eyes.

It is encouraging and perhaps ironic that newer scholars have in a sense completed a circle, reading all Freeman's works and going beyond the restrictions of "woman local-color writer" and "photographer" to find the variety and artistry that her contemporaries enjoyed. Of course, today's critics see differently from those of the late nineteenth and early twentieth centuries; for example, the character of Lucy Ayres in *The Shoulders of Atlas* was described by one unhappy critic as a "nymphomaniac"; today she is seen as a young woman conditioned by her culture to believe that an unmarried woman is a failure, and desperate for marriage in its social, rather than sexual, context.

Mary R. Reichardt's recent and thorough bibliographic essay, "One Hundred Years of Criticism," reflects the changing viewpoints and discusses possible reasons for Freeman's loss of popularity.[67] Since its publication in 1987 there have been several other studies; particularly notable are Elizabeth Meese's chapter on Freeman in her recent book, *Crossing the Double-Cross,* and Lorne Fienberg's "Mary E. Wilkins Freeman's 'Soft Diurnal Commotion': Women's Work and Strategies of Containment."[68] Looking at her work, including the lesser-known stories and her novels, newer critics are finding different ways to read her, are seeing her creativity, and are accepting her as something other than a "local-color realist," or at least finding that label less narrowing. Influenced perhaps by Susan Allen Toth's breakthrough essay, "Defiant Light: A Positive View of Mary Wilkins Freeman" (1973), more recent criticism is not afraid to contradict the established readings and finds a welcome variety of approaches, examining, for example, gender attitudes and relationships, women, the tension between the individual and a coded society, class, work, and other elements long neglected. In the original essays in this volume the authors have examined a wider range of texts and read them in a variety of ways. It is significant that while many of the conclusions contradict each other as well as earlier work, Freeman's texts will support many interpretations.

Compiling a collection of criticism on Mary Wilkins Freeman, or any literary figure, is a matter of making choices. While there is not a great mass of Freeman criticism, there is certainly too much to be included in one volume. Much had to be left out, often with regret.[69] The choices for this collection were designed to show the conventional approach to Freeman and to emphasize newer ways of looking at her, as well as to examine works like her novels that have been ignored in the past.

A great deal remains to be done. Besides further examination of her stories and novels, Freeman badly needs a new biography, although Brent L. Kendrick's collection of her letters, *The Infant Sphinx: Collected Letters of Mary E. Wilkins Freeman,* with its informative and straightforward introductory sections, provides a wealth of material about her life and work, presented with scholarly integrity. Not strictly a biography, Kendrick's well-researched and unbiased text should be read by anyone attempting to do work on Freeman. Although, as Kendrick points out, her letters are not "literary," they present no mere recorder of facts but, rather, a conscious artist with thoughts about and dedication to her craft; a woman who was intelligent, well read, and a competent manager of her business affairs; and a writer who possessed both sensitivity and a wry, subtle sense of humor.

For the Freeman scholar, texts of the short stories are available; nearly all the collections have been reprinted in the Short Story Index Reprint Series or the American Short Story Series.[70] These reprints include, of course, only the collected stories. Several more recent collections are useful for teaching: *Selected Stories of Mary E. Wilkins Freeman*, with an introduction by Marjorie Pryse; *The Revolt of Mother, and Other Stories*, with an afterword by Michelle Clark; and *Selected Short Fiction of Sarah Orne Jewett and Mary Wilkins Freeman*, edited by Barbara H. Solomon.[71] An edition of *Pembroke*, with an introduction by Perry D. Westbrook, was brought out in 1971.[72]

Certainly there is room for more critical studies: unbiased exploration of the relationship between Freeman's life and her work, particularly after she married and left New England; examination of her strong themes (guilt, attempted murder, euthanasia); study of her technique, her handling of narrative, and other elements by which literature is analyzed. It is to be hoped that the current revival of interest in her work will move Freeman from the margins back into the mainstream of American literature.

A work of this kind could not be completed without assistance. I am grateful as always to Theodore E. Kiffer, Dean, College of Liberal Arts, Penn State University, for both moral and financial support. Dennis Marnon of the Houghton Library went out of his way to help me find elusive information, and I thank Andrea Lewis, who searched the stacks; Ruth Witman of the Penn State Berks Campus Library; and the Inter-Library Loan staff of Pattee Library, Penn State, for their help.

Notes

1. Mary E. Wilkins Freeman, "The Girl Who Wants to Write," *Harper's Bazar* 47 (June 1914): 272.

2. Letter to Fred Lewis Pattee (25 September 1919), in Brent L. Kendrick, *The Infant Sphinx: Collected Letters of Mary E. Wilkins Freeman* (Metuchen, N.J.: Scarecrow Press, 1985), 385.

3. *The Best Stories of Mary E. Wilkins*, ed. Henry Wysham Lanier (New York: Harper's, 1927). The obituary is in *Publishers Weekly* (22 March 1930): 1685. Even the more accurate obituary by Willis Boyd Allen in the *Boston Evening Transcript*, 20 March 1930, 17, dwelt on character and personal qualities rather than on her work.

4. John Macy, "The Passing of the Yankee," *Bookman* 73 (August 1931): 612–21.

5. "The Shadow Family" won a prize of $50 dollars from the *Boston Sunday Budget*.

6. Frank Luther Mott, *History of American Magazines* (Cambridge, Mass.: Harvard University Press, 1957), 4: 43.

7. Willis Boyd Allen, *Boston Evening Transcript,* 20 March 1930, 17. He says also that "the editor of a well-known rival magazine offered her Harper rates for everything the latter should reject."

8. William Dean Howells, "The Editor's Study," *Harper's Monthly* 75 (September 1887): 639–40; *Harper's Monthly* 83 (June, 1891): 155–56.

9. *A Humble Romance* and *A Far-Away Melody* (Edinburgh: David Douglas, 1891).

10. *Critic* 17, n.s. 14 (23 August 1890): 101.

11. *Saturday Review of Politics, Literature, Science, and Art* 69 (10 May 1890): 576.

12. *Spectator* 68 (2 January 1892): 11–12; *Bookman* (London) 1 (December 1891): 102–03.

13. Sylvia Townsend Warner, "Item: One Empty House," *New Yorker,* 26 March 1966, 131–38.

14. *Critic* 18 n.s. 15 (May 1891): 286; *Athenaeum* 98 (18 July 1891): 93.

15. *Athenaeum* 99 (12 November 1892): 660–62.

16. *Critic* 22, n.s. 19 (22 April 1893): 256, and 22 n.s. 19 (29 April 1893): 276–77.

17. *Nation* 56 (February 1893): 166.

18. *Bookman* 3 (January 1893): 129; *Godey's Magazine* 126 (February 1893): 232.

19. Letter (28 October 1894), in *Untriangulated Stars: Letters of Edwin Arlington Robinson to Harry DeForest Smith 1890–1905,* ed. Denham Sutcliffe (Cambridge: Harvard University Press, 1947), 174–75. Robinson was not always approving; in an earlier letter (11 December 1892, p. 78) he grumbled about "Miss Wilkins' imitation of the French pastel. It is not as bad as the drool she had in the November Harper's, but I cannot say I look forward to the day when the pastel will be a recognized form of American literature." Four of Freeman's "pastels" are in *Harper's Magazine* 86 (December 1892): 147–48, titled "Pastels in Prose"; the same volume includes Brander Matthews, "A Cameo and a Pastel," 130–35.

20. Laurence Hutton, "Literary Notes," *Harper's Monthly* 89, supplement 3–4 (June 1894): 162.

21. "Chelifer," *Godey's Magazine* 134 (March 1897): 223–24. This is one of the few challenges to Freeman's creation of the New England character.

22. Horace E. Scudder, *Atlantic Monthly* 74 (August 1894): 272–74.

23. *Edinburgh Review* 187 (April 1898): 392–97.

24. *Spectator* 72 (23 June 1894): 858–59; *Critic* 25, n.s. 22 (21 July 1894): 35.

25. Horace E. Scudder, *Atlantic Monthly* 78 (August 1896): 269–70.

26. Laurence Hutton, "Literary Notes," *Harper's Monthly* 93, supplement 1 (July 1896): 324; *Bookman* 10 (June 1896): 84; *Saturday Review* 82 (4 July 1896): 16–17; Mary E. Wardwell, *Citizen* 4 (April 1898): 27–28.

17. Charles Miner Thompson, *Atlantic Monthly* 80 (December 1897): 857–59.

28. *Dial* 24 (1 February 1898): 79; Laurence Hutton, "Literary Notes," *Harper's Monthly* 95, supplement 1–2 (September 1897): 648.

29. *Bookman* (London) 14 (August 1898): 138.

30. *Saturday Review* 85 (25 June 1898); 854; *Outlook* 59 (2 July 1898): 588.

31. *Spectator* 83 (14 October 1899): 535; *Critic* 35 (August 1899): 745–46.

32. Cornelia Atwood Pratt, *Critic* 37 (September 1900): 276; *Bookman* 19 (November 1900): 59.

33. Frank Norris, "An American School of Fiction?" in *The Responsibilities of the Novelist* (New York: Doubleday and Page, 1903), 197–98.

34. Octave Thanet, *Book Buyer* 23 (December 1901): 379–80.

35. Henry Mills Alden, "The Editor's Study," *Harper's Monthly* 102 (March 1901): 646–47; Laurence Hutton, "Mary E. Wilkins Freeman," *Harper's Weekly* 47 (21 November 1903): 1879–80.

36. *Independent* 54 (6 February 1902): 345–46; Miriam Reese Edmondson, *Bookman* 15 (March 1902): 70.

37. Letter to Fred Lewis Pattee (5 September 1919), in Kendrick, *The Infant Sphinx,* 382. This is the same letter quoted earlier.

38. Mary E. Wilkins, "Emily Bronte and *Wuthering Heights,*" in *The World's Great Women Novelists* (Philadelphia: Book Lover's Library, 1901), 85–93.

39. *Book Buyer* 26 (April 1903): 253; *Saturday Review* 96 (4 July 1903): 20; *Bookman* 14 (November 1901): 306; *Times Literary Supplement,* 22 May 1903, 160; *Dial* 34 (1 June 1903): 376.

40. James MacArthur, *Harper's Weekly* 48 (30 July 1905): 1177.

41. *Bookman* 24 (July 1903): 150.

42. Anonymous, "An Unpleasant Masterpiece," *Public Opinion* 40 (17 February 1906): 217.

43. *The Independent* 59 (7 December 1905): 1340; *Harper's Weekly* 48 (30 December 1905): 1940.

44. Walter de la Mare, *Bookman* 31 (March 1907): 269.

45. *Atlantic Monthly* 100 (July 1907): 132–33; Herbert W. Horwill, "Present-day Tendencies in Fiction," *Forum* 38 (April 1907): 538–53; R. C. T., *Dublin Review* 140 (1907): 422–24.

46. *Nation* 84 (31 January 1907): 110.

47. *Saturday Review of Politics, Literature, Science, and the Arts* 103 (April 1907): 498.

48. *Independent* 62 (17 January 1907): 158.

49. *Nation* 86 (9 January 1908): 39.

50. *Nation* 87 (9 July 1908): 35–36; *New York Times,* 18 June 1908, 400.

51. *Athenaeum* 4211 (11 July 1908): 38.

52. *Literary Digest* 37 (5 September 1908): 325–26.

53. "The *Whole Family* and Its Troubles: Co-operative Novel by Twelve Leading Literary Lights Achieves an Impression of the Comedy of Confusion," *New York Times,* 24 October 1908, 590; for an excellent account of the writing of the novel, see Alfred Bendixen's introduction to the reprint (New York: Ungar, 1968), xi–li. The other authors were William Dean Howells, Mary Stewart Cutting, Mary Heaton Vorse, Elizabeth Jordan (the editor), John Kendrick Bangs, Henry James, Elizabeth Stuart Phelps, Edith Wyatt, Mary R. S. Andrews, Alice Brown, and Henry van Dyke.

54. *Nation* 90 (13 January 1910): 36–37.

55. *Literary Digest* 40 (22 January 1910): 152; *New York Times,* 1 November 1914, 475; *Dial* 66 (22 March 1919): 316–18.

56. Edwin Francis Edgett, "The New England of Mary E. Wilkins," *Boston Evening Transcript,* Book Section, 19 March 1927, 2. See also Nathalie Sedgewick Colby, "Simultaneous Differences," *Saturday Review of Literature* 3 (May 1927): 819; Laura Benet, "Mary E. Wilkins's Stories," *New York Evening Post Literary Review,* 9 April 1927, 10; *Spectator* 138 (21 May 1927): 915. It is interesting that Lanier calls her Mary E. Wilkins, dropping the Freeman, and that she apparently did not object.

57. *Times Literary Supplement,* 29 March 1928, 239.

58. Fred Lewis Pattee, *A History of American Literature since 1870* (New York: Century, 1915), 240; see also his "The Terminal Moraine of New England Puritanism," *Side-Lights in American Literature* (New York: Century, 1922), 175–209. For information about Pattee, see James J. Martine, *Fred Lewis Pattee and American Literature* (University Park, Pa.: Penn State Press, 1973).

59. Perry D. Westbrook, *Acres of Flint* (Metuchen, N.J.: Scarecrow Press, 1981; 1951), 97; see also *Mary E. Wilkins Freeman* (New York: Twayne, 1967).

60. See John Macy, "The Passing of the Yankee" (cited above). See also Abigail Ann Hamblen, *The New England Art of Mary Wilkins Freeman* (Amherst, Mass.: Green Knight

Press, 1966). This monograph is a blend of biography and criticism, and it too stresses the doomed-society approach. Even the essay by F. O. Matthiessen (included in this volume) is colored by this limitation.

61. Van Wyck Brooks, *New England: Indian Summer* (New York: World Publishing, 1946), 464–65.

62. Brooks, *New England: Indian Summer,* 473. See also the note on p. 465, in which he states that the characters in *The Jamesons* "were almost totally absurd, but Miss Wilkins only partially saw this." My contention in my essay (included here) is that Freeman knew exactly what she was doing.

63. Kendrick, *The Infant Sphinx,* 6, supports this view: "From the beginning of her career on up to the present day, they [critics] have tagged her as a local color or regional writer, thereby limiting her significance as well as her appeal, and they have seen her almost exclusively as a social historian: the grim recorder of New England decline. As a result, her more positive and decidedly universal themes as well as her stylistic and technical contributions to the short story tradition have been relegated to the background." I disagree only in thinking that Freeman's contemporaries were less limited in their perceptions than were the scholarly critics.

64. Edward Foster, *Mary E. Wilkins Freeman* (New York: Hendricks House, 1956). The book does include a fairly complete bibliography and a list of her collected short stories. She is also included in *Bibliography of American Literature,* ed. Jacob Blanck (New Haven, Conn.: Yale University Press, 1955) 3: 224–43.

65. Ann-Janine Morey, "American Myth and Biblical Interpretation in the Fiction of Harriet Beecher Stowe and Mary E. Wilkins Freeman," *Journal of the Academy of Religious Thought* 55 (Winter 1987): 741–63.

66. Frederick Houk Law, "Introduction: Eight Great Short Stories from American Literature," *Independent* 90 (April 1917): 172.

67. This excellent and thorough bibliographical review appeared in *Legacy: A Journal of Nineteenth-Century American Women Writers* 4 (Fall, 1987): 31–44, just as I was beginning work on this collection. It seemed foolish to duplicate Reichardt's work, and I am grateful for permission to use it as an introduction to the critical essays.

68. Elizabeth Meese, "Signs of Undecidability" (chapter 2) in *Crossing the Double-Cross: The Practice of Feminist Criticism* (Chapel Hill: University of North Carolina Press, 1986); Lorne Fienberg, "Mary E. Wilkins Freeman's 'Soft Diurnal Commotion': Women's Work and Strategies of Containment," *New England Quarterly* 62 (December 1989): 483–504. I regret that for reasons of time and space Fienberg's essay could not be included here. See also Thomas A. Maik, "Dissent and Affirmation: Conflicting Voices of Female Roles in Selected Stories by Mary Wilkins Freeman," *Colby Library Quarterly* 26 (March 1990): 59–68, and Elaine Sargent Apthorp, "Sentiment, Naturalism, and the Female Regionalist, *Legacy* 7 (Spring 1990): 3–21.

69. Some of the decisions were influenced by availability: most libraries have Van Wyck Brooks's *New England: Indian Summer* and Perry D. Westbrook's *Mary E. Wilkins Freeman* and his *Acres of Flint.* Pattee's work may be less available, but his points are developed by Westbrook and others.

70. The Short Story Index Reprint Series is published by Books for Libraries Press (Freeport, New York); the American Short Story Series is published by AMS Press (New York). *Books in Print* for 1989–90 lists several collections and a few of the novels as available in reprints: I have not seen any of these titles other than those in the Short Story Index Reprint Series.

72. *Selected Stories of Mary E. Wilkins Freeman,* ed. Marjorie Pryse (New York: W. W. Norton, 1983); *The Revolt of Mother and Other Stories,* ed. Michelle Clark (Old Westbury, N.Y.: Feminist Press, 1974); *Short Fiction of Sarah Orne Jewett and Mary Wilkins Freeman,* ed. Barbara H. Solomon (New York: American Library, 1979).

72. *Pembroke,* ed. Perry D. Westbrook (New Haven, Conn.: College and University Press, 1971).

REVIEWS

◆

The Editor's Study

William Dean Howells

September 1887

Take, for instance, a number of studies like *A Humble Romance, and Other Stories,* by Miss Mary E. Wilkins, and you have the air of simple village life as liberally imparted as if all the separate little dramas were set in a single frame and related to one another. The old maids and widows aging and ailing and dying in their minute wooden houses; the forlorn elderly lovers; the simple girls and youths making and marring love; the husbands and wives growing apart and coming together; the quarrels and reconciliations; the eccentricities and the heroisms; the tender passions and true friendships; the funerals and weddings; the hates and spites; the injuries; the sacrifices; the crazy consciences; the sound common-sense—are all suggested and expressed in a measure which, we insist, does not lack breadth, though each sketch is like the sentences of Emerson, "an infinitely repellent particle," and will have nothing to do with any other, so far as community of action is concerned. Community of character abounds: the people are of one New England blood, and speak one racy tongue. It might all have been done otherwise; the lives and fortunes of these villagers might have been interwoven in one texture of narrative; but the work would not necessarily have gained breadth in gaining bulk. Breadth is in the treatment of material, not in the amount of it. The great picture is from the great painter, not from the extensive canvas. Miss Wilkins's work could hardly have given a wider sense of life in a Yankee village and the outlying farms if it had greater structural unity. It has unity of spirit, of point of view, of sympathy; and being what the author intended, we ask no other unity of it; many "broader" views lack this unity which is so valuable. Besides, it has humor of a quaint, flavorous sort, it has genuine pathos, and a just and true respect for the virtues of the life with which it deals. We are tempted to give some passages illustrative of a very remarkable freshness in its description; they are abundant, but perhaps we had better content ourselves by referring the reader to the opening of the touching sketch, "A Far-away Melody." What is notable in all the descriptions is the absence of literosity; they are as unrhetorical as so many pictures of Tourguénief's, or Björnson's, or Verga's, and are interesting proofs of the fact

Reprinted from *Harper's Monthly Magazine* 75 (September 1887): 639–40.

that the present way of working is instinctive; one writer does not learn it from another; it is in the time, in the air, and no critic can change it. When you come to the motives of these little tales, the simplicity and originality are not always kept; sometimes they ring false, sentimental, romantic; but even then they are true in the working out of character, though this does not redeem them from the original error. For the most part, however, they are good through and through, and whoever loves the face of common humanity will find pleasure in them. They are peculiarly American, and they are peculiarly "narrow" in a certain way, and yet they are like the best modern work everywhere in their directness and simplicity. They are somewhat in the direction of Miss Jewett's more delicate work, but the fun is opener and less demure, the literature is less refined, the poetry is a little cruder; but there is the same affectionate feeling for the material, a great apparent intimacy with the facts, and a like skill in rendering the Yankee parlance. We have our misgivings however, about "thar" and "whar" on New England tongues, though we are not ready to deny that Miss Wilkins heard them in the locality she evidently knows so well.

JUNE 1891

. . . Such is the manner and such the matter of the latest advice to *Gentlemen*. We had our doubts in reading it, whether the author was not laughing in the sleeve of that body-coat which nothing would induce him to remove in the presence of ladies; but on the whole we incline to think he is not joking. To turn from this great world of *Gentlemen*, to the small, lowly sphere where Miss Wilkins's humble folk have their being, is a vast change, but there is a kind of consolation in it. Here at last are real interests, passions, ambitions; and yonder there do not seem to be any. The scenes of *A New England Nun and Other Stories* are laid in that land of little village houses which the author of *A Humble Romance* has made her own. The record never strays beyond; there is hardly a person in the drama who does not work for a living; the tragedies and comedies are those of the simplest and commonest people, who speak a crabbed Yankee through their noses, and whose dress and address would be alike shocking to *Gentlemen*. Still they may be borne with, at least in the hands of an artist such as Miss Wilkins has shown herself to be. We are not sure that there is anything better in this volume than in her first; we note the same powers, the same weaknesses; the never-erring eye, the sometimes mistaken fancy. The figures are drawn with the same exquisitely satisfying veracity; but about half the time we doubt whether they would do what they are shown doing. We have a lurking fear at moments that Miss Wilkins would like to write entirely romantic stories about these honest people of hers; but her own love of truth and her perfect knowledge of such life as

Reprinted from *Harper's Monthly Magazine* 83 (June 1891): 155–56.

theirs forbid her actually to do this. There is apparently a conflict of purposes in her sketches which gives her art an undecided effect, or a divided effect, as in certain of them where we make the acquaintance of her characters in their village of little houses, and lose it in the No Man's Land of exaggerated action and conventional emotion. In the interest of her art, which is so perfectly satisfying in the service of reality, it could almost be wished that she might once write a thoroughly romantic story, and wreak in it all the impulses she has in that direction. Then perhaps she might return to the right exercise of a gift which is one of the most precious in fiction. But perhaps this could not happen; perhaps the Study is itself romantic in imagining such a thing. It may be that we shall always have to content ourselves with now a story of the real and unreal mixed, and now one of unmixed reality, such as Miss Wilkins alone can give us. At any rate her future is not in the keeping of criticism, to shape or direct. Who can forecast the course of such a talent? Not even the talent itself; and what we must be grateful for is what it has already given us in the two volumes of tales, which are as good in their way as anything ever done amongst us; that is, among any people. In form they instinctively approach that of the best work everywhere in the fine detail of handling; but in spirit they are distinctively ours. The humor is American, and they are almost all humorously imagined, with a sort of direct reference to the facts of the usual rustic American experience. The life of the human heart, its affections, its hopes, its fears, however these mask themselves from low to high, or high to low, is always the same, in every time and land; but in each it has a special physiognomy. What our artist has done is to catch the American look of life, so that if her miniatures remain to other ages they shall know just the expression of that vast average of Americans who do the hard work of the country, and live narrowly on their small earnings and savings. If there is no gayety in that look, it is because the face of hard work is always sober, and because the consciousness of merciless fortuities and inexorable responsibilities comes early and stays late with our people.

Mary E. Wilkins

BY THE AUTHOR OF "QUAKER COUSINS"

We have yet another writer of tales of New England. No country of a like area ever produced so many novelists as that rocky land. Hawthorne, Mrs. Stowe, Miss Alcott, and a host of others have given the world pictures of New England life. The soil still remains fruitful, and we are eager as ever to welcome its new productions, and to learn all that may be said about a life so near to us in many ways, so far from us in others. Miss Wilkins's tales are no imitations nor re-echoes. They are as fresh and original as were ever "Mosses from an Old Manse" or "The Pearl of Orr's Island" in their day. The present writer can recall the delight of reading the former when it first appeared, and remembers the outburst of enthusiasm with which those pictures of New England of a past century were received here. Modern New England was untouched by Hawthorne; his was a mystic semblance of the past, full of beauty, but not the reality of to-day. Miss Wilkins's stories are realistic in the true sense of that much misused word. They are not mere collections of facts, more or less unpleasant, but a faithful chronicling of such details of human affairs as have a real meaning. Every character has the tone and air of New England, of the people who accept no tradition, yet are stiff with inborn prejudices; who unite the last "ism" and spasm of modern ideas with ultra-Scotch Calvinism; who grew up on their hard soil, and under a severe and oppressive sky, always independent, often eccentric, with the virtues and the faults of a vigorous race. Miss Wilkins knows the New Englander, what he thinks, what he feels, what he loves and hates, the food he eats and the air he breathes. She paints the village life, the people on farms and in workshops and workhouses; and in all, whatever may be the setting, she sees those things which are of perennial interest—the pathos and beauty of simple lives. Here is true excellence, native born, uncopied and untaught, but, one suspects, kept at its high level by contact with the best literary models.

How it may be with others we know not, but we must confess to a feeling of reluctance in discussing personal matters relating to the writer of these tales. Not because we would not willingly know much about one who has given us a new and lasting pleasure, but rather because there is about these three little volumes a certain touch of a fine and delicate soul which

Reprinted from *Bookman* (London) 1 (December 1891): 102–3; excerpted in *Critic* 20, n.s. 17 (2 January 1892): 13.

turns curiosity away, a little shamefaced. The few words of preface to "A Humble Romance" are spoken with such unassumed modesty, with such a retirement of the person behind the work, that we would accept that demure "M.E.W." gratefully, as all that is vouchsafed us. We know that Miss Wilkins is young, that she is New England descended, born, and bred, and further, that the few who have the privilege of being her friends, recognise in her the mirror of the quiet humour, the pathos, and the compassionate insight of her tales. It is told that Miss Austen used to hide the brilliant pages of "Emma" and "Pride and Prejudice" under a bit of blotting paper. We could imagine that this little trick of the blotting paper was Miss Wilkins's also, and we would not disturb the modest quiet which we feel sure enshrines the writer of "A Far-Away Melody" and "A New England Nun."

Miss Wilkins gives in her tales variety in sameness, character after character, fresh in its originality, yet still of one type. She draws many pictures of the American girl—not the rather attenuated smart person which we may meet fresh any month in Mr. Howells's pages—not the brilliant omnipotent belle of fashionable life, but the fair, delicate, nervous, independent flower of New England, the girl who "teaches school," works at dressmaking, or on the farm, whose slender form and pink and white complexion cover a resolute will and sensitive nerves. But it is in her pictures of middle-aged women that Miss Wilkins excels, and she has done what no other writer has ever dared to do in making them the heroines of her stories. Whoever heretofore brought tears to the eyes over the small trials, the little heroisms and silent sorrows of old maids and hardworked wives? There is an endless gallery of these curious portraits of aged maids and matrons, drawn with all the detail and clearness of Holbein's old women. And how delightful they are!—the "Old Arithmetician," who sits up all night working out the problem which has baffled minister and schoolmaster, and whose tender heart is torn with remorse over her neglected household duties; the poor "Village Poetess," dying meekly, broken-hearted, with her despised verses in a tea-pot beside her. The gentle old Anne Millet, almost driven to unbelief by the loss of her cat—with what sympathy one reads of her mental struggles! What a breath of relief one draws when the cat is found, and we hear her lift up her heart in self-reproachful joy! "I've been an awful wicked woman. I ain't been to meetin', an' I've talked an'—Them squashes I threw away! It's been so warm, they ain't froze, an' I don't deserve it—I hadn't orter hev one of 'em; I hadn't orter hev anything. I'd orter offer up Willy. Lor' sakes! think of me sayin' what I did, an' him down cellar." Then those two proud old sisters, who share one gala dress between them, hiding their poverty from their neighbours, yet incapable of lying, even when pressed by impudent curiosity—who does not rejoice when their vulgar enemy is brought to her knees over the "sizzlin' " fire-crackers?

The men of the stories are, as they would themselves express it, "of less account" than the women; and they are more sparsely scattered through the pages, as they are in reality fewer in number in a country suffering so much from male emigration as New England. But where they appear, they fill the space appointed them with true masculine vigour.

Here is a new view, a fresh sweetly-scented field of fiction, as racy of the soil as are Tourgenieff's short tales of Russian life. The thread of the narratives, however simple, always leads to some climax full and complete, leaving the reader satisfied, often taken by surprise, so skilfully hidden is the hand of Fate which guides it. The curtain descends without apparent signal, and one sentence frequently reveals the inevitable—often beautiful—solution. This young writer, dealing with the commonplaces of life, sees the eternal harmony of goodness explaining and softening all—in the homely doings, the potato settings, the dish washings, the going to meetin'; and amid all the ruthlessly exact details, there is a meaning which the divining eye of the poet sees. "Like all common things," says Miss Wilkins of "Christmas Jenny's" candle, "it had and was its own poem." This might be the motto of all her writings, and her gift is that of Jean François Millet, to see the symbolism of homeliness, the sacred pathos of the daily toil of dutiful lives. When a writer is endowed with this power, it is not necessary to seek strange situations, monstrosities of character, or tortuous and complicated passions to excite emotion; and there is the comfortable sense of reserve power which might say more than it does. She rarely touches the ghastly or horrible. If she does, a vague detail, far reaching in its significance, is sufficient. Here is an instance: a charitable woman takes a pillow to a miserly sick old man and his wife, who live alone with a ruffianly underpaid farm-servant. She finds the house still and deserted; her growing terror is described when to her repeated calls no answer comes. "The silence seemed to beat against her ears. She went across the kitchen to the bedroom. Here and there she held back her dress. She reached the bedroom and looked in." No more is told, only how she sped homeward, arriving there half-fainting. " 'Now tell me about it,' said Mrs. Ansel. 'What did you see first? What was you going there for?' 'To carry the pillow,' said Luella, pointing to it. 'I can't talk about it, Maria.' Mrs. Ansel went over to the lounge and took it up. 'Mercy sakes! What's that on it?' she cried in horror 'I s'pose—I—hit it against the wall somehow,' Luella replied. 'I can't talk about it, Maria.' " The horrible scene of the murder is somehow flashed upon us by that oblique stroke. Here is another swift and effectual touch. An honest young fellow has suddenly been dismissed from work by the foreman—no reason given. He stands with his handsome wife in the garden the same evening, and the foreman goes by. "She was standing close to her husband clinging to his arm when he got to the front of the house, just when he had his eyes fixed full on her. She even leaned her head against David's shoulder. She knew why she did it, though her husband did not; she knew also why this foreman had turned him off, and this was her method of stabbing him for it." In two lines, the key to the whole story.

Miss Wilkins paints the surroundings in her stories with much care and much felicity, and she knows how wisely to omit. She has the same careful eye for scenery as for moral niceties. The little vignettes of roadside and garden, field and sky, play their part in the picture as successfully as the "foreground" in a fine etching. In "The Solitary," two figures, the big and surly misanthrope, and the half-starved, miserable carrier, stand out against a background of a snowy night. We see the snow-covered woods, the clearing sky before the oncoming of the bitter night, the hush of death as the frost deepens. "The snow creaked under foot; the air was full of sparkles, there were noises like guns in the woods, for the trees were almost freezing. The moon was full, and seemed like a very fire of death, radiating cold instead of heat."

We might be tempted to compare these tales with the short tales of Mrs. Gaskell, which deal with the class of small farmers and working people of Lancashire. It would only be to point out the differences between them. The sombre colouring, the tragic speed and force of such tales as "The Crooked Branch," "The Heart of John Middleton," or the "Sexton's Story," are not here. Miss Wilkins's stories would not be true pictures of New England life if they were. American life is not tragic or sombre. The great future before it—the great prosperity of the American nation—determines the national mood and makes it cheerful, in spite of individual sorrows. American literature reflects a serene sky, and there is in it none of that deep undercurrent of passionate feeling born of the memories of oppression and struggle, a long history of endurance of evil, and battles lost and won, which flows under our best gaiety and content. Miss Wilkins's tales have the freshness of youth about them, though their theme may often be sad. Their pathos has in it a gentle sweetness, not far removed from happiness and hope.

Reviews of
A New England Nun, and Other Stories

THE NATION

Miss Wilkins's new volume is in the vein of her earlier one, and goes far to prove it inexhaustible. The poor, dingy old New England women have lost none of their bleakness, the young ones nothing of their pathetic attempt at youth under difficulties. The kitchen operations go on as before, and over all this dismal life float rosy clouds of faith, loyalty, and heroism, without which one would feel that nothing was left but suicide. The delicacy of Miss Wilkins's hand never fails, any more than does her fertility of resource in incident. With all the monotony of entourage, a tender surprise is in every story. It is not strange that this patient monotony, these stories of self-immolation, warm the cockles of the hearts of New Englanders the world over, and prompt the feeling that martyrdom has first found its fitting garments in faded gingham.

THE CRITIC

What can we say that will express our sense of the beauty of Miss M. E. Wilkins's *A New England Nun and Other Stories?* So true in their insight into human nature, so brief and salient in construction, so deep in feeling, so choice in expression, these stories rank even with the works of Mrs. Stowe and Miss Jewett. It is the marvellous repression of passion and feeling in the New England character that Miss Wilkins has drawn with such technique. Beneath the icy surface of demeanor she has looked into the heart of this strong self-contained people and has seen boiling and bubbling wells of fervency. It is chiefly from New England women that she has made her studies, and there is nothing in their narrow, sad, colorless life that has escaped her observation. Here are twenty-four stories so complete in form, so exquisite in texture, so fine that to single out any one, such as "A New

Reviews of *A New England Nun, and Other Stories* reprinted from *Nation* 52 (11 June 1891): 484; *Critic* 18, n.s. 15 (May 1891): 286; *Athenaeum* 98 (18 July 1891): 93.

England Nun," "Calla Lilies and Hannah," or "The Revolt of Mother" for especial praise means simply that there are times when the author has surpassed the even beauty of her literary style.

THE ATHENAEUM

In her stories of New England life Miss Wilkins has shown a great deal of skill and a power of observation which almost amounts to originality. She is in danger of settling down to a fixed manner and of exaggerating that quality which has brought her success. *A New England Nun* is too much after the style of *A Humble Romance,* and it requires a tough appetite to get through the two dozen stories of the more recent volume. The writer has many a time gone on elaborating details after her picture is finished. The austere and not very attractive types of character she deals with have often afforded her good material for really artistic work, but in many cases she has forgotten that elaboration which does not go directly toward heightening the pathetic or human interest of her stories is merely tedious.

Reviews of
Jane Field

LAURENCE HUTTON

Miss Wilkins has done no better descriptive writing than her picture of Amanda Pratt's cottage in the first chapter of *Jane Field*. It was like holding a shell to one's ear to enter Amanda Pratt's parlor. "The whole room in this little inland cottage, far beyond the salt fragrance of the sea, seemed like one of those marine fossils sometimes found miles from the coast. It indicated the presence of the sea in the lives of Amanda's race. Her grandfather had been a seafaring man, and so had her father, until late in life, when he had married an inland woman, and settled down among waves of timothy and clover."

Amanda Pratt and her neighbors are as real as if they had been painted by some Yankee Meissonier, as true to life as if they had been photographed by Sarony or by Cox. Or rather not photographs, not portraits, but breathing beings are they one and all.

The words "to be continued," at the end of "Jane Field," in *Harper's Magazine* for May last, came as a surprise, almost as a shock, to many readers. Miss Wilkins was so closely identified with the great art of writing short stories that the intimation that she was to try her hand at a novel of what the English call "the ordinary three-volume length" excited no little attention. And "Jane Field," as a study of Yankee character, is in many ways far in advance of anything Miss Wilkins has yet written. It is more than a study of character, it is a study of conscience and a study of soul. Even Hawthorne himself has never surpassed the description of the night of awful lonesomeness and morbid haunting fancies spent by Jane Field in the deserted house she had stolen from its rightful heirs. She sat bolt-upright and in total darkness through the long hours. She folded her hands primly and held up her bonneted head like some decorous and favored caller who might expect, at any moment, to hear the heavy step of the host upon the creaking stair, and his voice in the room. "She sat there so all night . . . she sat there and never tired until morning broke." And what she saw and heard and thought, realizing fully "the fact which underlay everything that she had sinned, that she had gone over from good to evil, and given up her soul for a handful of

Reviews of Jane Field reprinted from Laurence Hutton, "Literary Notes," *Harper's Magazine* 86, supplement 1 (February 1893): 486; *Nation* 56 (23 February 1893): 146; *Godey's Magazine* 126 (February 1893): 232.

gold," are depicted by Miss Wilkins with a vividness and an introspective power which are very remarkable in a writer so young in years and in experience.

THE NATION

The admirer of Miss Wilkins's stories opens with some misgivings her novel. If a writer can make a supremely good short story in a wholly new field, is it not a pity to depart and join the congested ranks of novel writers? Moreover, is not Miss Wilkins's genius essentially that of the episode-teller? Situations but not plot, impressions but not analysis, would seem to be her strong points, as well as detail to an extent which, while perfect within narrow limits, would run the risk of becoming petty if multiplied to the requirements of the novel's size. Such misgivings assail the mind of one about to read *Jane Field,* and assail it in proportion as one already cherishes the unique genius of Miss Wilkins. Great, therefore, is the reader's gratification to find that the new work is no less interesting than the old, while being, strange to say, of the same quality. That it is a conventional novel is hardly true; what is surprising is to find that the miniature-painting expands so well into scene-painting. The story, to which brevity, one would have said, was vital, pulsates with intensity through nearly three hundred pages; the grim, hard-shell, soft-hearted old women move with entire appropriateness through their larger field of action; the pathos which never was wanting from the little tales becomes here a touch of tragedy, still homespun but terrible. In the unexpected pleasure of finding that the dainty has borne enlarging into a feast, we may, perhaps, ask whether we shall be satisfied with small portions again, and whether Miss Wilkins has not established an incovenient claim upon her own pen.

GODEY'S MAGAZINE

For stories which are at the same time serious and humorous commend us to New England authors of the present day and generation. *Jane Field* is an illustration; the character of the heroine, a woman with a hard lot and a child whom she idolizes, is as minutely drawn and analyzed as if by Hawthorne; so is the course of the mental and moral gradation by which she became a thief, all for the sake of her child, and miseries which were hers as her daughter, who came to know her mother's secret, learned to abhor her parent. And yet, side by side with the details of this painful story, are scores of amusing suggestions from New England life; there is also much light thrown upon the apparent contradiction in one old type of New England character—the keeping of a warm heart under a cold, hard exterior. Few Yankee stories are so well worth keeping as this.

Reviews of
Pembroke

Laurence Hutton

Another writer of short stories who is a credit to her generation, to her sex, and to her country, is Miss Mary E. Wilkins, so essentially a short-story writer that her "Jane Field" is nothing more than a long short story, while her "Pembroke" is nothing less than three short stories in one. The simple fact that a romance is "to be continued in our next" does not make it a novel, and although it be extended to a hundred chapters, to a dozen parts, and to three volumes, a short story will be a short story still, pungent and concentrated even when it is not brief.

The great promise exhibited in Miss Wilkins's first effort at the expansion of a short story has been more than fulfilled in the trilogy of short stories which she now presents to her friendly public. *Pembroke* opens with a courting scene in New England, at about that historic period when Zekle crep' up quite unbeknown an' peeked in thru' the winder; and although the Huldy of this case is, unfortunately, not all alone, and although in the beginning of her career there was a disagreeable father nigh to hinder, Miss Wilkins's Barnabas Thayer and Charlotte Barnard suggest in many ways, sad though their story is, the familiar hero and heroine of Lowell's poem, and perhaps they are intended to be an elaboration of the characters upon whom the poet merely touches. " 'Twas kin' o' kingdom come to look on sech a blessed cretur as Charlotte was, and none in the whole country couldn't quicker pitch a ton nor drov' a furrer straighter than could Barnabas himself, who was not only clear grit and human natur', but was, as well, six foot o' man."

While it is pleasant to think of "The Courtin' " as a prelude to Miss Wilkins's drama, and to fancy that we are following the careers of Huldah and Ezekiel in the three love-stories which run along, side by side, in "Pembroke," the drama is much more than a sequel to the prologue, and is quite able to stand upon its own merits. It has all the qualities which were so conspicuous in "Jane Field" and in its author's many shorter tales; humor, pathos, homely devotion, Yankee contrariness and stubbornness, and, above all, the portrayal of that intensity of suppressed feeling which distinguishes

Reviews of *Pembroke* reprinted from *Harper's Monthly* 89, supplement 3–4 (June 1894): 162; *Saturday Review of Politics, Literature, Science, and Art* 77 (23 June 1894): 667–68; *Critic* 25, n.s. 22 (21 July 1894): 36–37; *Edinburgh Review* 187 (April 1898): 392–97.

the children of the Pilgrim Fathers even to the present day. It is hard to find in the whole range of modern fiction anything much more touching and tender than that early chapter in which Barnabas is seen all alone in the unfinished little cottage he is building for his promised wife, and when he thought how the very room, because she was to occupy it, seemed warm from floor to ceiling. " 'Her rocking-chair can set there,' said Barnabas, aloud. The tears came into his eyes, he stepped forward, laid his smooth boyish cheek against a partition-wall of this new house, and kissed it. It was a fervent demonstration, not towards Charlotte alone, nor the joys to come to him within those walls, but to all life and love and nature, although he did not comprehend it. He half sobbed as he turned away, his thoughts seemed to dazzle his brain, and he could not feel his feet."

The second pair of lovers in Pembroke are older, if not more experienced, than the first, and they, too, will appeal to all mankind by whom lovers are loved. There is something of Ezekiel in Richard as well as in Barnabas, and not a little of Huldah in Charlotte's Aunt Sylvia, who waited in her own sitting-room, and in patient maidenhood, eighteen years for her beau to up and kiss her. It will be remembered that Richard, on one famous occasion, had stood a spell on one foot first, then stood a spell on t'other, before he had the courage to sit by Sylvia's side on the haircloth sofa, his only demonstrative exhibition in fifty-two times eighteen Sunday evenings; and when we are told in Chapter II that Richard had a fine tenor voice, and had sung in the choir ever since he was a boy, we can imagine how he used to make Old Hundred ring in Sylvia's ears and heart.

The history of the third pair of lovers—William and Rebecca—is the most tragic of all; and the story of their courting, delicately told by Miss Wilkins, leads them into deeper and muddier waters than Miss Wilkins has ever sounded before. To say why gals acts so or so, or don't, 'ould be presumin', even in fiction; and from these two we turn, all teary 'round the lashes, to the better, although long deferred, fates of their cousins and their aunts; all smily 'round the lips when we learn that Sylvia's journey towards the poor-house and Barney's painful walk to Charlotte's door are to end in their both being cried lawfully in meetin', on the last Sunday we pass in Pembroke.

THE SATURDAY REVIEW OF POLITICS, LITERATURE, SCIENCE, AND ART

It is difficult to withstand the temptation to speak in terms of mere indiscriminate laudation of Miss Mary Wilkins and her works. She is undoubtedly a fine writer with a remarkable power of creating character, and a wonderful gift of insight into human nature; but, perhaps, she appears even greater than she really is, owing to the contrast between her work and that of the majority of the novel-writing herd of today. Five ladies, besides Miss Wilkins, help to provide the supply of fiction which we review this week, and they are no worse than most of the persons who devote themselves to this modestly lucrative branch of commerce; as it happens, none of them is notably nasty or very strikingly fatuous, and this is something to be thankful for after many recent feminine productions. The worst that need be said about them is that they are all about as capable of adding anything to literature as the average reader is of appreciating it. This seems to be considered no disqualification for turning novelist nowadays, and the reviewer only thinks it worth mentioning on the rare occasions when the work of an artist of fiction is in his hands. After the critic has got over his first feelings of unmixed appreciation upon reading *Pembroke,* it is probable he will not discover much in it to find fault with. All those qualities which have won our hearts and judgments in Miss Wilkins's tiny masterpieces of New England life are displayed here on a larger canvas, and the other elements necessary to the success of a work on a bigger scale are not lacking. "Pembroke" is the name of the village in which all the *dramatis personae* dwell; but it is not, as is too often the case, a mere local circumstance which secures the unity of Miss Wilkins's work. The central thread of the novel is the history of Barney Thayer and Charlotte Barnard, whose betrothal is broken by a quarrel over politics between the young man and Charlotte's father. Both are sullenly proud, and the feud goes on for years, though Charlotte is not in the slightest degree responsible for it. One of the chief characteristics of all Miss Wilkins's descendants of the Puritans is a tough endurance mixed with a marvellous personal pride, which at times takes the form of intense reserve or dignity, at times degenerates into rigid stubborness. With Barney, who cannot get over the insult put upon him by Charlotte's harsh old father, even after the offender and everybody else have made all possible atonement, this passion of duty to oneself is a disease; in spite of the skill with which the workings of his nature are delineated, we find it difficult to have patience with him or even to be altogether satisfied of his reality. Much more impressively convincing is his mother, Deborah Thayer, the sternly religious hardworking woman whose absolute devotion to her narrow interpretation of the Eternal Truths makes her life a wreck and ruins the happiness of those dearest to her. The reader sympathizes with and understands the conscience-driven tyrant and her victims equally; with the soft-hearted old husband and the roguish invalid boy who are so happy together when she leaves them alone, and with the stern Deborah whose terrible sense of an ever-threatening Deity forces her to cow the old man and torment the lad for their soul's health. The one stroke of the rod which she inflicts, in spite of the doctor's prohibition, on her peccant child is followed instantly by his death (of heart disease), and it is as if we were assisting at the visible acts of destiny. Hardly less impressive are the discovery by the wretched Deborah of her daughter's fall, and its effect on the girl, who, for years after her marriage to her lover, remains a shame-stricken

shadow of her bright healthy maidenhood. Grim as many of the incidents of
the book are, and crabbed as are the temperaments of some of the chief
characters, we must not leave our readers with the unjust impression that the
general tenor and effect of it is gloom. Laughter and tears are closely intermin-
gled in Miss Wilkins's presentation of life, and assuredly there is in *Pembroke*
no lack of mirth either of the pathetic or the sunnier kind. The description of
the cherry picnic is an idyl of happy youth and rustic merriment; the tale of
the weakling boy's last and crowning frolic makes one glad (though forebod-
ingly) to think that the poor little rascal had such a "real good time" for once;
and over the mingled comedy and pathos of sweet Aunt Sylvia's long drawn-
out wooing angels might smile and weep. No one has ever treated the whole
race of "old maids" with such tender truth as Miss Wilkins. But love is
always a very beautiful thing with this writer, though generally a serious one.

THE CRITIC

Miss Wilkins has achieved a distinct success—one that carries her farther in
her literary career than anything she has heretofore accomplished. While the
book, as a novel, in no way approaches the harmonious splendor and fulness
of Nathaniel Hawthorne's art, it gives us in its own kind the same wonderful
pictures of New England life—pictures that are at once a revelation of the
depth and steadfastness of human nature and the capacity for dogged, passion-
less suffering born and bred in the Puritan temperament. It is a suffering that
strikes one dumb with the chill of death, that freezes and kills expression
instead of softening and opening one's nature to beauty and tenderness—it is
the suffering of repression and insanity—the useless suffering that seems
wicked to the sane mind, because it is imposed by earth, and not by Heaven.
Wonderful in concentrated intensity, tremendous in power, this record of the
heart tragedies of a dozen men and women of the village of Pembroke is not
surpassed in our literature for its beauty of style, the delicacy of its character-
delineation and the enthralling interest of its narration. That a man like
Barney Thayer should refuse, when his house was nearly built, to marry the
girl of his choice, because he and her father had a dispute in which the latter
ordered him to leave his house, and that, in spite of the most tender loyalty
on his betrothed's part and a consuming love on his own, he should persist in
this course for ten years, is inconceivable to anyone unfamiliar with the
terrible power of will developed in that bitter Calvinistic atmosphere. It
shows a hardness of heart and purpose that throws a spell over the reader, as it
unmistakably has done over the writer—a spell to shake off whose benumb-
ing influence one rushes out into the sunny summer air, or reaches out to
touch some beloved familiar object.

The story of Barnabas and Charlotte is duplicated in another situation,
where, after twenty years of courtship, it is only the sight of the faded and

broken woman being taken to the poor-house that stirred the man's heart to any sense of obligation and protection. In fact, to review the characters of the book—mothers and daughters, fathers and sons,—is to summon before one a community where each tender nature seems to be yoked with one whose flint-like hardness can most cruelly wound it, and where each harsh and domineering one is in a position peculiarly adapted to wreck the lives of every one about it, and yet, where, in spite of it all, a rugged self-respect keeps the one from being crushed and the other from a wanton abuse of power. And through it all there is a stern rectitude and integrity that make one wish never to see unvarnished truth again. In "The Mill on the Floss" and "Adam Bede" George Eliot has given us pictures of communities of narrow, straight-laced folk; in "The House of the Seven Gables" and "The Scarlet Letter" Hawthorne has illuminated the Puritan character: but in each instance these authors have touched the wells of sympathy in their readers—and one feels, at least, that their people, though erring, are human. But there is something uncanny about the hardness of the characters in "Pembroke." And when Barnabas Thayer, because he sees Charlotte likely to be made a subject of disgrace and church discipline for having nursed him through a dangerous illness, conquers his old resentment enough to go to her father's house to reclaim her as his bride, we wonder whether, after all, miracles of the spirit can be performed any more than those of the body, and whether Charlotte, in marrying Barnabas, has not united herself to a nature as irretrievably warped and diseased in spirit as his body is bent and broken by work and rheumatism.

THE EDINBURGH REVIEW

Very different is the case of Miss Mary Wilkins, who has founded a school closely comparable to that which Galt inaugurated in the early days of this century, and Mr. Barrie has revived and glorified with the humour, force, and tenderness which he can lend even to his imitators. Miss Wilkins, however, is no one's imitator, though by a distant reflexion she sometimes recalls Hawthorne. She has studied her New England folk to the marrow of their bones, and she portrays them, as an artist should, unsparingly, yet lovingly; perhaps, in her artist's desire for unity of effect, insisting almost too much upon certain leading qualities. Yet the essential features of her New England folk are not merely local; one recognises behind the New England farmer that hard foundation upon which is built up the most composite of all types—the modern American. Will and conscience are the qualities which dominate in her stories like passions; they run to tragic or grotesque excesses, as in other races love or the fighting instinct will do; they merge into one another, and the passion for self-assertion becomes only another form of dogged resolution in carrying out a purely individual conception of duty. The American people are above all Nonconformist; one feels that in Mr. Harold

Frederic's merciless study of their religious phases; one feels it in Mr. Fuller's sketches of Chicago, with its riches won since yesterday, conscientiously endeavouring to invent social forms and adopt luxuries, yet ill at ease among them. The old Puritan breaks out in spite of deep carpets piled over him and butlers sitting on his head. One sees nonconformity even in Mr. Stephen Crane's sketches of American war, where every soldier in the ranks is a critic; but one sees it most of all in Miss Wilkins, and one realises from her that New England is the true matrix of the American type. Americans may have got from elsewhere their versatility, their calculating power, and their passion for novelty; but they took from New England the quality which they themselves call grit. The stiff long upper lip, the gaunt angular outline, express accurately enough Miss Wilkins's characters; these are attributes neither lovely nor endearing, but they inevitably command respect, and the race which has them in the end succeeds inevitably. How should it not? When people are so 'set'—it is the New England word—that a young man will sooner give up the girl he loves than go back upon a hasty word—when a father will sooner see his daughter live and die unmarried than speak a word of apology for a hot-tempered outbreak—this subordination of everything to an exaggerated self-esteem, this fetish worship of will, may be grotesque or tragic, but it is a terrible quality for an antagonist to possess, and it will make martyrs or heroes. Take the story of "Pembroke," the novel which in our judgement shows Miss Wilkins at her best; for, instead of presenting a single character or a single relation, it presents a complex of mutual interactions. It is, indeed, like several of her short stories blended into one; and the total result is to give a very curious and suggestive picture of the village community. You have here the story of Barney Thayer and of Charlotte Barnard, the story of William Berry and Rebecca Thayer, the story of Sylvia Crane and Richard Alger, and the story of Deborah Thayer and her invalid son. All these interlock, more or less, or at least combine to illustrate each other; and the whole book is a study of rigidity in character. The central figure in the book is Deborah Thayer, a terrible she-Puritan, who domineers in her own house, thin-lipped, notable, and unforgiving. And she has borne a son like herself—as "set" as she is. Barney Thayer is going to marry Charlotte Barnard; his new house is all but finished; and he goes for almost the last of many visits to court his sweetheart. But old Cephas Barnard is another of these unrelenting rulers, and he insists that Barney shall stay in the room with the rest; he provokes a discussion on politics, and the two men quarrel. The women try to keep the peace, but insults begin to fly. Cephas orders the young man out of the house and bids him never darken the doors again. " 'I never will, by the Lord Almighty,' returned Barnabas in an awful voice; then the door slammed after him." Charlotte pursues him, calling his name, but he never turns his head; then—for she is "set," too, in her way— she waits for long hours outside the house, thinking her father will have locked her out, and too proud to try the door. Meanwhile her aunt Sylvy

Crane, a tremulous pretty old maid, is detained by this trouble, and so, for the first Sunday evening for years, her door is shut when Richard Alger comes to see her. For years he had been coming—for years the village had been asking, When will Richard Alger marry Sylvy Crane? For years she had been hoping and palpitating while youth faded, but his life had grown "set" in its mechanical continuance, and he had never been able to depart so far from his habits as to speak. So when she gets back late, and finds that Richard Alger has come and gone, she knows that this is the end. On the last evening he had got almost out of his track; for the first time in all those years he had come to sit by her on her sofa; he had half begun a declaration; but the clock struck ten, and that was the invariable signal for his departure. So her absence on the next evening was an insuperable rebuff—he gave up coming.

Have these people blood in their veins at all? one asks oneself. Sometimes, it appears. Rebecca Thayer was in love with William Berry, whose father kept a grocery store, and a charming scene describes how the girl goes to make her purchases there, shy and half unwilling. Then comes the day when William's miserly old father authorises his children to invite the neighbourhood to a cherry party; and when the cherries are eaten the old man—it is a study of mania—comes to the guests asking payment for them. William Berry is nearly beside himself with shame, till Rebecca goes to him and throws her arms about his neck in a tumult of pity. She comes home late from her party, furtively radiant; but the terrible Deborah detects her. Deborah is furious because her son Barney has refused to go back and marry Charlotte; and now she deals straight with Rebecca: "You might jest as well understand it first as last; if you've got any idea of havin' William Berry, you've got to give it up." No one in the house but Barney attempts to stand against Deborah Thayer. Rebecca pines and in time grows languid; her mother, in a fit of maternal promptings, seeks to console her with a new dress; peremptorily tries it on the girl; and the truth is out. She orders Rebecca out of the house in a snowstorm; then, after some hours, goes to Barney and bids him find William Berry and make him marry Rebecca. The marriage takes place in a wayside house, while the little minister's wife, who is brought along for a witness, shrinks and quails before this unimaginable wickedness. Mr. Barrie's "Auld Lichts," stern as they are, are tolerant and human compared with these New Englanders. Marriage makes no atonement, and the girl pines, shut up by herself, unvisited, in a new house, and her child is born to her dead. Mrs. Thayer gives no sign of knowing that she exists, and no one dares mention Rebecca to her. But Deborah is broken down at last by a blow on her one tender spot. Her youngest child, a boy, has a weak heart, and the doctors have told her what that means. So he is shut up, forbidden to play, and held in a leash, drenched with detestable medicines, but not beaten; and, like a true urchin, he knows his advantage and keeps his heart ready for an excuse. His only playmate is his father, and Caleb Thayer is seldom allowed to play with his boy. But one night the other boys are "coasting" on sleds, and late, when his parents are asleep, Ephraim steals out to join them. Only one boy is left, and he soon goes, but Ephraim spends a delirious night coasting down hills and tugging the sled up again. He steals home at last with his heart beating till it chokes him, but jubilant in his emancipation; and in the intoxication of the moment he steals half a mince pie. Next day his mother goes off, leaving him with messages and injunctions about paring apples. But Ephraim's heart trouble is serious now; he is feeling weak; and when his father comes in and tempts him to play "holly-gull" he consents, and so the day is wasted. Deborah returns home and elicits confession; Ephraim is too ill to be afraid when she orders him to follow her.

> He and his mother stood together in the little bedroom. She, when she faced him, saw how ill he looked, but she steeled herself against that. She had seen him look as badly before; she was not to be daunted by that from her high purpose. For it was a high purpose to Deborah Thayer. She did not realise the part which her own human will had in it.
>
> She lifted up her voice and spoke solemnly. Caleb, listening, all trembling, at the kitchen door, heard her.
>
> "Ephraim," said his mother, "I have spared the rod with you all my life because you were sick. Your brother and your sister have both rebelled against the Lord and against me. You are all the child I have got left. You've got to mind me and do right. I ain't goin' to spare you any longer because you ain't well. It is better you should be sick than be well and wicked and disobedient. It is better that your body should suffer than your immortal soul. Stand still."
>
> Deborah raised her stick, and brought it down. She raised it again, but suddenly Ephraim made a strange noise and sunk away before it, down in a heap on the floor.

This rough analysis of the component parts shows sufficiently how Miss Wilkins conceives of will and conscience as they tyrannise among the Puritan villagers. The long struggle of Barney Thayer to shake off the fatal grip of his own stubbornness is vividly told, but it adds nothing to our point; and the curious piece of symbolism by which this kind of mental cramp is made to express itself in his body till the straight young man looks, to certain visions, bowed and twisted, is an ill-judged copying of Hawthorne. But Miss Wilkins has few failings in her sincere and genuine art. A strict limitation of range may be urged against her, but Miss Austen is liable to the same impeachment. We should rank her with Mrs. Gaskell—in our judgement no mean promotion. Her stories are old-maidish in temper—old-maidish even in the talk of her married women. An atmosphere of soap and water pervades her books, and the thing which most distresses one of her women when she cannot marry the man of her heart is to reflect upon the uncared-for state of his under garments.

There is certainly nothing old-maidish about Mr. Harold Frederic, whose masterpiece, "Illumination," next falls to be considered. Yet "Illumination" is also a story of New England life, and, to revert to our purpose of treating these novels as documents, a necessary complement to Miss Wilkins. The stories that Miss Wilkins writes make one feel the uniformity of American character; her people are all variations upon a single well-marked type. Mr. Frederic shows by implication that she has simplified the problem for herself in taking merely the life of villages. He treats not, indeed, of a great city, but of a small out of the world town in the backwoods, small enough for a clergyman's affairs to be a matter of general notoriety and interest, large enough to have a tramway and gaslight. Yet here, in the backwoods, you find that deep-rifted division which reaches through all American life, and the presence, side by side, of alien and incompatible races. The central figure of "Illumination" is a Nonconformist minister, the Reverend Theron Ware, and in his flock you recognise at once the hard-featured race whom Miss Wilkins presents, if not loveably, at least lovingly; but you recognise the unsparing portrait drawn by one who is intolerant of their intolerance. One recognises, in short, the fundamental qualities which go to make up the American. But the qualities are presented with their defects in strong relief; frugality is seen as greed, strength of will as fanaticism, intelligence as cunning, and conscience as an abiding desire to interfere with a neighbour's conduct. Over against this mass of Nonconformity is set the hostile camp of Catholicism; over against the Yankee, the Irishman; and between these two forces, which are at work gradually modifying each other, the Reverend Theron Ware is torn in sunder.

Review of
Madelon

Horace E. Scudder

It has sometimes been lamented, half whimsically, that there is no training-school for novelists, as there is for painters and sculptors; yet if the novelist has to master his art by untutored practice, he may have this resort, at least, that the writing of short stories offers a species of apprenticeship in the craft. Not that the short story may not be a worthy end in itself: sometimes the artist in this form reaches perfection here, and needs no larger canvas. But if one has it in him to draw his figures life-size, the short story may well serve for preliminary studies. Miss Wilkins has shown indisputably that her power in delineating life comes largely from the faculty of holding in a firm grasp the secret of a mastering impulse or principle. She has illustrated this in a large number of sharply defined personalities, drawn, so to speak, as individual figures, or in small groups occupied with quick incidents. With the growth of power the same kind of handling is apparent when she essays more considerable pieces, and carries the action over a longer time under a greater range of circumstances. She still has the unfaltering grasp impelled by clear insight, and the steady movement along direct lines. The concentration of power in her short stories is very great; it is even more noticeable in her longer tales. We had occasion to express our respect for her art when Pembroke appeared, and our admiration is not lessened by the new illustration of her artistic force in Madelon.

The heroine, Madelon herself, displays just this tenacious grip of an idea that we have recognized as the central fact in Miss Wilkins's art; so does Lot Gordon, the hero; so does Burr in a somewhat less degree; so does Burr's mother; and the same set, to use an expressive word, is what gives backbone to the otherwise invertebrate Dorothy Fair. Minor characters, like Richard, display a similar disposition, and at the close of the book the whole community is in peril of being swept into a Niagara of wrongheadedness. We think the culmination of Madelon is genuinely in the mere hint that is given of an impending disaster arrested by the suicide of the hero.

The book is, in fact, a most artistic portrayal of the *idée fixe* of the psychologist. We have no wish to enter the domain of the pathologist, yet we

Reprinted from *Atlantic Monthly* 78 (August 1896): 269–70.

would point out to the reader how much of Miss Wilkins's skill seems to lie in stopping just short of insanity in her characters. A little more, and every mother's son and daughter of them would be in the madhouse. Well, is not that the logical outcome of what is characteristic in New England country life, and is it not a tribute to Miss Wilkins's genius that she should have caught this temper and transferred it in all its fascination to the pages of her books? Heretofore, the type illustrated has been the New Englander of purest strain, such as may be seen in several instances in this tale; but in creating the Hautvilles Miss Wilkins has shown a not unfamiliar type, the English crossed by the French and Indian, and she has been unerring in her rendering of the rich, vibrant nature thus produced. But these, too, must have the dominant passion, and thus, though the author of their being takes a new clay in her hands, she fashions it again after her own image.

In the working out of her tragedy—for tragedy it certainly is—Miss Wilkins has shown dexterity in avoiding the grotesque while coming pretty near it at times, and there are fewer of those sudden gleams of beauty which gave relief in Pembroke. We suspect the explanation may lie in the somewhat artificial character of the central moment of the drama. The stab which she gives Lot Gordon when she mistakes him for Burr comes upon the reader almost before he is ready, and at once the whole story is pitched in a high key. There is scarcely a lowering of that key to the last. It is as if the author did not dare once relax, lest the note should not be recovered. The intensity thus is in the author almost more than it is in the tragedy itself, and for this reason the reader may take a somewhat more curious and less absorbing interest in the acting than might otherwise be the case. Yet if he comes upon few passages of clear beauty such as he had learned to hope for in this writer after reading Pembroke, he is impressed again by the extraordinary concentration of language of which Miss Wilkins is capable, and gives the highest praise to an art which makes language have the cold splendor of a winter sunset.

Review of
Jerome: A Poor Man

CHARLES MINER THOMPSON

A good way to judge the structure of a story is to examine it as if you intended turning it into a play. To do so is to ask about it two very searching questions: Is it well constructed? Is its theme strongly based upon the verities of human nature? Looking upon the story with the eye of the dramatist, you will see all its superfluities fade away,—all the "analysis of character," all the author's wise or humorous reflections, all the episodical incidents. Everything by which writers of novels are enabled to blind their readers to the structural weakness of their production, or to the essential improbability or triviality of their themes, seems to detach itself and vanish, leaving the substance and the form naked to the eye.

It is interesting to apply this test, which seems fair, although severe, to Miss Wilkins's latest story, *Jerome.* The plot, reduced to its simplest terms, is this: Jerome, a poor young man who is not likely ever to have any property to call his own, promises that he will give away to the poor of the town all his wealth if he ever becomes rich. Two incredulous rich men, taunted and stung thereto by the gibes of the company, declare that if, within ten years, Jerome receives and gives away as much as ten thousand dollars, they on their side will give away to the poor one fourth of their property. Jerome becomes possessed of a fortune, and does with it as he had promised to do. The two rich men thereupon fulfill their agreements.

This is the keystone of the novel, the central fact of the story which supports the whole structure. All that precedes is preparatory, all that follows is explanatory.

Now, to revert to the test of a play, this is not an idea upon which a serious drama could be founded. That such a bargain should be made and kept may be within the possibilities of human nature; few things, indeed, lie outside the possibilities of human nature. But it is not within the probabilities. Any serious play which should be based upon it would inevitably seem artificial. It is an idea for a farce, or, on a higher level, for a satirical comedy; for each of these species of composition may be based upon an absurdity, if, when once started, it is developed naturally and logically. A serious play, however, if it is not to miss its effect, must treat a serious theme; one of which no spectator for

Reprinted from *Atlantic Monthly* 80 (December 1897): 857–59.

an instant will question the reality. By such a test as this Miss Wilkins's novel fails because its theme lacks probability and dignity.

The theme, in fact, is of the right proportion for a short story, and this, indeed, is what Miss Wilkins has made; but she has prefixed to it a series of short stories and sketches dealing with preceding events, and has added another series of short stories dealing with subsequent events. These are all rather loosely bound together, and the result is that the reader, thinking over the story, does not have an idea of it as a unit; he thinks now of one part, now of another; and by the mere fact of his so thinking of it he confesses that he has not found it a good novel, but a bad novel by a good writer of short stories. Miss Wilkins applies in *Jerome* her short-story methods, and has not mastered the techniques of a larger structure. She is, as it were, Meissonier trying to paint a large, bold canvas.

The mention of Meissonier calls to mind the merits of the story, which, as any reader of her work may guess, are neither few nor small. There are many admirable human portraits in the book, many excellently dramatic bits of action, much strong, nervous, natural dialogue. Always the work is that of a keenly observant eye, and of the brooding type of mind that is most surely dowered with the creative imagination. A single excellent passage will illustrate our meaning. Jerome's mother is speaking to him of the report that he has given away all his wealth:—

> "I want to know if it's true," she said.
> "Yes, mother, it is."
> "You've given it all away?"
> "Yes, mother."
> "Your own folks won't get none of it?"
> Jerome shook his head. . . .
> Ann Edwards looked at her son, with a face of pale recrimination and awe. She opened her mouth to speak, then closed it without a word. "*I never had a black silk dress in my life,*" said she finally, in a shaking voice, and that was all the reproach which she offered.

The longer you consider Ann Edwards's comment, the more admirable you must think it.

One tendency shows itself in this latest novel by Miss Wilkins which should not pass without mention, and which must be lamented by every reader who wishes well to the literary art. The book, as may be guessed even from this brief synopsis of its plot, is a weak attempt to question the present economic system. It sets off the wickedness or selfishness of the rich against the virtue and helplessness of the poor after the manner of the sentimental socialist. A brief literary criticism is hardly the place to treat of economics, but one may pause to remark how odd it is that the novelist, since his business is particularly the study of human nature, and his capital a knowledge of it, should not perceive that the economic trouble lies, not in the present system of property, but in human nature itself.

Review of
Silence, and Other Stories

BOOKMAN

To describe Miss Wilkins' stories we borrow Miss Wilkins' phrase: they are "full of a grave and delicate stateliness." Their manner recalls that of some of her earliest and most excellent work—such as "A Far-Away Melody," and its companions—but shows, to our thinking, a distinct increase in power. They are not the kind of tales to be rushed through at breathless speed. They deserve and repay careful reading. The descriptions have a firm and cameo-like clearness. There is not a word of exaggeration, not a word out of place. They bear reading over and over again. The pathos is deep and tender, the more affecting because of the noble restraint of language. The writer does not throw herself and her whole stock of emotions at the reader's head. She gives an impression all through of reserve force. There are passages of quaint and touching humour, too, here and there—concerning Persis, for example, whose "very soul flagged" over the task of reproducing a landscape in cross-stitch, till at last an impious wish leaped up in her docile heart.

" 'I wish,' said Persis, quite out loud to herself when she was all alone in the front room—'I wish the trees had never been made, nor the roses, nor the river, nor the sky; then I shouldn't have had to work them.' Then she fairly trembled at her wickedness, and counted the stitches in a corner of the sky with renewed zeal and faithfulness."

The stories are chiefly about women, and about women of a strong and true womanliness, with whom dignity was an instinct and affectation an impossibility. It is a pleasure to read such a book, and a pleasure to recommend it to others. Perhaps it will be most highly appreciated by those who have tried to write themselves. We would strongly advise literary aspirants to read it. It belongs to the class of work which is at once their delight and their despair.

Reprinted from *Bookman* (London) 14 (August 1898): 138.

Mary E. Wilkins Freeman

LAURENCE HUTTON

It must be nearly twenty years ago that I first read "A Humble Romance" in a Scottish weekly, where it had evidently been purloined from the American periodical in which it originally appeared. The predatory editor who seized upon it may be forgiven his offence in view of the excellent judgment he showed in catering to his readers. Nearly twenty years ago, and yet the impression made by that story remains as clear and strong as an actual experience—clearer and stronger, as a matter of fact, for the circumstances of the time live only in association with the focusing point of the story, and fade away into insignificance beside its vivid memory. I can still see Sally stooping over the kitchen sink washing the breakfast dishes when the ringing knock came to the door and the tin pedler appeared. I can feel the thrill of Sally's tremulous response to the rough but skillful wooing of her first lover; I see her pride in him and her piteous fear as she is driven in the cart through the woods to Derby town; her determination to buy her wedding dress out of her scant savings; the wedding, the short honeymoon on the roads with the pedling cart, and the wrench that morning when Sally awoke and found her husband gone. Then the pathos of her simple faith in Jake, and the long waiting—"He told me to bear up, and I said I would bear up"—and the golden dawn of that morning in June three years later when the poor lonely pilgrim of love, driving through her old Arcadian solitudes, found her beloved swain, and she was crying in his arms: "Jake, I did—bear up—I did." It was some years later before the reader of that story came to know that the author had since then become famous through her short stories. It is difficult for a younger generation that has since sprung up to realize the widespread stir and excitement that these early stories of Mrs. Wilkins Freeman's caused throughout the country. She has so long been before the public as an author of established reputation that we have grown accustomed to her high estate in the world of letters, and her work is accepted as a matter of course. But she has placed herself in the strong citadel of a people's esteem and affection; her work in the past is held in grateful remembrance, and is a guarantee of good faith in her work of the future.

One other incident that I remember happened shortly after the publication of *Pembroke* in 1894. It was during Conan Doyle's visit to this country.

Reprinted from *Harper's Weekly Magazine* 47 (21 November 1903): 1879–80.

One day I heard him in the precincts of a club holding forth excitedly on the work of Miss Wilkins with the enthusiasm of one who has made a discovery and must tell it to the world. He had just read *Pembroke*. His admiration for her previous work was unbounded, but "this novel," he said, "is the greatest piece of American fiction since *The Scarlet Letter.*" I have found his opinion shared by other eminent critics since then, and in England especially is her name heard most frequently in connection with Hawthorne's.

I have mentioned these two incidents with good reason. The most remarkable quality about Mrs. Wilkins Freeman's stories is their indelibility, even to the minutest details. Years after you have read a story of hers, it will suddenly come back to you like a living thing, with the recollection of its pathetic incongruity and poignant humor. The absolute sense of truth and the self-unconsciousness of the artist are more strikingly evinced in her handling of character and circumstance than in any other of our short story writers since Hawthorne. It seems a supererogation to say aught in praise of her work now, but we are apt to take our literary benefactors so much for granted that we fail to realize their greatness, and fall short of that lively sense of appreciation which we accord the fresh and unaccustomed writer new to his laurels. Since "A Humble Romance" was written, other authors have come and gone, some have stayed, and will stay with honorable excellence, but to none do we owe so much during these years for that distinction and honor which upholds our literary ideals as to the name of Mary E. Wilkins.

It is seldom that an author who has excelled in the short story has shown equal power and mastery in the novel. Mrs. Wilkins Freeman has not always succeeded in maintaining the same high level of excellence in longer fiction, calling for sustained power and range and imaginative scope, as in her shorter pieces, but her stories, long or short, are always of absorbing human interest, and impregnated with a genuine human sympathy and insight. Two of her novels at least, *Pembroke* and *The Portion of Labor,* will live with the best New England fiction, and rank among the few memorable novels in American literature. Only one who has followed her work with careful interest can appreciate the steady growth of her powers, and their fine, full, strong expression in *The Portion of Labor.* Always simple and restrained, calmly benignant in tragedy or comedy, her feeling in this novel goes deeper and is more moving; her wisdom is nobler; her thought and style more refined and richer in quality. It is a drama of the people and lies very close to the soil. Yet in nowise is Mrs. Wilkins Freeman's imaginative power so strikingly demonstrated as in the noble play of sympathy and creative insight which takes this portion of the working-man's life, and lifts it from out the commonplace view on to a plane of understanding and nobility. The old reverence, the full, clear direct gaze on life, the fearless art, the delicacy, the poignancy, the humor, are there, but with a graver touch of majesty to the seriousness, and with a lighter touch of wit to the humor.

Review of
The Portion of Labor

Octave Thanet

It cannot be said that Miss Wilkins approaches her tremendous problem
lightly. Indeed—if one may risk a criticism which is more qualified than it
seems—she is so reverend she becomes timid; at times she gives the impression
of being afraid of her subject. However, timidity is so much preferable to the
all-knowing poses of some great artists that it seems almost unfair to prefer it as
a charge instead of a plea for merit. And in parts that direct, full, clear gaze
which has always been Mary Wilkins's most marvellous gift is turned on the
people and the life of her book; and they are described with illuminating power.

The tragic figure of Norman Loyd's [*sic*] wife is in Miss Wilkins's best
manner. It wrings the heart, and it is as true as death and heroism. The hero
himself is a fine, strong, natural, good fellow. Ellen is charming; a flowering
arbutus lifting its exquisite beauty (which seems so fragile and is of so hardy a
fibre) out of such meagre and chilly soil. And yet with all her charm, with all
the delicacy and the detail of her drawing, Ellen is not quite convincing. She
may have been, we think, not she *must* have been, like poor, limp, officious
Fanny and the violent Eva Loud. And powerful as are the pictures of the shoe
workers' life and the factory, grimly true and indescribably pathetic for that
truth, drawn with masterful strokes, *they* show only one side of the
problem—the workers'. We are taken inside their souls, but we have only an
outside (and not even a near outside) view of Norman Loyd. It may also be
conceded that it is a bit begging the question to extricate the fortunes of the
Brewsters by so time-worn a device as a beautiful girl's marriage; but *is* it?
Has it not another aspect as showing the vital quality of a democracy where
such a marriage can occur and not bring the social heavens down on the
audacious lovers? Is it not the most natural fate for a girl whose attraction is
spiritual and mental even more than physical; who seems, indeed, to have a
genius for attracting, to win love in her real, not her apparent, rank? She is a
lofty and delicate soul, so lofty and delicate and beautiful that she honors the
man of her choice beyond his deserts, be his pomp of living what it may.

And after we have emptied the quiver of our doubts and misgivings—
after we admit this is only a corner of a vast and dismal question, which is

Reprinted from *Book Buyer* 23 (December 1901): 379–80.

shown; after we agree that she gives us only the workers' statement of the question, not any answer even of hope—what then? Does it not remain, like every work of true and reverend art, a light in the darkness! The soul of the New England "shoe hand" is laid bare. That in itself is enough. It is great. It is terrible. It has a quality of reasonable and sober hope in its melancholy. The New England shoemaker in the factories, for all his discontent, is a right man. He lives in comfort. He has meat three times a day, and spends a great deal of money making his little parlor a shocking offence to taste; he can put money into a gold mine, and give his daughter a graduating present of a watch and chain. He is, to the bargain, generous, unselfish, fiercely independent, and cruelly honest. Conditions which allow such a man may be faulty, but they are neither degrading nor hopeless. They are infinitely better than the conditions, for instance, of Kingsley's mill operatives in "Alton Locke." The American-born workman's discontent comes out of the envy of a wider vision, not out of failing fortunes and oppression. Because he gets better wages and is better educated and has better ways of living than before, he is able to realize more keenly how much (which he sees others have) *he* lacks. He is more helpless, and needs more. Scan the talk of the "hands" when Loyd shuts down. They do not know how to retrench to the Continental standard. Of course the improvidence of their class appears; and the rank ignorance of the facts of industrial life, and the crazy visionary has his full share of the stage with his real New England logical elaboration of details to an impossible scheme; but what is most impressive? Is it not the chance brains have in the fight, coupled with the inadequacy of mere manual dexterity?

The Irish foreman "gets on," Brewster falls in the march. The Irish foreman, by the way, is deliciously done. So is the grandmother with her queer pride of station and her management of her pittance, and her conviction of the importance of the Brewsters. Of course there is a pair of ineffectual lovers—that goes without saying. A futile and self-destroying love affair seems as common as the east wind in New England villages. Risley, the lover, however, is a more amiable and engaging person than most of Miss Wilkins's patient but self-willed wooers who will not marry their sweethearts, neither will they leave them.

One observes in the novel the steady enriching and refining of Miss Wilkins's style. It has become statuesque as well as simple. She was always wise; now she is often witty. One could quote a score of epigrams. This one is of a poignant shrewdness: "Barriers of tragedy are nothing to those of comedy."

Some of the workers' barriers are of comedy, but there are plenty of tragedy, and the elderly workers' life grows more steadily tragic. Miss Wilkins has done nothing in this, her finest and strongest work, finer and stronger than her self-restrained and delicate but most pathetic portrayal of this part of the workingman's life, the time when his employers eye him askance for his gray hairs, the day when brains are at their best but the hand begins to falter.

Review of
The Givers

BOOKMAN

Mrs. Wilkins Freeman has a quality of allurement which is peculiarly her own. It is difficult to define, for other American writers have an equally finished simplicity of style. The author of "The Givers" adds to it an emotional power, a refined and subtle homeliness of affection which give grace to everything she touches. It is perhaps to a great extent her liking for simple-minded and plainly living men and women which attracts us, but it is even more the quiet intensity she flings into keeping anything uncomely or excessively violent out of her novels. To write of human creatures and not sooner or later introduce both sin and the sinner is practically impossible. But Mrs. Freeman deals with them as little as she can, seeming to be constantly arrested by gracious and touching personalities. When she does have to admit some black sheep into the fold, it is obviously painful for her to recognise absolute and genuine blackness, and they fade to a disarming greyness before one's eyes. In "The Givers," however, we have very few black sheep to deal with, but instead several of the elderly spinster ladies whom the writer represents with such comprehending tenderness. "The Reign of the Doll" is an almost perfect little study of two sisters, and the pathetic desire inherent in all women to love something, however unresponsive. "The Givers," which is the first of the series, is less sweet, but the touch of irony running through it adds a life-like element to the quaint scenes in the bare parlour of Sophia Lane's poverty-stricken dwelling. The book is essentially one to keep, because in its tranquillity and kindliness the feelings are never harrowed. Many novels actually more brilliant are impossible to read a second time. Mrs. Wilkins Freeman's would be a renewed pleasure on every fresh occasion.

Reprinted from *Bookman* (London) 26 (September 1904): 215.

Reviews of
The Debtor

PUBLIC OPINION

"AN UNPLEASANT MASTERPIECE"

Detachment—inexorable, unsmiling detachment from her characters and their actions—that is the keynote of Mrs. Freeman's work. Like a conscientious mother, she will have no favorites among her children, but sits critically watching them play about her house, never interfering in their quarrels or their joys. Somehow one gets the impression that she is merciless, like George Eliot, Mrs. Humphrey Ward, or Mrs. Wharton. Good company to be in, indeed; and one cannot class her elsewhere. The book here noticed is the story of a southerner transplanted north, forced by the rascality of another to live by his wits, and finally driven to that very last resort of a southern gentleman, Negro characterization in a New York music hall. Captain Arthur Carroll, of Kentucky, left with but one valuable asset out of his father's war-wrecked estate, a coal-mine, is cheated out of it by a shrewder man, after he has married and begotten children. He retaliates on the society which has fleeced him by fraudulent promoting of bubble companies and stocks. With his gentle wife, two winsome, sweet helpless daughters, and a sister, he settles in Banbridge, which the reader will easily recognize as any small New Jersey suburb of New York.

The book consists of nothing but the gradual revelation of the family's condition—hopeless, increasing debt, even starvation peeping around the arras. One can fancy a young literary aspirant reading this story and then giving up his purpose in despair at Mrs. Freeeman's unapproachable mastery of her method. The people are not attractive—how can we believe them so when the author has not a particle of sympathy for them? The subject itself is dreary—a hopeless struggle with debt. To pay the expense of his daughter's wedding, Carroll tries the music-hall turn, and after his daughter's presence alone has saved him from suicide, after he has gone through the spiritual furnace which burns away the dross of character, he brings himself at last to the vaudeville stage.

So much for the story; not worth telling in its bare outlines, it is made

Reviews of *The Debtor* reprinted from *Public Opinion* 40 (17 February 1906): 217; *Independent* 59 (7 December 1905): 1340.

into a masterpiece of Mrs. Freeman's method. It would be immensely more effective told as a series of short stories. It is worth reading, for people who care for that sort of thing. To make novel-reading an intellectual exercise nowadays—that is a feat, nothing less; but stories without humor or sympathy, stories in which all the loveable people are weak and all the strong characters unpleasant, can never be redeemed by any skill of method, even though it amount to genius, as in Mrs. Freeman's case.

THE INDEPENDENT

If any one would study the difference between the work of an author who adjusts himself obsequiously to his readers' lack of artistic sensibility, and one who considers simply and sincerely the business of interpreting certain types in a given situation, regardless of the popular demand for vaudeville features, he will find a remarkable example of the latter literary virtue in Mary E. Wilkins Freeman's new novel. It contains all the material out of which a sensational story might have been written, but she has kept her conception sane and true to life.

The elements of good and evil in the world are always the same. And in real men and women they show thru with a certain kind of temperance. We are hedged about with so many decencies that evil never can take entire, open possession of a man: and we are limited by so many native frailties that nobody gets to be perfectly righteous. But we know how it is in fiction. The villain is a character created expressly to be bad and to do wrong. All the author's faculties are engaged to produce a consistently evil mind. Such people rarely exist. No one has the magnificent power of concentration to hold steadily to the diabolical formula. And that which impresses the thoughtful reader of this novel is the fact that the Debtor is a villain working against the better nature which is in us all.

The exigencies of the story require that he act out virtue on the sly with a melodramatic flourish, but in the main it is a veracious interpretation of a man who is of average moral stamina but who handicaps himself along the way with a desire for revenge upon his enemy, with extravagant habits and with a grace at swindling which is fascinating. He had the "promoter's" temperament. He was courteous and magnetic by nature, and he had the power of inspiring confidence where another might excite suspicion. Now these are the elements of character and disposition which insure the success of good men. And come to think of it, good and bad men who succeed along their respective lines are endowed exactly alike. The difference is in which handle they take hold of in turning their wheel of life.

This truth is expressed or implied by the various men and women in the story. Some of the women hold aloof, daintily irresponsible to the last. And nothing is truer to life than their attitude. In every community these passing phases of incoherent femininity are to be found, women who are identified by their manners and clothes rather than by their morals or lack of morals. And, as is the case in this story, they are often the most unscrupulous people in it when it is a simple, savage matter of self preservation.

Other characters in the story are attractive and familiar. This is why each chapter is so peacefully interesting that we are in no hurry for the sequel, just as we are not morbidly curious to know the ultimate fate of the people with whom we associate from day to day. The love story flows in naturally, like the sun which fills in the dark places of the world with warmth and light. No better book of the honest, old fashioned kind has appeared this year.

Review of
"Doc" Gordon

THE SATURDAY REVIEW OF
POLITICS, LITERATURE, SCIENCE, AND ART

Miss Wilkins' delicate talent is incongruous with the wildness of her plot. She asks us to believe that, in order to save his sister's child from her wicked father, Dr. Gordon (a sane man) would all through her life pass off his own wife as another of his sisters. (We cannot help these complex relationships.) The end of the wicked brother-in-law is not unimpressive, but we feel that the character-sketches of rural New England are better stuff than the framework of the story. There is an unnecessarily harrowing discussion on the ethics of giving morphia to a tortured invalid whom it is sure to kill, and the solution of this particular question is a sharp anti-climax. Altogether, we look back regretfully to the middle-aged lovers and the engaging pet cats of the author's earlier stories.

Reprinted from *Saturday Review of Politics, Literature, Science, and Art* 103 (April 1907): 498.

Review of
By the Light of the Soul

THE ATLANTIC MONTHLY

I do not see how anyone can be greatly drawn to Mrs. Wilkins Freeman's latest novel, *By the Light of the Soul*. It seems to me to exemplify all that the temperamental novel should not be. One stands almost dazed by so gratuitously painful a plot: the futility of it, its barrenness of spiritual meanings. To be sure, everything might really have happened that way; each of the crucial events is very carefully protected. Maria Edgham, hyperaesthetic, self-conscious, forced by circumstances to be at odds with the world in which she lived and in which her girlhood was just beginning to blossom, might have been suddenly bound in a secret and merely nominal marriage with a boy under twenty, through the clumsy misunderstanding of a city parson; and if she had been, no doubt her life would have been shipwrecked much in the way Mrs. Freeman describes; yes, and the ultimate solution of it might have been Maria's deliberate disappearance from the scene under cover of pretended suicide, so that her younger sister might marry the liberated husband; but this seems a needlessly perverse and uninstructive complication. Suppose—and suppose—and suppose—what would have happened then? The conditions are too fantastic to have any important bearings, despite the author's endeavor to make the situation illuminate the meaning of sacrifice. It is useless to speak in this connection of Mrs. Freeman's gifts,—of the direct and uncompromising way in which she present her characters, of her impatience with mediocrity, of the stinging satire which she occasionally uses so effectively,—the pity is that she should not have put her ability to a more profitable employment.

Reprinted from *Atlantic Monthly* 100 (July 1907): 132–33.

Reviews of
The Shoulders of Atlas

THE ATHENAEUM

The new and deeper note of sin and mystery which Mrs. Wilkins Freeman strikes in her latest story militates against the atmosphere of old-world fragrance which is the special charm of her New England tales. The mysteries—for there are several, and they have no connexion with each other—are never satisfactorily solved—Sylvia Whitman, the middle-aged strenuous woman, with her yearning love for her husband and her young cousin Rose Fletcher, and her constitutional incapacity for being happy, is a striking figure, and one of those which the author delights to draw. Her husband, with a cherished grievance, which his wife's late-inherited legacy inconsiderately removes, is another excellent study of New England temperament. In Lucy Ayres, the girl who is "man-crazy," a painful element is introduced, but handled with infinite tenderness and sympathy. The burdens imposed upon the people of East Westland are, since the majority are self-made, scarcely to be compared to those of Atlas, and we cannot wholly forgive Mrs. Wilkins Freeman for allowing a sinister taint of mystery to rest upon so charming a heroine as Rose. This note of mystery is forced throughout, but none the less the book is full of human interest.

THE NATION

In the Aunt Sylvia of this tale Mrs. Freeman has produced another of her little masterpieces of New England portraiture. Sylvia and her mate are a grim, pathetic pair, troubled in their old age about many things, and about each other as much as anything. The story-teller, as usual, disdains to put a gloss upon their homeliness, their mental angularity, their reticence, their underlying emotional intensity. Henry's cherished grievance, Sylvia's almost savage fidelity to the course she has laid down for herself—of such tough

Reviews of *The Shoulders of Atlas* reprinted from *Athenaeum* 51 (11 July 1908): 38; *Nation* 87 (9 July 1908): 35–36.

strands the web of New England action is really woven. As long as Henry works in his shoe-shop and battles with his debts, he is reasonably contented with his grudge against the world. Solvency and a competency, depriving him of both work and grudge, make life a weary thing. As for Sylvia, she succumbs to a major temptation with the embittered thoroughness of her unco guid species. "Sylvia had the New England conscience, but, like all New England consciences, it was susceptible of hard twists to bring it into accordance with New England will." And the will is capable of altogether overbearing the conscience—for a time; for Sylvia's conscience inevitably triumphs, and her atonement is as thoroughgoing as the occasion deserves. The detail of her, the form and gesture and speech, are inimitable. A certain Miss Hart is suspected of poisoning a lodger:

> "Arsenic in the peppermint!" repeated Sylvia. "You needn't tell me Lucinda Hart put poison in the peppermint, though I dare say she has some in the house to kill rats. It's likely that old tavern was overrun with them, and I know she lost her cat a few weeks ago. She told me so herself. He was shot when he was out hunting. Lucinda thought somebody mistook him for a skunk. She felt real bad about it. I feel kind of guilty myself. I can't help thinking if I'd just looked round and then hunted up a kitten for poor Lucinda, she never would have had any need to keep rat poison, and nobody would have suspected her of such an awful thing. I suppose Albion Bennett right up and told she'd bought it, first thing."

This has the true ring of rustic comedy: Mrs. Freeman is, as usual, less successful with her urban characters. The Rose who arrives to trouble the conscience of Sylvia is an unreal person, an old jumble of the country maid and the woman of the world as seen in novels. She tries to borrow a lady's maid on her arrival at East Westland, and asks her astonished hostess if people are "formal" in that quiet village. For a time she is all upon the high horse, then suddenly lapses from her society lingo to such comfortable rural colloquialism as "You don't suppose he's taken suddenly insane or anything?" Her amour with the local high school principal is of very moderate interest; not so the daring and appallingly realistic study of the girl Lucy; a common type ignored by convention. Upon her frail shoulders the Atlantean burden of humanity assumes a peculiarly distressing form.

Review of
The Winning Lady and Others

THE NATION

This is altogether the best collection of short stories that Mrs. Freeman has published. It marks a definite return to her original theme and manner, with such development of both as time should naturally have brought. Her experiments in other fields, if they have seemed in themselves of comparatively little value, have no doubt served their disciplinary purpose. At all events, in these studies of rural New England character, her hand seems firmer than ever.

If it were not for her comparative indifference to the out-of-door setting, she would strike us as very closely comparable to Mr. Phillpotts. The grimly humorous aspects of rustic life have a similar attraction for her; and when she gives herself up to the pursuit of humor, she is equally likely to fall into the commonplace. "Billy and Susy," the story of a pair of cats who are quarreled over by two New England sisters on the ground of their supposed difference of sex, and who prove to be "both Susys," is the one story in the present volume which we could have done just as well without. The plot is not new, and the handling is rather clumsily farcical. In "The Selfishness of Amelia Lamkin" and "Old Woman Magoun," on the other hand, the writer is on her own ground. Amelia Lamkin is another case of over-developed "New England conscience"—a self-effacing type to be found on any Yankee countryside; while Old Woman Magoun is of a type hardly less common and not less difficult to portray—the Roman mother who stands ready to slay that which she loves for its soul's welfare. These are the pathetic or sombre aspects which Miss Wilkins was from the first most successful in presenting. The new thing in her—or the newer thing—is a vein of tender and unstrained sentiment which here yields a really beautiful study of what we rudely call "calf-love." "The Joy of Youth" represents the achievement of the writer who, because he is so faithful to the soil and the human beings he knows, succeeds now and then in creating something that the whole world must recognize as its own. So what in a narrow sense seems most provincial—a sketch of La Mancha, of Simla, or of Thrums—will turn out to be of more general appeal than all the vague and pretentious fictions that spring up year by year—whose scene is Everywhere, and whose theme is Everything.

Reprinted from *Nation* 90 (13 January 1910): 36–37.

The New England of Mary E. Wilkins

EDWIN FRANCIS EDGETT

Anyone who is inclined to think that the lapse of time from one generation to another, or the transition from one century to another, will throw into utter oblivion the literary best of its period is very much mistaken. The times may change, but we do not always or necessarily change with them. New modes, new methods, new forms, inevitably arouse an interest in those of an earlier day, it may be far away from our own time, or it may be near. A reading of an O. Henry, an Octavus Roy Cohen, and Edith Wharton, may, for instance, bring to mind and may cause us to turn to their immediate predecessors in the mastery of the short story. They are no better because they are of today.

Back in the late eighties, a young short story teller leaped suddenly into prominence. Miss Wilkins had predecessors, notably Sarah Orne Jewett, in the realistic and sympathetic depiction of the New England scene and character, but there was a new manner and a new touch in her writing. Her style was the simplest of the simple; her tales were of commonplace people and commonplace events, but there was nothing in them of the commonplace. Their scene was an inevitable part of their lives. They were literal transcriptions of what she herself had seen. She wrote with little pretence of art, but the art was there just as there is art in the work of the average photographer who calls the sun to his aid and asks that it tell nothing more than the truth. Back of Miss Wilkins's stories was the absolute truth. Sometimes it was agreeable, sometimes it was unpleasant, but always it was a perfect portrayal of the every day lives of these people whose world was bounded by the limits of a more or less secluded village life.

From year to year, Miss Wilkins wrote these short stories, until they have reached, if we may depend upon the accurate count of a tireless bibliographer, two hundred and twenty-seven in number. Their writing extends over a period of more than thirty years, from 1886 to 1918. The greater number of them came before the first year of the twentieth century, and in the midst of her work on them, Miss Wilkins also found time to write about a dozen novels, some verses, and a play. They have never lost their vitality or their simplicity, but it is safe to say that the best of her short stories are to be found in the magazine pages of the eighties and the nineties, and in the

Reprinted from *Boston Evening Transcript,* 19 March 1927, book section, 2.

earlier volumes into which they were gathered. But never is there absent from them anywhere that delicate, that sincere touch, which brought Miss Wilkins her first reputation.

The twenty-five tales selected by Mr. Lanier for his volume which he entitles *The Best Short Stories of Mary E. Wilkins* may be found scattered through her many volumes, from the first to the latest. The word best is a relative term, and much depends upon the personal taste as well as the judgment of the editor who uses it. Therefore we need have no quarrel with Mr. Lanier about his selective skill. He has chosen twenty-five excellent stories that are fully representative of Miss Wilkins's talent. Anyone else would of course have made a different selection, but it would not necessarily be a better selection. Any twenty-five of her stories chosen by anybody would do her full justice. Every one of these stories may be read with complete satisfaction, mingled with a certain amount of regret that she is now practically silent. The amazing thing is that the literary material about such a restricted district and lives seems to be unlimited.

It was to be expected that "A Humble Romance," "The Revolt of Mother," "A New England Nun" and "A Village Singer" would be included in this collection. They are the most characteristic, if not necessarily the best, examples of Miss Wilkins's vision of the New England way of life and thought and deed. The omission of "A Village Lear" is to be regretted, not only for itself, but because of its contrast with Turgenieff's Russian version of the same theme which is called in English "A Lear of the Steppes," a contrast which reveals the wide difference between the Slavic and the Anglo-Saxon temperament and the literary methods of expressing that temperament in fiction. We miss that story, however, but we cannot expect Mr. Lanier to offer us everything we want in what is only a comparatively small number of Miss Wilkins's stories.

All of the biographical material given by Mr. Lanier in his introduction is interesting and enlightening. Her early years were passed, partly in Massachusetts and partly in Vermont, in the midst of those people and scenes she has made the basis of her fiction, a fiction that is essentially fact as a whole and in practically all its details. She knows thoroughly the people of whom she writes, as Dickens knew his Londoners, Hardy his folk of Wessex, and Hamlin Garland his Middle Westerners. Her first ambition was to be a painter, and that aspiration coming to naught, she turned to the writing of verses, wherefrom she obtained much praise and a small amount of money. Her early verses, some of which were published in book form, today sell better, she says, than any of her books of stories. For her first story for grown-up people—she had been writing tales for young folks for that bygone juvenile magazine known as *Wide-Awake*— she received a fifty dollar prize. It was entitled "The Shadow Family," and it was, she says, "a poor imitation of Dickens." Then with the acceptance by Miss Booth of "Two Old Lovers," for which she received a twenty-five dollar check, and its appearance in

Harper's Bazar, she was over the threshold of her career. "After that very little was returned," she says. " 'A Humble Romance' was taken by Mr. Alden for *Harper's;* afterward he published my first novel, *Jane Field,* as a serial. I could not readily abandon my desire to be an artist. With a portion of that twenty-five dollars I bought paints, and started in to paint. I found I could mix colors but could not paint, and had sense enough to relinquish art." It was fortunate that she had that common sense. Her field of art lay elsewhere than in pictures on canvas.

It is decidedly unexpected to learn that so far away a critic as Arthur Machen has found pleasure in Miss Wilkins's work. His attitude and comment upon her is summarized by Mr. Lanier:

> He lays down, first, the measuring rod of ecstacy—"rapture, beauty, adoration, wonder, awe, mystery, sense of the unknown, desire for the unknown"; "if ecstacy be present, then I say there is fine literature"; and, after eliminating Thackeray, Jane Austen and Stevenson by this test, and placing at the summit *Pickwick, Don Quixote,* and *Pantagruel*—he finds Miss Wilkins almost unique among contemporaries. Not only are the tales "delightful," but he points out (with T. P. O'Connor) that there is no incongruity in finding "ecstacy" in these life episodes of reserved folk, for "passion does come through the reserve, and occasionally in the most volcanic manner." Also he discerns a remoteness and isolation of soul, each human being living a life of his or her own—strong, full of character, tense with feeling, however restrained, and "literature proceeds" from this lonely reverie and ecstacy.

We may or may not agree with Mr. Machen's theories, but we may praise him for his insight into Miss Wilkins's art.

Many phases of these stories might be emphasized. Miss Wilkins's keen sense of humor is too often overlooked, and so also is its frequent intermingling with pathos. In "The Revolt of Mother," forty years of suppression and repression under the marital yoke lead up to the final action that makes the story. At last, when a large and comfortable barn had been built on the very site where was to have been placed the house her husband had promised, she took matters into her own hands. During Adoniram's temporary absence, she moved herself, her children and their entire household belongings into the barn. He returned to find himself conquered, he who had always been the conqueror. "Adoniram was like a fortress whose walls had no active resistance, and went down the instant the right besieging tools were used. 'Why mother,' he said, hoarsely, 'I hadn't no idee you was so set on't as all this comes to.' " What better example of the New England character in word and deed can be found than this? Once in a while we get a story of pure comedy, such as "Billy and Susy," once in a while another all tragedy, such as "Old Woman Magoun," but frequently a mingling of the two, as in "A New England Prophet."

Anyone who doubts that the soul of a people may be found in fiction need only read these, or any other, stories by Miss Wilkins. Many a historian who has turned over numberless books in order to discover, to chronicle and expound New England, and to extract the essence of New England character, has achieved much less than has Miss Wilkins. With her, fiction and fact become one.

TWO ESSAYS BY
MARY WILKINS FREEMAN

♦

An Autobiography

MARY E. WILKINS FREEMAN

I am assuming that the various details relating to my life have appeared often enough already, and that it is unnecessary to repeat them. Bald facts are not especially interesting, and one cannot offer much besides bald facts unless one happens to be of the Mary MacLane type of writer.

It occurs to me that I have never read a severe criticism of an author's own work by the author, and that it may be an innovation. I am therefore proceeding to criticise the story by which I consider myself lamentably best known, and that is The Revolt of Mother. It was in an evil day I wrote that tale. It exposed me to much of which I could not dream. This very morning I have a letter concerning that story. Somebody wishes to use it in a book. I fear I am mostly known by The Revolt of Mother. My revolt against the case is perfectly useless. People go right on with almost Prussian dogmatism, insisting that The Revolt of Mother is my one and only work. It is most emphatically not. Were I not so truthful, having been born so near Plymouth Rock, I would deny I ever wrote that story. I would foist it upon somebody else. It would leave me with a sense of freedom I have not known since that woman moved into her husband's barn in print.

In the first place all fiction ought to be true, and The Revolt of Mother is not in the least true. When I wrote that little tale I threw my New England traditions to the winds and trampled on my New England conscience. Well, I have had and still have retribution. It is not a good thing to produce fiction which is not true, although that sounds paradoxical. The backbone of the best fiction is essential truth, and The Revolt of Mother is perfectly spineless. I know it, because I am of New England and have lived there. I had written many true things about that cluster of stainless states and for a change I lied.

Sometimes incessant truth gets on one's nerves. It did on mine. There never was in New England a woman like Mother. If there had been she most certainly would not have moved into the palatial barn which her husband had erected next to the mean little cottage she had occupied during her married life. She simply would have lacked the nerve. She would also have lacked the imagination. New England women of that period coincided with their hus-

Reprinted from "Who's Who and Why: Serious and Frivolous Facts about the Great and the Near-Great," *Saturday Evening Post*, 8 December 1917, 25, 75–78.

bands in thinking that sources of wealth should be better housed than consumers. That Mother would never have dreamed of putting herself ahead of Jersey cows which meant good money. Mother would have been to the full as thrifty as Father. If Mother had lived all those years in that little cottage she would have continued to live there. Moving into the new barn would have been a cataclysm. New England women seldom bring cataclysms about their shoulders.

If Mother had not been Mother, Father would never have been able to erect that barn. Instead there would have been bay-windows on that cottage, which would have ceased to be a cottage. Ambitious New England women do not like cottages. They wish for square rooms on the second floor. Women capable of moving into that barn would have had the cottage roof raised to insure good bedrooms. There would have been wide piazzas added to the house, and Father would simply not have dared mention that great barn to Mother. Father would have adored Mother, but held her in wholesome respect. She would have fixed his black tie on straightly of a Sunday morning and brushed his coat and fed him well, but she would have held the household reins. As a rule women in New England villages do hold the household reins, and with good reason. They really can drive better. Very little shying or balking when Mother drives. Father is self-distrustful, and with facts to back him, when it comes to managing the household.

Mother usually buys Father's clothes for him. He knows he would be cheated were he to attempt it. Besides, he is shy of chewing an end of fabric to test the color. Mother is valiant.

It is a dreadful confusion, but that woman called "Mother" in The Revolt of Mother is impossible. I sacrificed truth when I wrote the story, and at this day I do not know exactly what my price was. I am inclined to think gold of the realm. It could not have been fame of the sort I have gained by it. If so I have had my punishment. Not a story since but somebody asks "Why not another Revolt of Mother?" My literary career has been halted by the success of the big fib in that story. Too late I admit it. The harm is done. But I can at least warn other writers. When you write a short story stick to the truth. If there is not a story in the truth knit until truth happens which does contain a story. Knit, if you can do no better at that than I, who drop more stitches than any airplane in Europe can drop bombs. You can at least pull out the knitting, but a story printed and rampant is a dreadful thing, never to be undone.

Emily Brontë and *Wuthering Heights*

MARY E. WILKINS

It may possibly be considered as scarcely fair to characterize a writer of only one book as a great novelist, but after all, the proof of the labor lies not in the quantity but in the quality. Perhaps, going even farther, it lies not so much in achievement as in promise. There seems little doubt that had Emily Brontë lived, and had her genius been somewhat toned and crystallized, she might have surpassed her great sister, Charlotte. There are certainly forces at work in *Wuthering Heights* beyond those in *Jane Eyre, The Professor, Villette,* and *Shirley.* While the book is offensive, even repulsive, it has the repulsiveness of power. Charlotte Brontë's books are unmistakably those of a woman—a woman fretting at and scorning the limitations of her sex and her day, yet in a measure yielding to them. But Emily fairly takes the bit between her teeth and overleaps the barriers, and yet with such an innocence of power and necessity as to make one lose sight of the unwontedness.

There is in *Wuthering Heights* the pitilessness of genius, not only toward the sensibilities of the reader, but toward those of the writer. All that Emily Brontë is intent upon is the truth, the exactness of the equations of her characters, not the impression which they make upon her readers or herself. She handles brutality and coarseness as another woman would handle a painted fan. It is enough for her that the thing is so. It is not her business if it comes down like a sledge-hammer upon the nerves of her audience, or even if it casts reflections derogatory to herself. She is an artist after the manner of the creator of the Laocoön. She uses the scalpel as unflinchingly as the brush. She displays naked nerve and muscle unshrinkingly, and has no thought for graceful curves of flesh to conceal them. Had she lived longer she might have become equally acquainted with the truth and power of grace; she might have widened her audience; she might have attracted, instead of repelled; but she could not have written a greater book, as far as the abstract quality of greatness goes. *Wuthering Heights* from first to last is an unflinching masterpiece. There is evident no quiver of feminine nerves in the mind or hand. The utter fearlessness of the witness of the truth is upon her. She hedges at nothing. She has no thought for her womanly frills. She clears walls at a bound. She mixes her colors not to please and allure, but because of the facts of creation.

Reprinted from *The World's Great Women Novelists* (Philadelphia: Book Lover's Library, 1901), 85–93.

Wuthering Heights is almost inconceivable, taken as the work of a woman, still more as the work of a woman living an isolated life in a country parsonage in the midst of barren moorlands. How she ever came to comprehend the primitive brutalities and passions, and the great truth of life which sanctifies them, is a mystery. The knowledge could not have come from any actual experience. The book is not the result of any personal stress. She had given to her a light for the hidden darkness of human nature, irrespective of her own emotions. A lamp was set to her feet in the beginning. If a girl of twenty-eight could write a novel like *Wuthering Heights,* no other conclusion is possible.

Taken as a love story there is nothing in fiction to compare with the savage, irresistible cleaving to one another of Heathcliff and Catherine. It is almost unearthly. Married although Catherine was, and her lover not her husband, one gets a strange sense of guiltiness from this unrestrained might of love. It is made evident as one of the great forces of life; it is beyond earthly consideration; it survives death. It does not deal with the social problem; it is beyond it. It is a fusion of two souls under a law as unchangeable and uncontrovertible as any law of chemistry. While one condemns, one admits the inevitable. One might as well think of questioning the resistless plunge of the rapids toward the brink of Niagara. It is difficult to recall a heroine who, loving a man other than her husband, gives one such a sense of innocence and stern purity. She seems almost to hold a sword against her own heart, even in that wild love scene a few hours before her death. Perhaps this is the principal touch in the book which betrays the woman writer. Perhaps only a maiden woman could portray a scene of such passion and innocence. Perhaps only a woman could have in her brain the conception of such forces and not make them a part of her own life.

We all know the story of those Brontë sisters—the life of those gifted souls in that lonely parsonage in Yorkshire, their spurring one another to further effort—but our wonder as to them never grows less. In these days we say that knowledge of the world, and contact with those who best represent the tendency of the times and its progress, are necessary to success in any work of art. We mention this man or that as coming closely in contact with the true spirit of his day and generation, in most cases seeming to gain his power by unlimited opportunities for knowledge. All the gates of humanity have been unbarred to him. In this time of ready transit and contact, there are for a man few obstacles which he cannot overcome in the way of knowledge of his kind; it is still somewhat different for a woman. But the Brontës wrote over half a century ago, and they were women hedged about with great spaces of loneliness and insuperable barriers of religion, in an isolated parsonage with more of the dead than the living for neighbors. How did they gain this knowledge?

The *how* is very pronounced in the case of both Charlotte and Anne Brontë, perhaps still more in the case of Emily. How this girl knew the truths, the savage but undeniable truths which she had never been taught, the strength of the passions which she had never known and which she would doubtless have held as a shame to her maiden soul, is the question. Who taught her to strike nails on the head as with the hammer of Thor? It seems a case of downright subjective genius utterly removed from any question of personal experience or outside influence. Even granting that there had come within her observation some such savage and primeval characters as those in *Wuthering Heights,* how did she know how to develop them, and without a flaw in her premises? Her two and two always make four. There is never a slip. We condemn her characters, yet we acknowledge them and their might of personality.

Moreover, all the time we feel that we have to do with them, not with Emily Brontë. The personality of the author is entirely in the background, so entirely that it seems almost an impossiblity to dwell upon it, even to think of it without tearing down, as it were, the wall of imperishable work which she has placed before herself. In *Wuthering Heights* we have to deal with Heathcliff and Catherine, and Isabella and Earnshaw, not with the woman who put their histories upon paper. She wrote about them, that was all. She was not in the least responsible for their wild rebellion and revolt against the existing order of things. She saw these souls revolving unto death in a whirlpool of primitive emotion, and she depicted them, not omitting one oath or one shade of savagery and horror. It is like a great battlefield described by one posted on some calm tower of observation, with a soul so far removed from selfish emotions that it shrinks at nothing. What was it to Emily Brontë if her heroines were beaten, so they *were* beaten? One cannot imagine her weeping over that sad cut in the luckless Isabella's fair neck, though after all she may have wept. It is never safe to judge an artist by his work. He may write with ice or fire, and none but himself know; but *Wuthering Heights* gives the impression of impersonality on the part of the author, if ever a book did. It is far different in that respect from Charlotte Brontë's work. There is the nervous throb of a woman's heart through *Jane Eyre* and *Shirley,* but in *Wuthering Heights,* if the throb be there we do not feel it.

Wuthering Heights is the one novel of a woman, dead over half a century, and it is a book which offends and repels, but for all that it is the great work of a great woman novelist.

ESSAYS

◆

Mary Wilkins Freeman:
One Hundred Years of Criticism

MARY R. REICHARDT

Despite the hundred years and the changes in literary style and criticism that have distanced us from her earliest (and many contend her best) published works, Mary Wilkins Freeman remains an anomaly in the American literary tradition: no one quite knows where or even if she fits in. Over the years, various aspects of her work have been seized upon by sympathetic and unsympathetic critics alike, each with an eye towards fitting her into his or her own critical bias or into the popular critical mode of the time. Freeman's early success with her rural New England subjects in such volumes as *A Humble Romance and Other Stories* (1887) and *A New England Nun and Other Stories* (1891) was much a product of the literary climate of her time and place; she remained a popular author when she continued to capitalize on her public's demand for more of the same. Her many experiments in different modes—her plays, for example, or her novels concerning urban or political issues—were considered "deviations" by her reviewers, who tolerated them but complained nevertheless: they accused her of abdicating her single area of mastery. Having molded her in one particular way, then, her reading public refused to allow her to change.

Yet between 1887 and 1914 the social and cultural atmosphere around Freeman was rapidly and radically changing. Rural New England, "female" homey and domestic ideals, the Calvinistic conscience: these subjects were passé—naive—in the mental and moral upheaval surrounding World War I. New and exciting were the daring and decidedly masculine fictions of Dreiser, Crane, and Norris. In fact, the social climate in general in the period just before and after the First World War included a sharp reaction against America's legacy of Victorian feminine values. Social Darwinism, Muscular Christianity, and Teddy Roosevelt's "big stick" policy all were influences on or manifestations of a period which led what Ann Douglas in *The Feminization of American Culture* has called a "militant crusade for masculinity" (397).

In literature, the new naturalism's emphasis on determinism, force, and free expression of the "baser" human instincts reduced to mockery Howell's "smiling aspects of life," now scorned as indicative of a weak and overly-

Reprinted, with permission, from *Legacy: A Journal of Nineteenth-Century American Women Writers* 4 (Fall 1987): 31–44.

genteelized America. "Observe the condition in which we are now," Van Wyck Brooks wrote in 1934. "Sultry, flaccid, hesitant, not knowing what we want. . . . [We] stand in mortal fear of letting loose the spiritual appetites that impede our pursuit of a neat, hygenic and sterile success" (*Three Essays* 169). Likewise, Malcolm Cowley's 1936 *After the Genteel Tradition* condemned writers in the Howellsian tradition as timid, "false and life-denying" and applauded the current "bold and passionate" young generation of writers that "has untied itself from their stepmotherly apron-strings" (14). "Flaccid," "sterile," "life-denying": clearly, the verbal metaphors of the time indicate a disdain for, if not downright hostility toward, all things not aggressively "masculine," and therefore, by definition, weak or "feminine."

A 1919 male reviewer's vitriolic attack on Freeman's *The Copy-Cat and Other Stories* (1914) shows the disfavor her feminine subject matter already evoked only 30 years after her initial widespread success. After explaining that the content of the collection's title story concerns a young girl's school experiences, the critic fairly seethes: "This in the year of our Lord 1914! This in the year when blood began to flow as it has never flowed before; when free peoples everywhere awoke to the presence of Black Evil on earth; when big, generous America with all her faults was not exactly likely to be thrilled or touched or enlightened by the recital of how a plain little girl finally got up enough gumption to wear pink ribbons instead of blue. . . . But it is wretched stuff, really" (Overton 200).

Freeman's critical acceptance thus altered considerably in her own lifetime due in large part to the changing attitudes of her generation toward her female subject matter. The resurgence of interest in this author in our own generation, moreover, indicates a further shift in our expectations of and attitude toward such subject matter in literature: we are now, it seems, reacting against the anti-feminism which so dominated the first half of this century. Indeed only in the last 20 years or so has the woman's movement succeeded in validating the importance and efficacy of many facets of women's lives heretofore considered immaterial or trivial in comparison with those of men. In short, we are now able to return to Freeman's long-neglected works and reevaluate them for their artistic and literary merit without, one hopes, a previous generation's bias against "effeminate" subject matter.

A study of the history of Freeman criticism is both enlightening and puzzling: each generation has highlighted particular elements of her work which, when taken together, nevertheless fall far short of a composite picture of this writer's many abilities, yet significant weaknesses also. Every passionate attack on her style or subject matter has been met with an equally exuberant commendation. Few critics have attempted a thorough analysis of any one of her works, and no critic has considered her merit as a writer on the basis of her entire corpus of fiction. What is surprising, however, is that this lack of comprehensive study of her works continues. Perhaps, given Freeman's large, varied, and uneven corpus, the job is simply too demanding. Difficulty also arises in obtaining primary material: despite several recent reissuings, nearly all of her works are long out of print. Moreover, at least 70 of her short stories were never collected at all. More likely though, scholars doubt the efficacy of such an undertaking given Freeman's still dubious reputation. Is she worth it? Clearly, much work remains to be done in establishing Freeman's position in the canon of American literature.

In presenting the following summary of secondary material on Freeman, I have attempted (1) to identify and group several of the major trends in this criticism throughout the years, and (2) to focus specifically on critics who, both in her lifetime and especially in the last 20 years, have agreed that Freeman's outstanding feature is her careful and perceptive characterization of women. I indicate, moreover, how this evaluation of her women has altered considerably over the years. As far back as Freeman's first publications, reviewers, many of them women, acknowledged a "certain something" in her works that attracted them. The emergence of feminist criticism and psychology has given critics of both sexes the necessary authority and vocabulary to account for this heretofore inexplicable quality of Freeman's work and its special appeal to women readers. Examining the history of Freeman criticism, therefore, not only allows us insight into the specific areas of attention given this author over time, but also serves as a kind of barometer of our cultural attitudes toward gender in the 100 years that have elapsed since Freeman embarked on her literary career in 1887.[1]

I

Most secondary material written about Freeman in her lifetime and up through the 1960s focuses on five major areas: (1) the novelty of her subject matter; (2) the objective, frank realism of her style; (3) the faithfulness with which she records elements of the New England decline; (4) her interest in the Puritan conscience and will, seen as a legacy from Hawthorne; and (5) the inner strength or "spirituality" of her characters that accords her work a universal rather than merely local appeal.

By 1887 William Dean Howells was well established as the founder and chief practitioner of the new "realism" movement in American fiction, a mode of narrative he himself defined as "telling the truth" of "the motives, the impulses, the principles that shape the lives of actual men and women." As the former editor-in-chief of the *Atlantic,* and as a monthly contributor to *Harper's,* he kept his literary eye ready to spot, and used his enormous influence to promote new young writers whose literary aims seemed to mesh most fully with his own deeply held convictions. Critics agreed that Mary Wilkins, one of his protégées, was producing stories sympathetic with the major tenets of Howell's ideology. "She makes us exclaim with admiration over the novelty, yet truthfulness, of her portraitures," one early review stated (Scudder 848), and another, "She paints the village life, the people on farms and in workshops and workhouses. . . . She sees those things which are of perennial interest—the pathos and beauty of simple lives" ("Mary E. Wilkins," *Bookman* 102). Yet within these simple lives, a moral or spiritual value was implicit. This also attracted Howells: for him, as for Henry James, life and morality were virtually synonymous terms. Scudder's 1891 article cited above goes on to state that "she touches a very deep nature, and opens to view a secret of the human heart which makes us cry out that here is a poet, a seer" (848), and several years later, Charles Miner Thompson's "Miss Wilkins: an Idealist in Masquerade," recognizes that "back of all her work is the idea, the sense of the mystery of human life, the question, 'Why is this?' and she gently pushes selected incidents and characters before you, as if filled with the desire to learn . . . the meaning of these problems—clues doubtless, each one in its degree, to the answer to the Great Problem" (675).

Freeman's style also was new and exciting in 1887. "A singular fascination lies in this style of hers, which is after all rather the absence of style—direct, simple, without a superfluous word," says one critic (Wardwell 27), and another, her "short, terse sentences, written in the simplest, homeliest words, had a biting force" (Thompson 669). A third early commentary on Freeman's style is significant also because it establishes the connection continuing today between Freeman's work and that of Sarah Orne Jewett. Julia R. Tutwiler in 1903 calls Freeman's art "Gothic" as opposed to Jewett's "Grecian" art "in the somber rigidity of its moral ideals, and in a union of childlike directness and reticence that embroider economy of phrase with delicate and intricate suggestion." "Where Miss Jewett suffuses you with a delightful melancholy," this critic concludes, "Mary E. Wilkins makes your eyes smart with tears that refuse to fall" (419, 424).

When Freeman ventured away from short story writing to try her hand at longer forms of fiction, however, critics complained sharply about her prose. As a whole, she was urged that both in terms of style and subject matter she was better off sticking with short fiction. "Inelegant," "in bad taste," and "clumsy," were only a few of the condemnatory adjectives a reviewer of *Madelon* applied to her style in his article entitled "Concerning Good English" (1896). He sees in this novel a "striking" example of "the possibilities of indirection and obscurity in our own language," so much so that "the work becomes a curious study in literary awkwardness and affectation" (Preston 361). Thompson summarizes succinctly the view of critics towards Freeman's longer fiction in general: calling it "regrettable" that Mary Wilkins was beginning to venture into novels, he concludes that she "thinks in the length of the short story . . . she has never been able to see the larger proportions of the novel in their proper perspective" (672). A 1904 reviewer agrees that "Miss Wilkins is a great artist, but she is not an artist of the big canvas" (Courtney, *Feminine Note* 212). One often repeated comment is, in fact, that Freeman's novels tended to read as if they were merely hastily spliced together short stories.[2]

Freeman was roundly commended for her accurate portrayal of New England life, especially in its physical and spiritual decline. Rollin Hartt's two-part article "A New England Hill Town," appearing in the 1899 *Atlantic Monthly*, takes a satirical and critical, yet extremely revealing look at mythological "Sweet Auburn," a prototypical New England village. After discussing the village's overall decay in culture and character, Hartt commends Freeman's truthfulness in her delineation of the life found there: "I have heard Miss Wilkins censured for caricaturing New England. No conceivable criticism could be more unjust. Were I to pass judgement upon Miss Wilkins's work, I should say that it is a little deficient in artistic audacity; she understates the case . . . her fantastic types exist . . . they abound in the hill towns" (569). As late as 1951, Perry D. Westbrook, in his *Acres of Flint: Writers of Rural New England, 1870–1900,* concurs that "two or three volumes of her early short stories and one or two novels, all written before 1900, form as valuable a study of New England rural and village life as we have" (97).

Freeman indeed gives us much insight into custom and ritual, into daily life and habits in her world, her "Wilkinston."[3] Critics have pointed out that her major interest is not so much in setting and scene as in character. "To her the New England mind was a complex of morbidly sensitive conscience and overdeveloped will," Westbrook says (*Acres* 98). As such, Freeman was considered a successor of Hawthorne. Paul Elmer More's "Hawthorne: Looking Before and After," written on the centennial of Hawthorne's birth in 1905, traces a "regular process" of inheritance "from the religious intolerance of Cotton Mather to the imaginative isolation of Hawthorne and from that to the nervous impotence of Mrs. Freeman's men and women" (180). "If I am not mistaken, the real progenitor of Miss Wilkins is Nathaniel Hawthorne," another critic stated a year earlier. "She is inspired by the same ideals and appears to be capable of similarly delicate and exquisite workmanship" (Courtney 204). Although Freeman failed in the eyes of many of her critics to live up to this early optimism, she continues to be equated with Hawthorne in her intense yet objective probing of the Puritan conscience.[4] In his 1931 "The Passing of the Yankee," John Macy credits her with simply adhering to the truth of the New England she knew so well: "The gentle woman merely records a grimness for which she is not responsible, in limited and thwarted lives which she understands but does not wilfully create" (617).

Finally, several early critics set the stage for later Freeman criticism by touching upon the inner strength, determinism, and often, spirit of revolt that informs many of her characters and directs their lives. "The center of her art, the beginning and the end of it, is humanity, the individual soul," said Fred Lewis Pattee in a chapter from his 1922 *Sidelights on American Literature* entitled "On the Terminal Moraine of New England Puritanism." "Her favorite theme is revolt. . . . Often it is internal. On the surface of the life there is apparent serenity and reserve, but beneath there is an increasing fire" (201, 207). F. O. Matthiessen's "New England Stories" in John Macy's *American Writers on American Literature* (1931) concurs: "Courage supports a great many of Miss Wilkins's characters, the courage that is born of loneliness. The struggle of the heart to live by its own strength alone is her constant theme, and the sudden revolt of a spirit that will endure no more from circumstance provides her most stirring dramas" (408).

This inner turmoil and spirit of revolt, however, seen as a positive human strength by these critics, was considered "depressing" by reviewers of a different temperament. Thompson, for example, sees each character in *Pembroke* as "a monstrous example of stubbornness—of that will which enforces its ends, however trivial, even to self-destruction" (665). Years later, as we shall see, this opinion prevails in such articles as Alice Glarden Brand's 1977 "Mary Wilkins Freeman: Misanthropy as Propaganda." Brand sees Freeman's fiction as a "taxonomy of disappointments," and "disillusioned and cynical," full of characters who "faithfully lived out frustrations." "She was a civilized critic of destructive human behaviors," Brand concludes (100).

After Freeman's initial success, critics continued in her lifetime and in the next few decades to argue her merit as a writer; if deemed worthy of a place in American literary history at all, she was usually grouped with such diverse writers as Bret Harte, Sarah Orne Jewett, and George Washington Cable under the heading "local color literature." The bulk of commentary from this period up to 1931 is just that: commentary. Little attempt was made to evaluate critically her worth as a writer based on her entire corpus of work. Reviewers in Freeman's lifetime touch on the plot of a new work, yet make little attempt to assess both its strengths and weaknesses in the context of her previous writing. The exceptions here are two articles mentioned above: Thompson's "Mary Wilkins Freeman: An Idealist in Masquerade," and Pattee's "On the Terminal Moraine in New England Puritanism." No student of Freeman should ignore these two thorough critical essays. In addition, a third article already cited, Rollin Hartt's "A New England Hill Town," provides an interesting and informative background to the moral and cultural atmosphere of Freeman's settings, albeit mentioning the author and her works only in passing. Finally, Matthiessen's "New England Stories" is a brief but perceptive early summary of the woman and her works.

Although Freeman's literary output remained fairly high up to 1930, her declining popularity beginning after the First World War rendered her work unread and thus uncriticized between 1930 and 1960. Brief mentions only were accorded her in several important works on the history of American fiction. Few new insights, however, either positive or negative, were generated. A few examples will illustrate this. Arthur Hobson Quinn, in his 1936 *American Fiction: An Historical and Critical Survey,* begins the chapter "The

Development of Realism" with Freeman, and concludes that "she belongs, in the history of fiction, not to any local color school but to a wider field, that which reveals to the understanding the inner workings of the heart" (440). Ima Herron's 1939 *The Small Town in American Literature* devotes several pages to Freeman, calling her work "a major contribution" in the literary use of the New England town (88–95). And Van Wyck Brooks's *New England: Indian Summer: 1865–1915* (1940) considers her "an eminent artist" whose strength lies in her "fierce and primitive" view of life and in the "sublime will to live" her characters evince (464–65).

One exceptional study came out of this period in Freeman criticism: Babette May Levy's "Mutations in New England Local Color" (1946). A breakthrough in identifying and classifying women's local-color writing, this article, discussed in more detail below, paved the way at this early date for later renewed interest in Freeman. In the next 20 years or so that interest remained a small but growing one. Westbrook's 1951 *Acres of Flint* devotes a chapter to Freeman, placing her, as Levy does, with her contemporaries Sarah Orne Jewett, Alice Brown, and Rose Terry Cooke among others, and discussing several of her stories under such headings as "The New England Conscience," and "The Crooked Will." Westbrook's discussion, like Levy's, is of value because it also begins to establish the connections continuing today among nineteenth-century New England women local-color writers.

The most substantial work to come out of this period, and one which, though largely outdated in critical style, remains our most valuable source for biographical material on Freeman, is Edward Foster's monograph, *Mary E. Wilkins Freeman* (1956). Foster's work grew out of his own unfinished dissertation of several decades earlier; at that time he had the benefit of personally interviewing surviving members of Freeman's family and circle of friends. In terms of thorough criticism of all her writings, however, the work falls far short: several of her novels, for example, are summarized in a mere sentence or two. Likewise, Westbrook's TUSAS volume, *Mary Wilkins Freeman* (1967), purporting to be a critical biography, is far from "critical." Rather, both studies rely too much on calibrating the chronology of the woman with that of her works; at best, they provide the literary critic with a general overview and background to Freeman's life and career.

II

In the history of Freeman criticism we can identify several distinctive periods. For approximately 25 years, between 1887 and 1914, her writings, especially her short stories, were immensely popular. Critical commentary in this period is largely laudatory and concentrates primarily on her adherence to the tenets of the new realism. Though many of her stories were published in women's magazines such as *Home-Maker* and *Ladies' Home Journal,* Free-

man's association with both Howells and the Harper's firm established for
her a widespread male audience during this time as well. However, the anti-
feminist mood of our culture after World War I resulted in criticism by
reviewers of both sexes becoming increasingly negative or merely dropping
off altogether. Freeman simply was no longer read: only nine of her 41
volumes of works were in print the year she died. Through the 1950s,
scholars were concentrating primarily on a canon of nineteenth-century
American authors which included Hawthorne, Melville, Whitman, Twain,
and James, but scarcely acknowledged women writers coming from the same
period.

Increasingly, however, the proliferation of feminist criticism resulting
from the women's movement added to the new interest in Freeman spawned
by Foster's and Westbrook's studies. Focus on Freeman's work now shifted to
her many women characters: they were recognized as holding the key to
Freeman's primary themes and concerns. The women's movement of the last
two decades, therefore, has been largely responsible for rediscovering female
writers such as Freeman whose women's themes rendered them "uninteresting" in the period up to the mid-twentieth century.

It is important here to trace the origins of this focus. For even in
Freeman's time, several perceptive critics of both sexes were already noting,
albeit in passing, the predominance and importance of female characters in
her fiction. These early reviews divide rather evenly into positive and negative reactions. An unsigned article in the January 2, 1892, *Critic* is the first
to note that "[Mary Wilkins] draws many pictures of the American girl . . .
whose slender form and pink and white complexion cover a resolute will and
sensitive nerves. But it is in her pictures of the middle-aged women that Miss
Wilkins excels. . . . Whoever heretofore brought tears to the eyes over the
small trials, the little heroisms and silent sorrows of old maids and hardworked wives? . . . The men of the stories are, as they would themselves
express it, 'of less account' than the women . . ." ("Mary E. Wilkins" 13).
Thereafter, reviewers often commented on a "certain something" in Freeman's works which appealed, many agreed, particularly to the woman reader.
Henry Alden felt it was "not a literary quality, but something indefinable,
yielding to the test of sensibility, but not to that of analysis" ("Editor's
Study" 646). Mary Moss, in "Some Representative American Story Tellers"
(1906), the first substantial article to deal almost exclusively with Freeman's
women, identifies this quality as Freeman's focus on minute, concrete detail:
"Her scope may be limited, but within it she *knows*. . . . With unerring
elimination she seizes the telling detail" (21). Moss's perceptive article further describes the condition of life for, and the psychological atmosphere
surrounding, Freeman's many types of women.

Another generally positive early assessment of Freeman's women is
Blanche Williams's "Mary Wilkins Freeman," a chapter from her *Our Short
Story Writers* (1920). Williams identifies and discusses several categories of

women in Freeman's stories: the young girl, the spinster, the middle-aged woman. She notes especially that the old women "show . . . a strength of character, a kind of masculine determination, which somewhat controverts the theory that they live in a man-ruled world" (165–66).

Around the turn of the century, both male and female critics began to forecast Freeman's decline by deeming her concentration of women and women's concerns a liability to her art. Freeman's "stay-at-home" stories lacked the adventure and vigor of the "masculine" times, they said; increasingly, Americans of both sexes were uncomfortable with her portrayals of "bony figures of aging spinsters" (Brooks 469). Although Thompson's 1899 article mentioned above is in most other respects a balanced and fair account of Freeman's early writings, he holds to the typical attitude in this period toward a woman's world and the possibilities of its representation in fiction: narrow and restricting, it was simply not particularly interesting. "Had [Miss Wilkins] been a boy," he tells us "she would have roamed the fields, gone fishing and hunting, had the privilege of sitting in the country store and listening to the talk of the men of evenings . . . [she would] have learned to look at life as the men look at it, with the larger and more catholic view which is theirs. . . . As she was a girl, her outlook was confined to the household; her sources of information were the tales of gossiping women, which would naturally relate mostly to the family quarrels and dissensions that are the great tragedies of their lives" (668).

Too bad, says Thompson in effect: born and raised a woman among women, Mary Wilkins necessarily had produced and would continue to produce second-rate art. Thompson is explicit in his opinion here; more common are critics such as Grant Overton who, while not specifically calling Freeman's womanhood detrimental to her art, nevertheless consider her concerns "trivial" in the new, fast-paced, and male-dominated "business" world of the 1920s. Overton thus takes umbrage with those who "insist upon the literary value of such writing as Mrs. Freeman's. . . . There are no literary values, there are only values in life. And what is Mrs. Freeman's value in life? Slight, reminiscential, pleasing, sometimes entertaining . . . but never for a moment revealing anything unexpected . . . her stories are cordially welcome and likeable (in general) without having the slightest relation to the business of living" (199).

Though female reviewers tended, on the whole, to be more sympathetic to Freeman's works, at least one woman, Mary E. Wardwell, roundly chastised Freeman not for her use of women characters in general, but for her use of a particular kind of woman, which in 1899 Wardwell sees as outmoded. After briefly commenting on the "sorry" male characters in her stories, Wardwell states that "The women are still more unfortunate. Patience and endurance, which in the struggling days of the colonies two centuries ago were noble qualities, reappear again and again in forlorn old maids and long-suffering wives" (27–28). Wardwell condemns Freeman for failing to portray, or even acknowledge, the "new woman," whose recent entrance into society, she says, is rapidly displacing older values:

> We have sometimes been inclined to deplore her entrance on the scene, but after a course of these depressing village experiences no one can doubt that her mission is heaven-born. To the remotest nook of farthest Vermont and New Hampshire she will penetrate with her clubs and her fashion-books and her scientific housekeeping. There will be no more old maids in many-times turned gowns, living alone with a cat and a poor little memory of some faithless swain . . . but a busy, cheerful set of women, well-dressed, well-fed, and perfectly happy though single. It would be less quaint, less picturesque, less to her taste, but most interesting if Miss Wilkins would take us back amongst some of her plain-song people after they have been stirred by the broad and vivifying influences of the time. (28)[5]

"Her characters mostly are unmarried women," Pattee said in his 1922 *Sidelights on American Literature.* "With such material there are infinite possibilities for depressed realism" (206–7). Trivial, trite, not worth much attention, because women, or at least these kind of women, were not worth much attention: this opinion continued to dominate Freeman criticism until the mid-1960s. One exception, already mentioned, is noteworthy. In 1946, Babette Levy's "Mutations in New England Local Color," published in the *New England Quarterly,* grouped Freeman with Stowe, Jewett, and Cooke not by virtue of their New England heritage alone, but because of their similar conviction of the validity and meaningfulness of a woman's world: "Although [these women's] stories occasionally concern family life, they are nearly always told from the woman's point of view . . . typically, the wife and mother wins her point against her selfish, parsimonious husband by feminine persistence, prayer, or trickery. . . . Nearly all the main women characters, whatever their age or social position, display that New England characteristic called 'faculty.' . . . [T]he reader, particularly the female one, feels a kindly kinship with these women, perhaps because of their very human ambitions in life—a home of their own, a best parlor, a good silk dress, a little comfort . . ." (340–41).

Levy's article goes on to discuss the four women writers' individual responses to their common environment, concluding that Freeman's tragedies arise most often from the "besetting sin of pride" that isolates her protagonists. Anticipating by several decades widespread interest in not only women's regional writing but in all women's writing as well, Levy's article opened the door for more recent studies such as Ann Douglas Wood's "The Literature of Impoverishment: The Women Local Colorists in America 1865–1914" (1972) and Josephine Donovan's *New England Local Color Literature: A Woman's Tradition* (1983), which seek to establish artistic and thematic connections between women writers of a particular region; hence, a "tradition" of women's fiction. In writing of women's New England regional works, Levy and each of the critics to follow her lead have positioned Freeman's writings at a pivotal point in this tradition: a culmination of her centuries' romantic and idealistic elevation of womanhood's virtues, Freeman's stories, influenced by the changing attitude toward women in her times, nevertheless subvert such idealism by documenting the decay of the "woman-centered, matriarchal world" of her predecessors (Donovan 119).

The mid-1960s with its growing feminist concerns saw the first real burgeoning of modern Freeman criticism. Since that time, the majority of that criticism has focused on her women characters, clearly the theme in her fiction of most interest to us today. In 1965 an article by a male critic about one of Freeman's more popular stories initiated, largely because of its reactionary comments on women, vibrant new interest in Freeman's themes. David H. Hirsch's "Subdued Meaning in 'A New England Nun' " caused a stir that continues today. A new-critical and Freudian reading of the text, Hirsch's article concludes that protagonist Louisa, suffering from an "obsessive neurosis" exhibited by her quest for order, rejects "life"; that is, marriage to long-time fiancé Joe Dagget, because of her inherent fear of the "disorder" of sexuality. A throw-back to this century's earlier view of women, this interpretation commenced a re-reading of many of Freeman's better known stories and initiated a dialogue of sorts between those (usually male) critics who agree with Hirsch's thesis, such as Larzer Ziff who, in *The American 1890s* (1966) calls a Freeman spinster "imprisoned" because she is "deprived of what Mrs. Freeman considers to be her birthright—a man" (293), and feminist critics such as Marjorie Pryse who insist that, far from "rejecting" life in her decision not to marry, Louisa actually asserts the value of a woman's life and the possibility of self-fulfillment away from marriage and motherhood. As Pryse explains in her "An Uncloistered 'New England Nun' " (1983), "When Louisa Ellis reconsiders marriage to Joe Dagget, she aligns herself against the values he represents. Her resulting unconventionality makes it understandably difficult for historians . . . to view her either perceptively or sympathetically. . . . In analyzing 'A New England Nun' without bias against solitary women, the reader discovers that within the world Louisa inhabits, she becomes heroic, active, wise, ambitious, and even transcendent, hardly the woman Freeman's critics and biographers have depicted. In choosing solitude, Louisa creates an alternative pattern of living for a woman . . ." (289).

Feminist critics such as Pryse have likewise turned to Freeman's stories of women's rebellion against authority or tradition to illustrate Freeman's conviction of the value of a woman's inner beliefs. Susan Allen Toth's "Defiant Light: A Positive View of Mary Wilkins Freeman" (1973) discusses such stories as "A Village Singer," "A Church Mouse," and "An Independent Thinker," and concludes that "Freeman puts . . . emphasis on the positive drive towards fulfillment that motivates her strong characters, a fulfillment of what they believe to be their own true selves" (90). Michele Clark's

"Afterword" to *"The Revolt of 'Mother'" and Other Stories* (1974) calls these female rebels "heroic": "their demands may be small, but it is impossible to renege on them. . . . The issues change in each story, each circumstance, but the ability to evaluate, choose, and then act according to inner convictions remains essential" (194–95). And Alice Glarden Brand, in "Mary Wilkins Freeman: Misanthropy as Propaganda" (1977) sees Freeman's rebellious women as indicative of her personal anger towards men: "Freeman's stories were an exposé: an exposé of contempt for men's impotence, incompetence, and aggression and for women's passivity, dependence, and rage. . . . As Freeman becomes angrier and bolder, her women become angrier and bolder" (83–84).

Feminist critics have also emphasized the positive, nurturing quality they see depicted in Freeman's mother-daughter relationships or in women's relationships with each other. "Women's primary relationships are to each other rather than to men," Clark states. "Wilkins's women are fiercely protective and respectful of other women in their communities" (195). Donovan also considers this "one of the dominant themes in her work," yet notes that because Freeman "seems to have imbibed a moral atmosphere which assumes the male prerogative," her plots often retain a measure of "incongruity," "where intense relationships between women are simply dropped with no explanation" (129). Going a step farther, Leah Blatt Glasser's "Mary E. Wilkins Freeman: The Stranger in the Mirror" (1984) draws on Clark's earlier suggestion of a "latent, hidden homosexuality" in several of Freeman's works in discussing the inner conflict and self-division between submission and rebellion of the woman protagonist in the short story "A Moral Exigency."

While invaluable in its contribution to the "rediscovery" of Freeman's works, such feminist criticism, like other Freeman criticism throughout the years, has nevertheless unwittingly distorted our views of the author and her themes. Basing their arguments on a small number of stories from one period of Freeman's long and varied career, feminist critics have often sought to fit Freeman too neatly into a niche as a prime illustration for larger feminist issues.

Hence, those today with a "lay" person's knowledge of Freeman's works are likely to regard her as an early feminist herself—a creator of strong, independent, "rebel"-like women who defy social convention in order to maintain their own integrity. On the basis of her handful of popular stories—"A New England Nun," "The Revolt of 'Mother,'" "A Village Singer"—this conclusion is sound. However, it falls flat when one considers these stories in the context of Freeman's entire corpus of work: Freeman's rebellious women, rather, constitute only one image, and a relatively limited one, in her overall portrait of women and womanhood. Her writing probes equally as sharply into the lives and sensibilities of women who accept the Victorian "true womanhood" ideal of wife and mother; women rejected by lovers who feel their lives are now worthless; women frustrated with and yet submissive to the confines of marriage; women whose sole means of solidarity with other women is through self-aggrandizing gossip; and women who must deal with the twin hardships of advancing age and loneliness.

Along with feminist interpretations of Freeman's works in the last 20 years has come a number of more specialized studies and a handful of dissertations focusing on Freeman's women. Several articles have sought to explicate hitherto unknown short stories with women protagonists: for example, Susan Allen Toth's "Mary Wilkins Freeman's Parable of Wasted Life" (1971), concerning "The Three Old Sisters and the Old Beau"; John W. Crowley's "Freeman's Yankee Tragedy: 'Amanda and Love' " (1976); and Sarah W. Sherman's "The Great Goddess in New England: Mary Wilkins Freeman's 'Christmas Jenny' " (1980). A few specific studies also deserve brief mention. Marilyn Davis DeEulis, in " 'Her Box of a House': Spatial Restriction as Psychic Signpost in Mary Wilkins Freeman's 'The Revolt of "Mother" ' " (1979) looks at the "fusion of house and personality" in this story which "defines the narrowness of [the woman protagonist's] existence" (52). Joseph R. McElrath, Jr., a year later considers the "artistry" Freeman employs in the same story, concluding that it has "one of the most complicated trick-endings in all of nineteenth-century American short fiction" (261). Aliki Barnstone's "Houses Within Houses: Emily Dickinson and Mary Wilkins Freeman's 'A New England Nun' " (1984) sees a "striking" similarity between the poet's "house of consciousness" and the story writer's depiction of physical surroundings. Finally, Susan Oaks's "The Haunting Will: The Ghost Stories of Mary Wilkins Freeman" (1985), and Alfred Bendixen's "Afterword" to a reissuing of Freeman's stories of the supernatural, *The Wind in the Rose-Bush* (1986), both take a long overdue look at this forgotten genre. Oaks's thesis is that in these stories as well, "Freeman continues to explore the theme that is basic to all of her fiction—the operation of the individual will" (206); Bendixen sees the terror in these tales arising from "the perversion of the home, the distortion of normal family relationships" (247).

Brent L. Kendrick found 12 unpublished dissertations dealing solely or in part with Mary Wilkins Freeman in 1975, but he called the majority of them "discouraging" in quality since they continued to focus primarily on her recording of the New England decline ("Mary E. Wilkins Freeman" 255). To date 13 years later the pronouncement "discouraging" may still obtain, for only seven of the current 24 dissertations concern Freeman exclusively and most of these continue to discuss her as a local colorist along with Harriet Beecher Stowe, Sarah Orne Jewett, Alice Brown, or others. Only two of the seven dealing with Freeman alone focus on her women characters: Rosamond Smith Bailey's "The Celebration of Self-Reliance in the Fiction of Mary Wilkins Freeman" (1975), and Leah Blatt Glasser's " 'In a Closet Hidden': The Life and Work of Mary Wilkins Freeman" (1982).[6] Bailey's purpose is to present an optimistic Freeman who parodies the time-worn sentimental heroine and melodramatic plot in order to "celebrate" life's nonconformists and outcasts. She concludes that Freeman is a "quiet feminist," one who "slashes through romantic stereotypes" in order to expose their destructive effect on a woman's personal integrity and self-worth. Glasser's study examines the contradictory forces of "repression and rebellion" in Freeman's own life and applies them to the ambivalence often manifest in her characters' actions. Freeman's women are "battlegrounds" of inner conflict, she concludes; though we often see them in defiant revolt, they nevertheless are haunted by deep-seated guilt, insecurity, and anxiety.

Several other recent dissertations focussing on women's issues deal in part with Freeman. Colleen Davidson's 1975 "Beyond the Sentimental Heroine: The Feminist Character in American Novels, 1899–1937" discusses the conscious use of the "decidedly unsentimental" heroine in a number of female American authors; Marjorie Ann Romines's 1977 "House, Procession, River: Domestic Ritual in the Fiction of Seven American Women, 1877–1972" is especially interesting in its discussion of the metaphoric implications of houses in Freeman's stories; Barbara Johns's 1979 "The Spinster in Five New England Women Regionalists" examines the different roles and attitudes Freeman among others gives to unmarried women in fiction; Mary Ellen Ellsworth's 1981 "Two New England Writers: Harriet Beecher Stowe and Mary Wilkins Freeman" looks at how these two authors differ in portraying a woman's relationship to God, to her church and minister, and to her community; and Laraine Flemming's 1983 "Women of More than Local Color" evaluates Freeman's and Jewett's role in changing the themes and styles of women's writing around the turn of the century.

The most substantial recent work in Freeman scholarship is Brent L. Kendrick's *The Infant Sphinx: Collected Letters of Mary E. Wilkins Freeman* (1985). A reworking of his dissertation of a few years earlier, this volume is carefully annotated and documented, and serves to correct several misconceptions about Freeman that have been popular over the years.[7] Despite the fact that much of Freeman's private correspondence is unavailable to us—it has either been destroyed or is privately owned—one is struck upon reading through the 510 letters collected here not so much by what Freeman says, but by what she leaves unsaid. "Myself is an object of such intense, vital interest to myself," she once stated (Kendrick 57), but a private and reticent person all her life, that self was, one comes to realize, conveyed primarily through the "safer" medium of fiction. Nevertheless, Kendrick's volume of Freeman's correspondence allows us an invaluable insight into the daily life and habits of a disciplined and determined woman author.

In summary, then, criticism on the works of Mary Wilkins Freeman in the 100 years since the publication of her first collection of short stories has varied considerably in emphasis and evaluative content. From early commendations for her use of new realistic techniques in style and subject matter and her Hawthorne-like concentration on New England Puritan themes, Freeman's stories fell into disfavor not because she "lost" her talent as some maintain, but because her era lost its taste for overtly feminine subject matter. Our renewed interest in Freeman today, albeit growing, has been slow to develop. The definitive study of the woman and her writing—including her neglected children's works, plays, and poetry—has yet to be written.

Yet it is primarily through her short stories that Freeman has touched women for nearly 100 years. We have rediscovered Freeman in her rebel figures, but we must not stop there. Her strength as an artist lies in her ability to draw pictures through language of the unspoken aspirations, desires, fears, sorrows, and joys which make up many women's lives. For this reason, she warrants reevaluation as a woman artist who rightly deserves a place in the American literary canon not only for her pioneering technique in realism or local color fiction, but because her women's themes render her work universal appeal. As Sylvia Warner, a British critic visiting New England for the first time in 1966, remarked, Freeman's stories, full of a "riveting authenticity," continue to compel women of every generation: "though I could not have defined what I had found [in her stories]," Warner muses, "I knew it was what I had wanted. . . . If I had the courage of my convictions downstairs, when everyone was talking about Joyce and Pound and melting pots, I would have said, 'Why don't you think more of Mary Wilkins?' " (134).

Notes

1. My essay here does not aim at completeness, but rather selects and discusses some of the more representative Freeman criticism published over the years. A complete bibliography of secondary material on Freeman can be found in my recent dissertation, " 'A Web of Relationship': Women in the Short Stories of Mary Wilkins Freeman," U of Wisconsin-Madison, 1987.

2. A thorough discussion of the problem of form in Freeman's writing can be found in an unpublished dissertation, Thomas Knipp's "The Quest for Form: The Fiction of Mary E. Wilkins Freeman," Michigan State, 1966.

3. Freeman's stories, while not usually overtly related in character or subject matter, can be read as a composite picture of a single New England village much akin to Masters's *Spoon River Anthology* or Anderson's *Winesburg, Ohio*. Michele Clark uses this term in the "Afterword" to her collection of Freeman's stories (195).

4. Freeman has at least two pieces, also, which closely parallel Hawthorne stories in content and imagery: "The Slip of the Leash" is much like "Wakefield," and "The Three Old Sisters and the Old Beau" resembles "The Wedding Knell." However, Freeman denied Hawthorne's influence on her work: "I do not know if I am 'akin to Hawthorne,' " she once told Fred Lewis Pattee. "I do not care for him" (Kendrick 385).

5. After 1900, Freeman portrays several thoroughly "modernized" women in her novels and short stories; almost always, however, she satirizes their concerns with fashion and social clubs as petty and superficial. Margaret Edes of *The Butterfly House* (1912) and Mrs. Bodley of "Mother-Wings" (1921) epitomize this type of "new" woman for Freeman.

6. My own dissertation on Freeman's women adds to this list. It closely analyzes the

various ways Freeman defines her women characters through relationship in her entire corpus of 220 short stories (see Works Cited for complete reference).

7. Two of these are the statement "I have never been fond of people" which Freeman was erroneously quoted as saying, and the facts behind the success—or lack thereof—of her marriage (Kendrick 145, 264).

Works Cited

Alden, Henry. "Editor's Study." *Harper's Monthly* Mar. 1901: 644–48.

Bailey, Rosamond. "The Celebration of Self-Reliance in the Fiction of Mary Wilkins Freeman." Diss. Alberta, Canada, 1975.

Barnstone, Aliki. "Houses Within Houses: Emily Dickinson and Mary Wilkins Freeman's 'A New England Nun.' " *Centennial Review* 28.2 (1984): 129–45.

Bendixen, Alfred. Afterword. *The Wind in the Rose-Bush and Other Stories of the Supernatural.* Chicago: Academy Chicago, 1986. 239–53.

Brand, Alice Glarden. "Mary Wilkins Freeman: Misanthropy as Propaganda." *New England Quarterly* (1977): 83–100.

Brooks, Van Wyck. *New England Indian Summer, 1865–1915.* New York: Dutton, 1940.

———. *Three Essays on America.* New York: Dutton, 1934.

Clark, Michele. Afterword. *"The Revolt of Mother" and Other Stories.* New York: Feminist Press, 1974. 165–201.

Courtney, William L. "Miss Mary Wilkins." *The Feminine Note in Fiction.* London: Chapman and Hall, 1904. 199–224.

Cowley, Malcolm. *After the Genteel Tradition: American Writers Since 1910.* New York: Norton, 1936.

Crowley, John W. "Freeman's Yankee Tragedy: 'Amanda and Love.' " *Markham Review* Spring (1976): 58–60.

Davidson, Colleen. "Beyond the Sentimental Heroine: The Feminist Character in American Novels, 1899–1937." Diss. U of Minnesota, 1975.

DeEulis, Marilyn Davis. " 'Her Box of a House': Spatial Restriction as Psychic Signpost in Mary Wilkins Freeman's 'The Revolt of "Mother." ' " *Markham Review* Spring (1979): 51–52.

Donovan, Josephine. *New England Local Color Literature: A Women's Tradition.* New York: Ungar, 1983.

Douglas, Ann. *The Feminization of American Culture.* New York: Avon, 1977.

Ellsworth, Mary Ellen. "Two New England Writers: Harriet Beecher Stowe and Mary Wilkins Freeman." Diss. Columbia U, 1981.

Fisken, Beth Wynne. " 'Unusual' People in a 'Usual Place': 'The Balking of Christopher' by Mary Wilkins Freeman." *Colby Library Quarterly* (1985): 99–103.

Flemming, Laraine. "Women of More Than Local Color." Diss. State U of New York at Buffalo, 1983.

Foster, Edward. *Mary E. Wilkins Freeman.* New York: Hendricks, 1956.

Glasser, Leah Blatt. " 'In a Closet Hidden': The Life and Works of Mary Wilkins Freeman." Diss. Brown U, 1982.

———. "Mary E. Wilkins Freeman: The Stranger in the Mirror." *Massachusetts Review* 25 (1984): 323–39.

Hartt, Rollin. "A New England Hill Town." *Atlantic Monthly* Apr. 1899: 561–74; May 1899: 712–20.

Herron, Ima H. *The Small Town in American Literature.* Durham: Duke UP, 1939.

Hirsch, David H. "Subdued Meaning in 'A New England Nun.' " *Studies in Short Fiction* 2 (1965): 124–26.

Johns, Barbara. "The Spinster in Five New England Women Regionalists." Diss. U of Detroit, 1980.

Kendrick, Brent L. "Mary E. Wilkins Freeman." *American Literary Realism* 8 (1975): 255–57.

———, ed. *The Infant Sphinx: Collected Letters of Mary E. Wilkins Freeman.* Metuchen: Scarecrow, 1985.

Levy, Babette May. "Mutations in New England Local Color." *New England Quarterly* 19 (1946): 338–58.

Macy, John. "The Passing of the Yankee." *Bookman* Aug. 1931: 612–21.

"Mary E. Wilkins." *Critic* 2 Jan. 1892: 13.

"Mary E. Wilkins." *Bookman* 1 Dec. 1891: 102–03.

Matthiessen, F. O. "New England Stories." *American Writers on American Literature.* Ed. John Macy. New York: Liveright, 1931. 404–09.

McElrath, Joseph R. "The Artistry of Mary E. Wilkins Freeman's 'The Revolt.' " *Studies in Short Fiction* (1980): 255–61.

More, Paul Elmer. "Hawthorne: Looking Before and After." *Shelburne Essays* 2 (1905): 173–87.

Moss, Mary. "Some Representative American Story Tellers: Mary E. Wilkins." *Bookman* Sept. 1906: 21–29.

Oaks, Susan. "The Haunting Will: The Ghost Stories of Mary Wilkins Freeman." *Colby Library Quarterly* 21 (1985): 209–20.

Overton, Grant. "Mary E. Wilkins Freeman." *The Women Who Make Our Novels.* New York: Moffat, Yard, 1919. 198–203.

Preston, George. "Concerning Good English." *Bookman* 3 (New York) 1896: 358–62.

Pryse, Marjorie. "An Uncloistered 'New England Nun.' " *Studies in Short Fiction* 20 (1983): 289–95.

Quinn, Arthur Hobson. "The Development of Realism." *American Fiction: An Historical and Critical Survey.* New York: Appleton-Century-Crofts, 1936. 433–71.

Reichardt, Mary R. " 'A Web of Relationship': Women in the Short Stories of Mary Wilkins Freeman." Diss. U of Wisconsin-Madison, 1987.

Romines, Marjorie Ann. "House, Procession, River: Domestic Ritual in the Fiction of Seven American Women, 1877–1972." Diss. George Washington U, 1977.

Scudder, Horace. "New England in the Short Story." *Atlantic Monthly* June 1891: 845–50.

Sherman, Sarah W. "The Great Goddess in New England: Mary Wilkins Freeman's 'Christmas Jenny.' " *Studies in Short Fiction* (1980): 157–64.

Thompson, Charles Miner. "Miss Wilkins: An Idealist in Masquerade." *Atlantic Monthly* May 1899: 665–75.

Toth, Susan Allen. "Defiant Light: A Positive View of Mary Wilkins Freeman." *New England Quarterly* (1973): 83–93.

———. "Mary Wilkins Freeman's Parable of Wasted life." *American Literature* (1971): 564–67.

Tutwiler, Julia R. "Two New England Writers—In Relation to Their Art and to Each Other." *Gunton's Magazine* Nov. 1903: 419–25.

Wardell, Mary E. "About Miss Wilkins." *Citizen* Apr. 1898: 27–28.

Warner, Sylvia Townsend. "Item, One Empty House." *New Yorker* 26 Mar. 1966: 131–38.

Westbrook, Perry D. *Acres of Flint: Writers of Rural New England, 1870–1900.* Washington, DC: Scarecrow, 1951.

———. *Mary Wilkins Freeman.* New York: Twayne, 1967.

Williams, Blanche C. "Mary Wilkins Freeman." *Our Short Story Writers.* New York: Moffat, Yard, 1920. 160–81.

Wood, Ann Douglas. "The Literature of Impoverishment: The Women Local Colorists in America, 1865–1914." *Women's Studies* 1 (1972): 3–40.

Ziff, Larzer. *The American 1890s: Life and Times of a Lost Generation.* New York: Viking, 1966.

Two New England Writers—In Relation to Their Art and to Each Other

JULIA R. TUTWILER

Sarah Orne Jewett and Mary E. Wilkins are New England writers in the color, atmosphere, and spirit of their work as distinctively as in their birthplace. They have both chosen to depict New England village and country life and character, they are both realists, both have failed in the historical novel, and both have done their finest work, not on the large canvas that demands a broad brush and bold modeling, but against a background limited to effects produced by low relief in line and color.

And yet these broad and easy parallels only emphasize the oblique divergence of their gifts and ideals of expression, their definition of the art of the Short Story, and what they have read in and into the face that life has turned upon them. Miss Jewett's inspiration is Greek in its love of beauty, its serene optimism, and its copious simplicity; while Mary E. Wilkins' art is essentially Gothic in the sombre rigidity of its moral ideals, and in a union of childlike directness and reticence that embroider economy of phrase with delicate and intricate suggestion.

Their very realism roots in alien soils and bears flowers that blow to opposite points of the compass. Mary E. Wilkins' is purely objective. Her detachment reminds one of Bastien Lepage; she has no personal feeling, but she has immense personal insight. Miss Jewett is a realist in the sense that Millet is a realist. She is concerned with the people and happenings of life's little days, and with nature's unobtrusive moments, and she makes them as distinct and complete to the reader's vision as they are to hers, but she puts her own spirit into whatever she sees and romance is the native air of this spirit. This sympathetic subjectivity imbues everything she writes with the charm of personality and is the redeeming virtue of her earliest sketches; for, unlike the author of "A New England Nun" and "A Humble Romance", whose first published work reached the high water mark of achievement in the Short Story, there is a meagreness in Miss Jewett's first stories which fills one with admiration for the discernment that perceived in them the promise fulfilled by "A Dunnett Shepherdess," "Martha's Lady," "A Marsh Island," and more than one other piece of delicate and finished workmanship. Writ-

Reprinted from *Gunton's Magazine* 25 (November 1903): 419–25.

ing done almost from childhood, and apparently with the spontaneity of a child, has developed out of inherited culture grafted upon a rarely beautiful nature the intellectual and spiritual distinction which removes "A Tory Lover" from the plane of ignoble failure and makes Sarah Orne Jewett's best work exquisitely inimitable. Any tyro might catch her phrase of expression, but no amount of copy could reproduce the soul that makes the phrase individual.

Again, this sympathetic subjectivity narrows her creative horizon to what she has felt in seeing and enlarges her vision within the limits of this horizon. Although she has traveled and observed in many countries, it is of her own that she writes, deliberately or unconsciously substituting depth of feeling for breadth of scene and character. She discerns and describes what escapes Mary E. Wilkins' perception or interest, and gives a sense of space composition and full, quiet breathing to the most restricted life and situation. This may be because her vision is colored by the large and tender spirit that sees beauty and matter for rejoicing in people and lives unconscious of either; and because she explicitly portrays character and situation where Mary E. Wilkins leaves them to utter their own speech. With the younger writer, the flesh is the obstacle through which the soul stutters half articulate; with the other, it is merely the medium, the accident, as it were, of the soul's expression.

For Miss Jewett is not so much an observer as she is an interpreter of nature's and life's spiritual potencies. She is sensitively alive to nature's kinship with the human soul; but she sees the one apart from the other, each is dear to her as an individual existence, and from each she receives a message which the other could not deliver. Mary E. Wilkins, on the contrary, with all her power of vivid and delicate description, sees nature always in its relation to human passion. It is what the cinnamon roses symbolize to Elise Mills, the elm tree to David Ransom, the balsam fir to Martha Elder, that appeals to her imagination, not the entity of the rose or tree.

The large, beneficent independence of nature that Miss Jewett delights in and rests upon, is for Mary E. Wilkins absorbed into its point of contact with human inclination. One secret of the unity and concentration of her work is that nature is only the background of the drama which moves, compact and complete, across the stage of her imagination. She herself remains always the spectator whose interest in the play and the players eliminates her own personality. You know her quality of mind, her poignant realization of the tragedy of life—there is a saturnine flavor even in her humor—her interest in certain social problems; but the woman is as great a stranger to you when you have read all her stories as before you turned their first page. While with Miss Jewett, the woman speaks uninterruptedly through the author. You catch the loveliest glimpses of her when you least expect it; you know her religion, her personal tastes, her little prejudices; you are tenderly aware of her lack of humor, of what she feels as well as what she thinks; upon every page a loving and trustful nature throws wide its delicate doors of companionship.

And partly because of this irresistible personality, her comradeship with nature, her responsiveness to all the sweet and dear humanities of life, her instinctive rejection of the repulsive and the harsh, and in spite of distinction rare in its quality and gifts of insight and description, she is not in the modern sense either a novel or a Short Story writer. She lacks two essentials of both—concentration and constructive power. Her novels are moving pictures rather than one coherent, unified presentation of life; her shorter stories are impressions taken upon her imaginative sympathy, chapters out of her own life of emotion quite as much as out of the lives of her characters. The limitation of her gift—which is also its nobility—makes "A Tory Lover" flat and inconsecutive, and proves for the thousandth time that no amount of preparation or culture will take the place of historic imagination. Paul Jones is a feeble and ineffective shadow of the Paul Jones who lives "a man of like passions as ourselves" in Mr. Buell's admirable biography.

In her other stories, Miss Jewett strays into lovely byways of reflection and meditation, and we go with her gladly, hand in hand, companioned in spirit and example by Irving and Hawthorne, Thackeray and Charlotte Brontë, and a score of other illustrious artists. It is only when we have momentarily escaped from the influence of her grace and charm that we ask ourselves, Is her art the art of the Short Story of her own day and generation? Certainly "Andrew's Fortune"—and many others on her varied list—is the story that is short, a very different thing from the form of art technically classified as the Short Story; and even those exquisite etchings, "A Dunnett Shepherdess" and "The Queen's Twin" are linked psychologically with the hour that precedes their own moment of existence. The last touches are put to William Blackett's portrait in "A Dunnett Shepherdess," but the first careful studies were made in "The Country of the Pointed Firs"; and it is our long established intimacy with Mrs. Todd which makes the hour with the queen's twin a sympathetic unit. Strictly speaking, much of Miss Jewett's most charming composition has neither beginning nor end—no skilfully ascending series of incident or emotion to a consistent and inevitable climax. Indeed, the very word "climax" is too emphatic, too sharply insistent for association with the tonal quality of her work, a work that stands apart from that of every other American writer of our time.

In curious contrast with the twentieth century unorthodoxy of her fervent creedless religion is the old-fashioned aroma permeating her style and thought—an aroma in no way dependent upon periods of time. In "A Tory Lover"—the only one of her stories which seems to have been made, not to have grown of itself—this aërial quality of suggestion is noticeably absent, while it lends a quiet distinction to her stories of modern and familiar setting. Reading "The Country of the Pointed Firs" is like opening one's grandmother's chest of spotless, lavendered linen, or spending a day in a deep forest glade within sight and sound of clear, softly flowing water, the sky blue above the pines and the air shot through and through with Indian summer sunshine.

There is no clinging sweetness of past fashions or ideals in Mary E. Wilkins' work. Lavender and thyme, however much she may choose to write about them, are not the flowers that grow in her garden of achievement. She is identified with the literary form of her own generation. Her theme is the interdictions of New England life and character, but it is the strenuous passion of the human filtered through the medium of the New England type that constrains her imagination. Her stories are about old-fashioned, provincial people, narrow conditions, the bleak dogma of isolated thought, and standards transmitted through tenacious, instinctive reproduction; but they are also finished examples of that form of literary art in which America ranks inferior to France alone, and inferior to France in bulk, not in the individual instance. Objectivity, the condensed phrase that suggests without explaining, ruthless excision of every word or incident not indivisible from the organic life of the unit, unswerving rapidity of movement to a climax psychologically and coherently ordained from the first tentative breath of conception, identify Mary E. Wilkins as a great twentieth century Short Story writer, and set as impassable a gulf between the form and spirit of her art and the art of Sarah Orne Jewett as her lack of distinction does. There is scarcely a story in "A New England Nun" or "A Humble Romance" which is not perfect or nearly perfect in form, and not one in which a happy ending is not the price of rending anguish, or the happiness itself a tragic commentary upon life's denials and tyrannies. The rounded completeness of old Hetty Fifield's ("A Church Mouse") Christmas opens out a terrifying vista of pinching monotony, and the consummation of Nancy Pingree's ("Old Lady Pingree") ambition hardens the lump in your throat that her renunciation has put there.

Though "The Portion of Labor" has the strength characteristic of her first volume of Short Stories, it is upon these stories that Mary E. Wilkins' claim to a permanent place in American Literature is based. "The Revolt of Mother" has the qualities of the classic, and deserves the rank in American Fiction awarded to two of Hawthorne's most inferior stories, "The Ambitious Guest" and "The Stone Face." "Understudies" is an example of the author's impassioned interest in the human to the exclusion of animal life, as "Six Trees" is an illustration of her subordination of nature to psychology. In "The Heart's Highway," she has made a cheap, if conscientious, effort to conform to the commercial demands of her profession, with the result that her historical novel, lacking the redeeming sincerity and distinction of Miss Jewett's ineffective story, falls without the pale of literary breeding that elevates even the inferior work of the older writer. Mary E. Wilkins' dramatic work is so far tentative, and no more enters into a serious consideration of her art than Sarah Orne Jewett's stories for children and girls and the verse written with the fluency of immature self-confidence form a coherent part of her contribution to literature. As to the charge of hackneyed types so often brought against both of these writers, it is the surface impression of readers who can not learn that to write about the same class and environment is not equivalent to writing about the same individual.

To sum up the relation of these New England writers to each other or to Fiction is not easy. Where Miss Jewett suffuses you with a delightful melancholy, Mary E. Wilkins makes your eyes smart with tears that refuse to fall. The one tells you that life itself is the reward of living; the other sends you freshly girded to the contest, but she never deceives you with the promise of extraneous victory; the guerdon of the battle is the way you bear yourself in it. Mary E. Wilkins has never done anything as exquisite as Mrs. Blackett, William, or old Elijah Willett's unconscious dedication to love's spiritual constancies; but Sarah Orne Jewett is incapable of writing any one of the Short Stories in "A New England Nun" or "A Humble Romance"; while at the same time her power to portray happy stillness, seclusion lovely and withdrawn, but not remote, the living that robs life of sordidness, is offset by Mary E. Wilkins' competent and coherent grasp upon the unities of incident, character, and emotion, just as her discovery, in literature, of old maidenhood as distinct from old maidism, is balanced by Miss Jewett's interpretation of old age. The inherent difference of their art makes invidious comparison of it impossible and places them side by side at the head of New England imaginative writers.

New England Stories

F. O. Matthiessen

Henry James's remark that it takes a great deal of history to produce a little literature is well illustrated in the chronicles of New England life which were written during the half century following the Civil War. The extraordinarily widespread desire to set down on paper the custom of the country and its exact local flavor can be attributed to many causes, most of which focus in two facts: the overwhelming majority of these recorders of the New England ebb-tide were women, and their characteristic mode of expression was in nearly every case the short sketch. The interpretation of these facts reveals the condition of the region: the period when it had seemed to hold within itself all the elements necessary for physical and spiritual well-being was at an end, the great shipping trade was long since dead, the farms were mortgaged, the provincial utopia that Emerson and Thoreau had not only dreamed but lived was shaken to pieces by the pounding machines in the textile mills, the men of vigor had already gone to follow the new energies of the country in the West, or were competing against the surging Irish immigrants in the towns. It is noteworthy that the one or two lesser men who turned their full attention to carrying on the literary tradition came from outside. Howells was drawn east from Ohio by his veneration for the earlier great names, and Aldrich did not return to Boston until all the formative years of his young manhood had been passed in New York. Meanwhile the women were left alone in their dwindling villages to their memories of a more spacious day.

Instinctively they turned to pen and paper; they were not fully conscious of the vast changes through which they were living, but they were aware, those of them whose childhood had lain before 1860, that they had glimpsed a kind of existence that was fast disappearing. Others, born a few years later, realized more acutely the strained uniqueness of the new environment, their world of a deserted village composed in large part of old women and children, retired captains who had not seen a ship for thirty years, eccentric characters of all sorts driven by too much isolation into humors and oddities, distorted old maids, and awkward girls over whose starved emotions already hung the shadow of a kindred distortion. It was natural that a

Reprinted from *American Writers on American Literature*, ed. John Macy. By Thirty-seven Contemporary Writers, by permission of Liveright Publishing Corporation. Copyright 1931 by Horace Liveright, Inc. Copyright renewed 1959 by Liveright Publishing Corporation, 319–413.

sensitive temperament living in such a community should want to write, either to give permanent shape to her memories, or to find through words the fulfillment of her nature that had been denied. Such writers were by no means purely literary in their motives; very often indeed they were hardly literary at all. Their needs were simpler and more immediate; they told what they knew about their surroundings. They had for the most part no very highly developed sense of form. They were not poets except in the intensity of their feelings, and when they wrote novels the story was generally clumsy and broke down into a number of loosely connected episodes. These episodes were their hearts' blood; they contained what life had taught them and were the moments in which their writers lived.

Harriet Beecher Stowe (1811–1896), a child of the earlier day not only in being the daughter of a theologian whose words were logic on fire and the sister of the greatest pulpit orator of his time, but also in the amazing scope of her own aspirations, played such a thrilling part in the struggle against slavery that it has overshadowed her other achievements, and has caused it to be forgotten that she was among the first to make articulate her reasons for writing about New England. Her preface to *Oldtown Folks* (1869) defines the path which many others followed, and the book itself has a particular significance since its description of what Mrs. Stowe called the seed time of New England, the opening generation of the nineteenth century, also accounts for the dominant elements in the New England character, and thus serves as a background to the work of a later writer like Miss Wilkins. To Mrs. Stowe her book was more than a story, and the way in which she writes about it reveals the throbbing purpose she had to feel in everything she did; it was her "resumé of the whole spirit and body of New England, a country which is now exerting such an influence on the civilized world that to know it truly becomes an object." Her passionate determination to make her mind "as still and passive as a looking glass" and to set down the facts of that existence precisely as they were is perhaps explained by one of the facts themselves; just as resolutely as the first settlers had "made their farms by blasting rocks and clearing land of ledges of stone, and founded thrifty cities and thriving money-getting communities in places which one would think might more properly have been left to the white bears, so resolutely they pursued their investigations amid the grim mysteries of human existence, determined to see and touch and handle everything for themselves, and to get at the absolute truth if absolute truth could be got at." To this she adds the burning comment that "they never expected to find truth agreeable." Portraying such lives she shows them deeply rooted in the unending struggle of thought against the tremendous and awful problems of the infinite, and therefore suffused with a profound and unutterable melancholy. The gloom of her picture is relieved only by the salty jocularity of such a character as Sam Lawson, the village do-nothing who as a fundamental revolt against the incessant steam power in Yankee life "won't be hurried, and won't work, and will take his ease in his own way, in spite of the whole protest of his neighborhood to the contrary."

Mrs. Stowe was by no means an isolated pioneer in chronicling the daily life of New England, since from its very opening number in 1857, the *Atlantic Monthly* carried Rose Terry Cooke's observing and frequently humorous if somewhat diffuse comments on up-country life near Hartford. But the recorder of Natick, Massachusetts, which is the scene of *Oldtown Folks,* and of a Maine fishing village of the mid-century in *The Pearl of Orr's Island* (1862), possessed a more vigorous sweep which was of great importance in its influence. Sarah Orne Jewett (1849–1909) dated the awakening of her own desire to write from the day when, in her thirteenth or fourteenth year, she first read this latter book about people living along the wooded sea-coast and by the decaying shipless harbors. Its first chapters made her see with new eyes, and follow more eagerly than before the old shore paths that led from one gray weather-beaten house to another along her own Maine coast at York and Wells. And although, turning back to Mrs. Stowe's books ten and twenty years later, she could perceive that they were practically never carried out with the strength of their original conception, and regretted that the harmony and simplicity of their natural descriptions were frequently vitiated by elements of high-strung melodramatic romance, she never forgot her original thrill and debt.

Miss Jewett and Mrs. Stowe present the contrast of two generations. In the life of the daughter of Berwick's country doctor there was never a sense of being at the center of burning issues. She could remember dimly the flood time of New England's energies as represented in the life of her grandfather, the sea captain whose ships had brought back from the West Indies the wealth that was symbolized in the handsome eighteenth-century house in which she always lived. But the lives that she observed as she rode beside her father on his visits to patients in fishing shacks and upland farmhouses were of waning power, lives that were no longer shaped in the bustle of the world but that slipped by in a long succession of eventless days, in quiet endurance, in resignation rather than in hope. There was something infinitely pathetic in their cheerful acceptance of frustration, but it was the cheerfulness rather than the frustration that touched Sarah Jewett's heart. She loved every inch of the countryside, every patch of wintergreen, every clump of bay and juniper, and the mysterious humming radiance which she felt in even the bleakest November days seemed to her to emanate from and enfold the people as well as the rocks and hills. She was always aware of the heritage of manners and customs that had been bestowed by the complex civilization that had built the great mansions, by the governors and judges and courtly ladies who had considered their standards of judgment to be on a level with those of Paris and London. And in their descendants' frequent poverty and hardship she could still read a secret of life unguessed by the mushroom growth of the manufacturing towns, a knowledge of being deeply rooted in the soil with its attendant dignity, reserve and self-respect, an inborn instinct for making an ordered pattern of their lives.

Consequently when she began to realize that her mission in life was to be a writer, the thing above all else that she wanted to do was to "help people to look at 'commonplace' lives from the inside instead of the outside, to see that there is so deep and true a sentiment and loyalty and tenderness and courtesy and patience where at first sight there is only roughness and coarseness and something to be ridiculed." The reflection of this desire is mirrored in her first book, *Deephaven* (1877), a series of sketches that had previously appeared in the *Atlantic Monthly,* to whose pages she had had access from the moment she had sent in her first contribution at the age of nineteen. *Deephaven* contained all her knowledge of her environment, a richer content than might seem to be suggested by that phrase when one perceives her extraordinary gift of observation, her awareness of every sight and sound, richer still when one realizes that by knowledge she never meant photographic recording, but "real knowledge . . . all my dreams about my dear Berwick and York and Wells—the people I know and have heard about: the very dust of thought and association that made me."

Sarah Jewett was a deliberate artist from the outset. She was in no sense untutored; she might lament the lack of any logical training of her mind, but the broad shelves of the library in the old house had put her in touch with the great masters of words from the day she could spell. She read not only Jane Austen and Thackeray, but Tolstoy and Zola; she glimpsed a purpose kindred to her own in that of Turgenieff, and kept two sentences from Flaubert pinned over her desk as a constant challenge to perfection. She did not want to write regular magazine stories; she had very little sense of plot. She emphatically did not want to write *about* life, but to suggest its fleeting essence, to make the reader feel her people "as one instinctively feels the character of the people one meets." Her laughing remark that the trace of French blood in her veins kept her always "nibbling all around her stories like a mouse" indicates her unflagging effort to give them shape, and her grasp of the subtle value of elimination. When John Burroughs spoke of "the clear human impression" conveyed by her first sketches, she was delighted, but it was not until many years later, years of much writing and transient successes, that she produced the title story of *The White Heron* (1886), and could really feel that she was no longer describing, but had caught the flavor of the land itself.

In the very next year appeared the first volume of stories by a writer who brought very different gifts from those of Miss Jewett. Mary E. Wilkins (1862–1930), the author of *A Humble Romance,* had encountered far more of the sharp angles of life, and had met them resolutely. Born in Randolph, Massachusetts, she moved in 1873 to Brattleboro, Vermont, where her father opened a small store. She had no recollections of what New England life might have been before the Civil War. The society she knew was undernourished and severe; it did not provide enough elements for the full normal development of any personality. Its too narrow customs had dug deep grooves in the road, grooves which held people in rigid isolation, and encased their thwarted emotions in grimness and silence and willful obstinacies, grooves from which one could generally escape only by a sudden violent upheaval which destroyed the repressions of a lifetime, and often the life itself. Miss Wilkins did not want to be a writer at all. A frail and sensitive girl, she dreamed from her seclusion of being a painter, but for lack of paint and canvas she turned to making verses which were printed in children's magazines when she herself was hardly more than a child. Her father died when she was twenty-one, a very short time after the deaths of her mother and only sister. She was now forced to work for her mere living, and her one resource lay in what had previously been her diversion. She turned to the short story because it seemed the simplest, most directly marketable form, easier for her to manage than a novel. People in every quarter of the United States were writing stories of "local color" in their native dialect, delineating the features of their region and its peculiar human types. Part of the product of the new scientific curiosity and of an increasing consciousness of the national resources, there appeared, during the very year that Mary Wilkins was beginning to write, Bret Harte's *On the Frontier,* Craddock's *In the Tennessee Mountains,* Edgar Howe's *Story of a Country Town,* Thomas Nelson Page's *Marse Chan, Huckleberry Finn,* minor books by Harris and Jewett, a volume of Cable's about New Orleans, and a series of Philander Deming's stark pictures of the Adirondacks. Miss Wilkins' first story won a fifty-dollar prize from a Boston newspaper; her second was accepted by *Harper's Bazar;* her third was *A Humble Romance.*

Although others had long been working in similar materials, Miss Wilkins was not shaped by any previous writer. In fact she would not read anything which she thought might influence her. She had not even read Miss Jewett. But whether she was conscious of it or not, her view of the New England temperament was very like Mrs. Stowe's. Yet there is this significant difference. Mrs. Stowe saw that the tragedy of New England lay in the relentless wrestling of the mind against the forces of evil. The abnormal struggle of the conscience cast a shadow across the lives of nearly every one who grew up here, the shadow in which Hawthorne dwelt and which formed the very substance of his romances. Miss Wilkins does not portray this struggle, but the result of generations of such a struggle. Her characters do not brood much upon the mysteries of sin and death, but the pattern of existence into which they are born has been warped and twisted by all the intense introspection of their ancestors. Mrs. Stowe thought of New England as the region which had cradled the destinies of America; Miss Wilkins simply sees the implications of life in a country town from which the high tide of achievement has long since fallen away.

Her vision is uncompromising; her extraordinary power comes from the unflinching directness with which she sets down even the harshest facts.

Unlike Miss Jewett she is never the detached spectator watching what is going on about her; she and her characters are one. She can present all the essential elements of a situation in a few blinding sentences the very blunt and awkward shortness of which intimates the kind of life she is creating. Her power of catching the actual cadences of speech is equally great; she conveys the baffled groping for words that resorts to well-worn idioms, the stupid reiteration of phrases which reveal a man's efforts to hide a sudden emotion or the cumbersome processes of his slow mind in reaching an unexpected meaning. The parts of her stories one remembers are these flashes of illumination: Deborah Thayer's discovery of her daughter's pregnancy while she is making her try on a new dress; the pathetic spectacle of old Polly Moss trying to play ball with the children—"she never caught the ball, and she threw it with weak aimless jerks; her back ached, but she was patient, and her face was full of simple childish smiles"; the sinister impression of the almshouse in the glimpse of a door flying open and a little figure running down the corridor "with the swift trot of a child. She had on nothing but a woolen petticoat and a calico waist; she held her head down, and her narrow shoulders worked as she ran; her mop of soft white hair flew out. The children looked around at her; she was a horrible caricature of themselves."

Mary Wilkins is unsurpassed among all American writers in her ability to give the breathless intensity of a moment. She does not build up to it laboriously. She rarely even uses the word which the situation carries to the reader. You know that Rebecca is pregnant simply by the way her mother pushes her violently away and stands staring at her. You discover that Oliver Weed and his wife have been murdered by the hired man only when Luella Norcross comes to bring a pillow stuffed with everlasting flowers that she has made for Mr. Weed's asthma.

> "Queer the barn door ain't open," she thought to herself. "I wonder what John Gleason's about, late as this in the mornin'?" . . .
>
> Luella heard the cows low in the barn as she opened the kitchen door. "Where—did all that—blood come from?" said she.
>
> She began to breathe in quick gasps; she stood clutching her pillow, and looking. Then she called: "Mr. Weed! Mr. Weed! Where be you? Mis' Weed! Is anything the matter? Mis' Weed!" The silence seemed to beat against her ears. She went across the kitchen to the bedroom. Here and there she held back her dress. She reached the bedroom door and looked in.
>
> Luella pressed back across the kitchen into the yard. She went out into the road, and turned towards the village. She still carried the life-everlasting pillow, but she carried it as if her arms and that were all stone. She met a woman whom she knew, and the woman spoke; but Luella did not notice her; she kept on. The woman stopped and looked after her.

How did a girl in her early twenties who had had little experience that could be measured in external events, and who had been shut in upon herself by delicate health, how did she contrive to know so much about life, to understand so accurately love and hate, to have penetrated souls that were consumed with cruelty and festering meanness, to have guessed the secrets of others that confronted the world with grim humor and silent courage? The answer is suggested in a passage she later wrote about Emily Brontë, with whom she had a very close sympathy, the subject of the only critical essay Mary Wilkins seems ever to have published:[1] "Hedged about by great spaces of loneliness and insuperable barriers of religion, in an isolated parsonage with more of the dead than the living for neighbors . . . how she ever came to comprehend the primitive brutalities and passions, and the great truth of life that sanctifies them, is a mystery. The knowledge could not have come from any actual experience. The book is not the result of any personal stress. She had given to her a light for the hidden darkness of human nature, irrespective of her own emotions. A lamp was set to her feet in the beginning. If a girl of twenty-eight could write a novel like *Wuthering Heights,* no other conclusion is possible." The circumstances of Mary Wilkins' own early life were so almost exactly parallel to those described here that these sentences tell us more of her own aspirations and achievement than the few bleakly awkward paragraphs which are all that her modesty ever permitted her to write about herself.

The readers of the eighties and nineties often found Miss Wilkins morbid and depressing. They asserted that her view of the New England nature was one-sided and distorted, that the people she drew were not typical but mere exaggerations. In one limited sense they were right. The sharply unexpected sentences with which she often ends her stories, as when she makes Candace Whitcomb, the village singer, ask her rival to sing for her as she lies on her death bed, and then gasp with almost her final breath: "You flatted a little on—soul"; the angularities and eccentricities of her characters sometimes remind us that she was working in the prevailing mode of the local colorists, which was the mode of Dickens and caricature. But such defects are on the surface. Mary Wilkins possessed what few of her contemporaries seem to have been able to understand, a deeply rooted feeling that life was a tragedy. She herself never fully explored the implications of this feeling; she never achieved a complete expression of it in any of her stories. But once again her remarks on *Wuthering Heights* come to her aid to illuminate her purpose: "All that Emily Brontë is intent upon is the truth, the exactness of the equations of her characters, not the impression which they make upon her readers or herself. She handles brutality and coarseness as another woman would handle a painted fan. It is enough for her that the thing is so. It is not her business if it comes down like a sledge-hammer upon the nerves of her audience, or even if it casts reflections derogatory to herself."

Actually the effect of Miss Wilkins's work is rarely depressing. The qualities that she emphasizes are to be seen in Delia Caldwell, the very characteristic heroine of *A Conquest of Humility.* Her tall, full figure stood like a young pine tree as if she contained all the necessary elements of support within herself. She would have been handsome except for her thick and dull complexion; there was a kind of stiff majesty in her attitude; she had the air of being one who could accomplish great things but might grind little ones to pieces. On the day of her wedding when the groom does not appear and she learns that he has been caught by a pretty face, she takes off her pearl-colored silk without a word, ties up the presents, and sends them back, and goes on with her daily routine as though nothing had happened. She allows herself only one remark, that Lawrence Thayer "has shown out what he is," and when his father agrees, "I don't blame you a bit for feelin' so, Delia," the quietness of her reply is deafening: "I don't see any other way to feel; it's the truth." She faces the world so unquiveringly that her mother finds her unnatural, but Delia Caldwell contains within herself a strange poise unknown to weaker natures. She is sustained by her self-respect.

Similar courage supports a great many of Miss Wilkins's characters, the courage that is born of loneliness. The struggle of the heart to live by its own strength alone is her constant theme, and the sudden revolt of a spirit that will endure no more from circumstance provides her most stirring dramas. Sometimes the revolt is violent, as when old woman Magoun feeds her granddaughter deadly nightshade rather than let her fall into the hands of her debauched father. More frequently it is gently pathetic. In a great many instances it gains a happy end, for beneath the surface of her realistic detail Miss Wilkins is burningly romantic: the girl manages by sheer force of will to support herself and avoid a man she does not love, or the lover returns from the West after many years to marry the old maid. Mary Wilkins knows that the solitary spirit ends in defeat, and the words which echo through her pages are those of crusty old Nicholas Gunn who, having been hurt by people, tried to live entirely apart from life and not let anything touch his sympathies. At the end he says: "Well, I was all wrong . . . I've give it all up. I've got to go through with the whole of it like other folks, an' I guess I've got grit enough. I've made up my mind that men's tracks cover the whole world, and there ain't standin'-room outside of 'em. I've got to go with the rest. Now we'll have breakfast."

It is staggering to realize that after her first two collections of stories, *A Humble Romance* (1887) and *A New England Nun* (1891), Mary Wilkins printed more than thirty-five volumes. She wrote novels, a detective story about the Borden murder, serials, a play, and sketches of New Jersey where she lived after her marriage in 1902. None of her later work has anything like the strength that I have been describing. It is commonplace, frequently sentimental, and lacking in any positive virtues of style. It makes her remark that she did not want to be a writer at all ring in one's ears. In retrospect it now appears that she told all she knew about life in those first stories. As stories they were frequently clumsy and stiff, fitted to a fairly ordinary pattern, owing their effect to single passages rather than to the shaping of the whole. She was not naturally an artist. She had the one great gift of poignant intensity, and a determination to face the truth.

Sarah Jewett once made the penetrating remark that in America we confuse our scaffoldings with our buildings, a remark that helps further to explain the unexpected burning out of such a talent as that of Miss Wilkins, and to contrast the difference of Miss Jewett's own later development. Bret Harte, Cable, Craddock, and most of the other local colorists all produced distinctive first volumes and spent the rest of their lives unsuccessfully trying to equal them. Sarah Jewett understood the reasons why: they drew authentic pictures, but they tried to make their material count for everything, and naturally it soon lost its freshness. "The trouble with most realism," she observed, "is that it isn't seen from any point of view at all, and so its shadows fall in every direction, and it fails of being art." She had grown to perceive the limitations of her own Deephaven sketches; they were accurate transcriptions, but she had stood too directly in the middle of her own experience, and had not been able to see it with any perspective. As her life expanded into wider contacts, and embraced her intimate devotion to Annie Fields, and her friendship with Aldrich and Howells and other of the Boston group, she realized that her books, if they were to be anything, must be the expression of a ripening personality. Amazingly close observation which had been able to echo the very rise and fall of nasal voices had given the sharp tang to her early work, but it was not enough. She had to wait for twenty years, looking back at her treasured scenes from afar, letting her memory dwell on them and re-combine them in new shapes, bathing them in the life-giving pools of her imagination, before she could write *The Country of the Pointed Firs* (1896).

The scope of this book is no different from that of *Deephaven*. It simply gives an impression of a summer's life in a fishing village: the subdued hum of daily existence that surrounds Almiry Todd, the famous herb-gatherer, and her old mother Mis' Blackett, alert and gracious for all her eighty-six years; the story of poor Joanna who, having been deserted by her lover, willed to live and die alone on Shell-Heap Island; the idle gossip along the shore; the great expedition up to the head of the bay for the Bowden family reunion. Miss Jewett is not a part of this life; she uses the somewhat pale device of regarding it through the eyes of a visitor to Dunnet Landing, but her visit is really a lifelong pilgrimage constantly to recapture the qualities that lie closest to her heart. She wrote the definition of her own achievement in a letter to her young friend Willa Cather: "The thing that tenses the mind over and over for years and at last gets itself put down rightly on paper—whether little or great it belongs to literature."

One gets a very exact sense of the way she lingered over her details in the limpid atmosphere that enfolds so many of her later pages: "It was evening again, the frogs were piping in the lower meadows, and in the woods, higher up the great hill, a little owl began to hoot. The sea air, salt and heavy, was blowing in over the country at the end of the hot bright day. A lamp was lighted in the house, the happy children were talking together, and supper was waiting. The father and mother lingered for a moment outside and looked down over the shadowy fields; then they went in, without speaking. The great day was over, and they shut the door."

This is the final passage in *The Hiltons' Holiday*, a story which was one of its author's own favorites, and which consists simply in the account of a trip to town made by a farmer and his two small girls. Sarah Jewett's most distinctive quality lies in her ability to enmesh the actual touch of the countryside, a whiff of salt air across the marsh, the flickering shadows over a field of grain. One thinks of the lambent coolness of her sketches in terms of a fresh June day when the lilacs have faded and the peonies are just opening and there is a breeze straight in from the sea; or of the August morning that carries the first hint of autumn when the swamp maple is suddenly a blaze of red.

But there is more to her sketches than atmosphere. She is not merely a poet of nature. She may not tell you many facts about her characters, but they embody a deeply interfused humanity. Her imagination breathes softly through them, and suggests the dimensions of life. You generally think of the stout figure of Almiry Todd as sitting heavily in the stern of a dory, or bent over in a patch of pennyroyal, loquacious, drolly positive, and disconcertingly downright. But in rare moments you also catch a glimpse, behind this daily bustle, of the uncharted depths of a heart that knows the full meaning of love and loss and suffering. Sarah Jewett did not have a sense of tragedy, a limitation which defines her sphere. The daughter of a country doctor was well aware of the stark elements of human nature, but in her temperament these were subordinated to tender pathos and humor. The characters she delineates are not torn by passions, but move on the fringes of life. They have had to give up a good many hopes, but they do not dwell on their hardships. They do not revolt; they do not try to escape. They have long ago settled down to cultivating the pattern of their narrow lives as well as their rocky squares of garden. They are as much a part of the soil they were born upon as the huckleberries and the pointed firs themselves. The style which Miss Jewett developed to convey their existence has a clarity and precision that suits it exactly to her quiet ends. It is not accidental that her language recalls Wordsworth's in the direct simplicity of its appeal. For her contribution is also one of emotion recollected in tranquility as she recites her gentle elegies of New England.

Miss Jewett and Miss Wilkins were by no means the only laborers in this vineyard. The other names would more than fill this page, names which are dropping farther and farther from sight every year, though once they bore a sweet fragrance: Elizabeth Stuart Phelps, Harriet Prescott Spofford, Annie Trumbull Slosson, Eliza Orne White. Their crop was abundant although it may have the thin taste of crab-apples. You can still bite into it anywhere and find the tart flavor of the daily life of the region. Celia Thaxter will be remembered for her picture of the subdued desolateness of the Isles of Shoals. Rowland Robinson, one of the very few men, brings in his speech the authentic twang of Vermont. Tom Bailey's Portsmouth escapades in *The Story of a Bad Boy* should find readers long after Thomas Bailey Aldrich's wanly literary poetry has been forgotten. Perhaps the latest figure to enter the field was Alice Brown, whose first book of New Hampshire stories, *Meadow Grass,* was published in the same year that *The Country of the Pointed Firs* was appearing in the *Atlantic Monthly,* and the best of whose work suggests the level of Miss Jewett, although such a comparison reveals it as less direct and somewhat over-written.

Since that time the center of creative life has moved even farther away from New England, and the strength of American prose has almost exclusively recorded other regions. It is significant that Mrs. Wharton's *Ethan Frome,* the outstanding story about New England written in the twentieth century, is the work of a woman whose life has been passed elsewhere. Willa Cather inherited much of her style but none of her material from Sarah Jewett, a style which, in the more ambitious projects of the later writer, always seems a trifle self-conscious, its classic restraint too manifestly cultivated to be able to suggest life as it does in Miss Jewett's more restricted sphere. The countrysides we are most familiar with to-day are Winesburg, Ohio, and the Minnesota woods of Ernest Hemingway. To be reminded of the essence of New England one turns to the poets, for Robert Frost and the Robinson of *Isaac and Archibald* carry on the older heritage.

The mention of these more immediate names makes the nineteenth-century story writers seem dim and far away, and one questions what there is in them to challenge our return. The answer lies in pursuing the remark of Henry James with which this essay began. It takes a great many years of living in a place to produce even a little tradition, and a great deal of tradition to give one the sense of being part of an adequate civilization. These New England writers have pictured variously an order of life which exists no longer, but which is ours none the less, since we are, at least partially, its result; and consequently through a knowledge of the aspects of that life we gain perspective on our own. But the value of Sarah Jewett and Mary Wilkins is greater than that of simply providing a link with the past. They not only reported life; each of them created, if not a world, at least a countryside of her own, the permanent endurance of which has enriched the American soil.

Note

1. I am indebted for this fact and many others to Mr. Fred L. Pattee's study of Miss Wilkins in *Side-Lights on American Literature,* 1922.

Subdued Meaning in
"A New England Nun"

DAVID H. HIRSCH

One of the most beautifully achieved scenes in the American "local color" fiction of the nineteenth century occurs in Mary Wilkins Freeman's "A New England Nun." The plot of the story is characteristically straightforward and uncomplicated. Louisa Ellis, who has waited fourteen years for her fiancé, Joe Dagget, to return from Australia, "where he had gone to make his fortune,"[1] greets his return with some apprehension. In fourteen years of waiting, Louisa has grown set in her ways. The prospect of immediate marriage fills her, quite understandably, with misgivings. As things turn out, Louisa's fears never materialize, for Joe Dagget, while unwilling to break his troth, nevertheless falls in love with a younger girl, Lily Dyer, his mother's maid. Louisa, unseen, happens to overhear Joe and Lily discussing their feelings for each other, whereupon she subsequently provides Joe an honorable exit, which he hesitantly takes, leaving Louisa in peace to resume her celibate existence.

The crucial scene I have in mind, which takes place while Joe and Louisa are still going through the motions of keeping their engagement, is impressive both in its economy and intensity. Its dramatic action exposes with superb efficiency a love affair never more than tepid at best, now grown cold:

> . . . Joe Dagget entered.
>
> He seemed to fill up the whole room. A little yellow canary that had been asleep in his green cage at the south window woke up and fluttered wildly, beating his little yellow wings against the wires. He always did so when Joe Dagget came into the room.
>
> "Good evening," said Louisa. She extended her hand with a kind of solemn cordiality.
>
> "Good-evening," returned the man, in a loud voice.
>
> She placed a chair for him, and they sat facing each other, with the table between them. He sat bolt-upright, toeing out his heavy feet squarely, glancing with a good-humored uneasiness around the room. She sat gently erect, folding her slender hands in her white-linen lap.
>
> "Been a pleasant day," remarked Dagget.

Reprinted, with permission, from *Studies in Short Fiction* 2 (Winter 1965): 124–36.

"Real pleasant," Louisa assented, softly. "Have you been haying?" she asked, after a little while.

"Yes, I've been haying all day, down in the ten-acre lot. Pretty hot work."

"It must be."

"Yes, it's pretty hot work in the sun." (pp. 3–4)

It is quite clear that in the fourteen-year interval the two lives (Joe's and Louisa's) have gone off on different tangents. Joe and Louisa have no talk for each other—no common problems whose importance both believe in. They are "realistically" portrayed serious, tight-lipped New England "types," with no ability or even desire to generate "charm," or to make witty small talk. Lacking any vital connection in their lives, they have nothing to say to each other: flirtation in the ordinary sense is out of the question for them.

At the same time, the scene, quite remarkably, does not suffer from the "imitative fallacy." That is, while the people portrayed are "dull," and while their actions in each other's presence are embarrassed and awkward, the scene itself is not dull at all. On the contrary, the scene pulsates with tightly controlled dramatic tension. Though Louisa and Joe are plain, inarticulate people who cannot reveal themselves to each other, nevertheless, their relationship is charged with an undercurrent of significance which reveals them to the reader in spite of their own silence and reserve. This undercurrent I would like to discuss in greater detail, but before doing so, it may be appropriate to consider first the relentlessness with which even the surface of the scene reveals the character of Louisa.

The naturalistic details are rendered so as to provide what is almost a case study of an obsessive neurosis, that is, a "neurotic disorder in which there are repetitive impulses to perform certain acts. Although the person sees that his ideas are unreasonable, he nevertheless feels compelled to carry out ritualistic behavior."[2] Louisa's neurotic compulsiveness becomes especially prominent after her meager store of conversation has been exhausted:

Presently Dagget began fingering the books on the table. There was a square red autograph album, and a Young Lady's Gift-Book which had belonged to Louisa's mother. He took them up one after the other and opened them; then laid them down again, the album on the Gift-Book.

Louisa kept eying them with mild uneasiness. Finally she rose and changed the position of the books, putting the album underneath. That was the way they had been arranged in the first place.

Dagget gave an awkward little laugh. "Now what difference did it make which book was on top?" said he.

Louisa looked at him with a deprecating smile. "I always keep them that way," murmured she.

"You do beat everything," said Dagget, trying to laugh again. His large face was flushed. (pp. 4–5)

Louisa must set the books in their proper order, but the order, as Joe's challenge makes clear, is arbitrary and useless. While Louisa's compulsive neurosis reaches a direct dramatic culmination in this scene, it appears as a recurring motif throughout the story. We are told, for example, when Louisa is stowing away her sewing equipment, that ". . . she quilted her needle carefully into her work, which she folded precisely, and laid in a basket with her thimble and thread and scissors. Louisa Ellis could not remember that ever in her life she had mislaid one of these little feminine appurtenances, which had become, from long use and constant association, a very part of her personality" (p. 1). Immediately following this, we read that, having picked some currants for tea, ". . . she sat on the back door-step and stemmed them, collecting the stems carefully in her apron and afterwards throwing them into the hen-coop. She looked sharply at the grass beside the step to see if any had fallen there" (pp. 1–2), a series of acts parallel, on the one hand, to her quilting the needle, and on the other to her examining the rug after Joe leaves (". . . she set the lamp on the floor, and began sharply examining the carpet. She even rubbed her fingers over it, and looked at them. 'He's tracked in a good deal of dust,' she murmured. 'I thought he must have.' Louisa got a dustpan and brush, and swept Joe Dagget's track carefully" [p. 5]). Just before Joe enters the room, Louisa removes her outer aprons, just barely managing to fold "the pink and white one with methodical haste" and remove it from sight. It takes Louisa ". . . a long time to prepare her tea; but when ready it was set forth with as much grace as if she had been a veritable guest to herself" (p. 2). Finally, I cite one more passage in which Louisa's compulsive personality is very explicitly and clearly set forth:

> Louisa had almost the enthusiasm of an artist over the mere order and cleanliness of her solitary home. She had throbs of genuine triumph at the sight of the window-panes which she had polished until they shone like jewels. She gloated gently over her orderly bureau-drawers, with their exquisitely folded contents redolent with lavender and sweet clover and very purity. Could she be sure of the endurance of even this? She had visions, so startling that she half-repudiated them as indelicate, of coarse masculine belongings strewn about in endless litter; of dust and disorder arising necessarily from a coarse masculine presence in the midst of all this delicate harmony. (p. 10)

In all this, it must be said, Mrs. Freeman does not seem to deviate greatly from the subject matter and methods of her sister writers in the New England local-color tradition. The story seems to be, no matter how skillfully done, one more among the "good many . . . tales [which] concern single women."[3] And especially does it resemble those fine tales of blighted romance so frequently found in the works of Sarah Orne Jewett. But what distinguishes the scene I have singled out, and, indeed, the entire story, from the pastoral tranquility of Miss Jewett[4] or from the sentimentality of Harriet

Beecher Stowe and Rose Terry Cooke, is the undercurrent I have already referred to.

That undercurrent provides an insight into the nature of Louisa's compulsive neurosis, but more important, antedating Freud, it anatomizes the nature of neurosis itself as a dynamic tension between conscious desire and unconscious, repressed fears. In Mrs. Freeman's story, this tension appears as an understated conflict between order and disorder, and is developed in images which become a pervasive and clearly recognizable pattern in the story.

At the outset of the scene I have chosen to analyze, for example, this conflict is immediately evident. Joe seems to "fill up the whole room" and his very presence is enough to waken the hitherto tranquil canary and send it into a frenzy. To Louisa and her domain at least, Joe represents a constant threat of potential chaos. He does not, indeed, cannot, belong in the established order of Louisa's home life and his intrusion into that life brings inevitable discord. Joe's function as an agent of discord dominates the action of the scene. After the impoverished small talk between Joe and Louisa has run its course, Joe literally upsets the established order of album and gift-book. Not only that—when Louisa attempts to restore order, Joe challenges her purpose in doing so. Next he stumbles over the rug, displacing it, and upsets Louisa's work basket in trying to recover himself. And this time, Louisa refuses to restore order until "after you're gone." Finally, we find that in addition to his gross blundering, Joe has also committed a more subtle violation of order, tracking in dust which is noticeable only under close scrutiny.

For the most part, the tension between Joe and Louisa remains beneath the surface, threatening to break out into the open only once, when, as the narrator informs us, Louisa "spoke with a mild stiffness. Either she was a little disturbed, or his nervousness affected her, and made her seem constrained in her effort to reassure him." Again, the surface detail is just right. Joe's nervousness communicates itself to Louisa, as one feels it inevitably would. But from all indications, Louisa is nervous in her own right, and her nervousness may be affecting Joe. What seems most noteworthy, then, is the sense of a clash between two opposed forces. Louisa, who feels herself responsible for the maintenance of order, is frustrated by Joe's presence. Joe is equally frustrated by Louisa's "fussing." And the underlying tension is, at the moment of Louisa's speaking with "a mild stiffness," converted into overt behavior. The clash appears explicitly, moreover, in Louisa's mind when she is contemplating her "orderly bureau-drawers," and imagines the "dust and disorder arising necessarily from a coarse masculine presence in the midst of all this delicate harmony."

Babette Levy writes that "No one in a Freeman story reads or has any intellectual interests . . . ," and although Miss Levy does not make the statement pejoratively, nevertheless it seems to suggest that the stories themselves may be somewhat deficient in intellectual content. This may explain to some extent why Mrs. Freeman's stories are so largely ignored.[5] What I would like to propose at this point is that "A New England Nun," far from being deficient in its ideational content, is actually charged with ideas, though they may not appear discursively.

In an impressive analysis of "The Fall of the House of Usher," Professor Leo Spitzer points out that the story, placed against the background of ". . . ideas concerning *milieu* and *ambiance* which were being formulated at the time, will appear to us as a poetic expression of sociological-deterministic ideas which were in the air in 1839. . . ."[6] Professor Spitzer's insight into the way in which cultural ideas may inform literature may help to illuminate "A New England Nun," which we then can see not only as a superb "realistic" representation of certain drab facts of nineteenth century New England life, but also as a poetic expression of psychological-deterministic ideas which were in the air in the 1880s.

These ideas, implicit in the imagery of order-disorder already mentioned, are further developed in what appears on the surface to be an irrelevant, humorously hyperbolic description of Louisa's one other pet (besides her canary), a dog named Caesar. "Caesar," we are informed, "was a veritable hermit of a dog. For the greater part of his life he had dwelt in his secluded hut, shut out from the society of his kind and all innocent canine joys." His incarceration "was all on account of a sin committed when hardly out of puppyhood." And although Caesar is now "fat and sleepy, . . . there was a neighbor who bore on his hand the imprint of several of Caesar's sharp white youthful teeth, and for that he had lived at the end of a chain, all alone in a little hut, for fouteen years." Despite his placidity, however, Caesar is still ". . . regarded by all the children in the village and by many adults as a very monster of ferocity. St. George's dragon could hardly have surpassed in evil repute Louisa Ellis's old yellow dog" (p. 10).

The most striking details here are first the fouteen years of imprisonment, which immediately suggests an association between Caesar and Joe Dagget, whose sojourn in a foreign land is also fourteen years, and second the linking of Caesar, however superficially and comically, with St. George's dragon. These two connections, moreover, are brought together somewhat later in the description, when the narrator asserts that "Caesar at large might have seemed a very ordinary dog, and excited no comment whatever; chained, his reputation overshadowed him, so that he lost his own proper outlines and looked darkly vague and enormous. Joe Dagget, however, with his good-humored sense and shrewdness, saw him as he was. He strode valiantly up to him and patted him on the head, in spite of Louisa's soft clamor of warning, and even attempted to set him loose" (p. 11).

That the allusion is more than mere ornament may be indicated by the courtly romance diction, the "strode valiantly" and "Louisa's soft clamor of warning." True, the connection is light-hearted and humorous, but humor itself may sometimes point to a deeper meaning. The story of St. George and the dragon has commonly been linked to the slaying of the sea-monster by Perseus; and as a matter of fact, just such a connection is made by Ishmael in *Moby Dick,* also humorously, in the chapter "The Honor and Glory of Whaling."

One need not, I think, try to push Mrs. Freeman beyond her natural depth by insisting that she was consciously manipulating what we have come to call Jungian archetypes and Melvillean symbols. Neither will it do to insist that Joe is actually St. George or, in good nineteenth century terms, a sun-god.[7] Still, even a casual consideration of the comic association between Joe and St. George-Perseus may be illuminating. In *The Anatomy of Criticism,* Northrop Frye speaks of the way in which "romance" has a tendency "to displace myth in a human direction." In a sense, the imagery in "A New England Nun" provides a superb example of this kind of "displacement." Frye describes the phenomenon as follows:

> The central principle of displacement is that what can be metaphorically identified in a myth can only be linked in romance by some form of simile: analogy, significant association, incidental accompanying imagery, and the like. In a myth we can have a sun-god or a tree-god; in a romance we have a person who is significantly associated with the sun or trees. In more realistic modes the association becomes less significant and more a matter of incidental, even coincidental or accidental imagery. In the dragon-killing legend of the St. George and Perseus family . . . a country under a feeble king is terrorized by a dragon who eventually demands the king's daughter, but is slain by the hero. This seems to be a romantic analogy . . . of a myth of a wasteland restored to life by a fertility god.[8]

What we find in Mrs. Freeman's story is the kind of "incidental" linking mentioned by Frye, but in the story here, the link is essentially ironic; and it is also, I think, more significant than Frye will generally allow in a "realistic" or "low-mimetic" work. In the myth-legend, Perseus-St. George saves the virgin by killing a sea-monster or dragon; when the hero saves the virgin, he also saves the society from decimation. But Louisa views her own "salvation" from spinsterhood as a prelude to the destruction of society. Joe intends not to kill the dragon but to release him. And it is this possibility, precisely, that terrifies Louisa, though, apparently, she does not apply the consequences of Joe's projected deed to herself alone, but to the town and the townspeople, that is, to society at large. Andromeda's salvation goes hand in hand with the slaying of the monster, Louisa's with the freeing of him. Contemplating what might happen should Joe succeed in releasing Caesar, Louisa

> . . . pictured to herself Caesar on the rampage through the quiet and un-guarded village. She saw innocent children bleeding in his path. She was

herself very fond of the old dog, because he had belonged to her dead brother, and he was always very gentle with her; still she had great faith in his ferocity. She always warned people not to go too near him. She fed him on ascetic fare of corn-mush and cakes, and never fired his dangerous temper with heating and sanguinary diet of flesh and bones. Louisa looked at the old dog munching his simple fare, and thought of her approaching marriage and trembled. Still no anticipation of disorder and confusion in lieu of sweet peace and harmony, no forebodings of Caesar on the rampage, no wild fluttering of her little yellow canary, were sufficient to turn her a hair's breadth. (pp. 11–12)

Once more the controlled surface irony is immediately evident in the disparity between Louisa's faith in the "ferocity" of Caesar and the actual senile harmlessness of the dog himself. But Louisa's vision of Caesar's brutal destructiveness, her seeing this destructiveness as a threat to the town rather than directly to herself, and her insistence on keeping him chained to a monkish existence (his "ascetic fare of corn-mush and cakes") all reveal something about the deep unrest at the core of Louisa's being. Her vision of "innocent children bleeding in [Caesar's] path," inspired by the "thought of her approaching marriage," suggests her sublimated fears of defloration. Similar fears are suggested by Caesar's imprisonment, which can be viewed as a symbolic castration: "The neighbor, who was choleric and smarting with the pain of his wound, had demanded either Caesar's death or complete ostracism." And it is Joe, of course, who threatens to commute the sentence. Finally, the last sentence of the quoted passage brings the essence of Louisa's conflict into the open. She is at a point of crisis because she has committed herself to a choice of "disorder and confusion in lieu of order and harmony."

If we consider, now, the wasteland myth underlying the Perseus-St. George legends, it is evident that the St. George link is not at all gratuitous in the story. And the way in which Mrs. Freeman invests mundane events with the myth-legend constitutes a piece of brilliant psychological insight. Joe—without being St. George or a sun god—stands as a sexual threat to Louisa; and it is quite fitting that she should associate him in her fantasies with fertility figures and fertility-sterility myths, even though Louisa herself may not recognize them as such. But whereas in the ordinary fertility myths the god is welcomed by the society because he brings with him the renewal of life, to Louisa, Joe is actually abhorrent because precisely what she does not want on at least one level of her psyche is the renewal of life and fertility that he promises, though she cannot consciously acknowledge or articulate her abhorrence.

The acuteness of Louisa's conflict is emphasized by the reintroduction of "the fluttering of her little yellow canary," in conjunction with her "forebodings of Caesar on the rampage." One thinks immediately of the lines from Edward Taylor's "Meditation Eight," which, of course, Mrs. Freeman could not have known: "When that this Bird of Paradise put in / The Wicker Cage (my Corps) to tweedle praise. . . ." The use of the bird in a cage as a symbol of spirit, however, is by no means limited to Taylor. Commenting on *Revelation,* 18:2 ("Babylon the great is fallen, is fallen, and is become the habitation of devils, and the hold of every foul spirit, and a cage of every unclean and hateful bird."), C. G. Jung remarks that "The birds are soul images."[9] The dog, on the other hand, especially when associated with dragons, is usually a death symbol,[10] and certainly the fictitious ferocity of Caesar tends to raise echoes of Cerberus (as does, also, his being fed with [honey?] cakes).

The conjoining of the two images—dog and bird—has further ramifications. In one sense, the images are parallel and intensify each other. That is, if dog is death, then Louisa's fear of seeing Caesar freed may be taken to indicate her fear of death. Moreover, if bird-in-cage is soul-in-body, then the fluttering of the bird in its cage could signify the desire of the soul to separate itself from the body: again, death. Finally, these two analogous actions work within the imagistic framework of order-disorder, too. For in both cases, Joe threatens to replace order with disorder, that is, life with chaos or death. In another sense, however, dog and bird can be taken as images of fertility and life. This is patent as regards Caesar, for he is associated with Joe, as we have seen, and his rampage through the town seems more bull-like[11] than dog-like. But the canary's flutterings, too, can be taken as the stirrings of life which Louisa has so forcefully suppressed. In both instances—dog-as-phallus, bird-as-soul—life itself has been denied.

What Mrs. Freeman does, then, with the aid of the imagery of order-disorder, sterility-fertility, is to portray contradictory impulses in Louisa that Louisa herself is not and cannot be aware of. Louisa does not want to leave her established ways; yet society, which insures fertility and continuance through the institution of marriage, seems to demand that she do leave them. Part of the problem, of course, is that in Western society, marriage itself is an ambiguous condition. At the same time that it is the very embodiment of social order it is also the consecration of anti-social Dionysian erotic impulses. Marriage is both a mundane and a "romantic" affair. For Joe it is the latter, for Louisa the former:

> Joe . . . had turned his face away from fortune-seeking, and the old winds of romance whistled as loud and sweet as ever through his ears. All the song which he had been wont to hear in them was Louisa; he had for a long time a loyal belief that he heard it still, but finally it seemed to him that although the winds sang always that one song, it had another name. But for Louisa the wind had never more than murmured; now it had gone down and everything was still. She listened for a little while with half-wistful attention; then she turned quietly away and went to work on her wedding clothes. (p. 8)

This passage, which occurs almost in the exact center of the story, echoes both the opening and closing paragraphs. In the former we are told that "It was late in the afternoon, and the light was waning. . . . Somewhere in the distance cows were lowing and a little bell was tinkling. . . . There seemed to be a gentle stir arising over everything for the mere sake of subsidence—a very premonition of rest and hush and night" (p. 1). And in the latter: "Outside was the fervid summer afternoon; the air was filled with the sounds of the busy harvest of men and birds and bees; there were halloos, metallic clatterings, sweet calls, and long hummings" (p. 17). For Louisa, sounds are always domesticated, always muted or off somewhere in the distance, remote whispers of death rather than the frenzied melodies of Dionysus.

This suppression of the Dionysian is developed in another set of order-disorder images, the alternation between garden and wilderness. Awaiting Joe's arrival, Louisa goes ". . . into the garden with a little blue crockery bowl, to pick some currants for her tea." For supper, she eats, among other things, ". . . a leaf or two of lettuce, which she cut up daintily. Louisa was very fond of lettuce, which she raised to perfection in her little garden" (p. 1). On the other hand, when Caesar has to be fed, "There was a little rush, and the clank of a chain, and a large yellow-and-white dog appeared at the door of his tiny hut, which was half hidden among the tall grasses and flowers." The one time that Louisa ventures out of her ordered world and cultivated garden is the time that she overhears Joe and Lily:

> There was a full moon that night. About nine o'clock Louisa strolled down the road a little way. There were harvest-fields on either hand, bordered by low stone walls. Luxuriant clumps of bushes grew beside the wall, and trees—wild cherry and old apple-trees—at intervals. Presently Louisa sat down on the wall and looked about her with mildly sorrowful reflectiveness. Tall shrubs of blueberry and meadow-sweet, all woven together and tangled with blackberry vines and horsebriers, shut her in on either side. She had a little clear space between them. Opposite her, on the other side of the road, was a spreading tree; the moon shone between its boughs, and the leaves twinkled like silver. The road was bespread with a beautiful shifting dapple of silver and shadow; the air was full of a mysterious sweetness. "I wonder if it's wild grapes?" murmured Louisa. (pp. 12–13)

It is in this totally alien atmosphere, in this untamed jungle suffused with the fragrance of "wild grapes," that Louisa discovers her "vocation." From the very heart of unchecked fertility and chaos she snatches the possibility of celibacy and order.

Thirty years ealier, Flaubert had anatomized a very similar neurotic crisis in *Madame Bovary*. Erich Auerbach, with his usual penetration, analyzes as follows the meal scene from *Madame Bovary* which represents the climax of Emma's dissatisfaction with her life at Tostes: "*Le Poele qui fumait, la porte qui criait, les murs qui suintaient, les paves humides*—all this, of course, Emma sees and feels but she would not be able to sum it up in this way. . . .

Flaubert does nothing but bestow the power of mature expression upon the material which she affords, in its complete subjectivity. If Emma could do this herself, she would no longer be what she is, she would have outgrown herself and thereby saved herself."[12] What Professor Auerbach says about Emma holds for Louisa as well. If she were able to articulate what Mrs. Freeman conveys through the imagery in Louisa's surroundings and in her mind, then she would very possibly no longer be the victim of her fate.

That fate is a spiritual death as certain as Emma's. But while Emma's neurotic paralysis arises out of her detestation of her present surroundings and her frustrated desire for an impossibly romantic existence, Louisa's issues from the threatened disruption of her present existence. Emma wants to flee from the filth and disorder of her immediate surroundings (a filth and disorder for which she herself is largely responsible) to an imagined order which she has created out of her reading of sentimental literature. Louisa, on the other hand, who has also created her own world, has created it as a world of tangible physical order, and she tries desperately to preserve it from the encroachments of romance. The world that Emma yearns to escape into is precisely the world that Louisa dreads, because she has already found a satisfactory escape in the immediate present—that is, in her "vocation" as a New England nun. But the irony of Louisa's calling is that it is the very opposite of spiritual fulfillment. For a person she has substituted things, for a "Thou" an "it." Her commitment is no longer to any human or divine values but to possessions: "Every morning, rising and going about among her neat maidenly possessions, she felt as one looking her last upon the faces of dear friends" (p. 8).

Louisa's acceptance of the price that must be paid for rejection of life is described as the story subsides into its deceptively placid conclusion:

> Now the tall weeds and grasses might cluster around Caesar's little hermit hut, the snow might fall on its roof year in and year out, but he never would go on a rampage through the unguarded village. Now the little canary might turn itself into a peaceful yellow ball night after night, and have no need to wake and flutter with wild terror against its bars. Louisa could sew linen seams, and distil roses, and dust and polish and fold away in lavender, as long as she wished. That afternoon she sat with her needle-work at the window, and felt fairly steeped in peace. Lily Dyer, tall and erect and blooming, went past; but she felt no qualm. If Louisa Ellis had sold her birthright she did not know it, the taste of the pottage was so delicious, and had been her sole satisfaction for so long. Serenity and placid narrowness had become to her as the birthright itself. She gazed ahead through a long reach of future days strung together like pearls in a rosary, every one like the others, and all smooth and flawless and innocent, and her heart went up in thankfulness. Outside was the fervid summer afternoon; the air was filled with the sounds of the busy harvest of men and birds and bees; there were halloos, metallic clatterings, sweet calls, and long hummings. Louisa sat prayerfully numbering her days, like an uncloistered nun. (pp. 16–17)

For Louisa, marriage is no longer a possibility; order has triumphed over confusion. Although the price of victory is not fully evident, some hint of it may be gleaned from the narrator's observation that "Caesar at large might have seemed a very ordinary dog, and excited no comment whatever; chained, his reputation overshadowed him, so that he lost his own proper outlines and looked darkly vague and enormous" (p. 11). If Caesar on the rampage can be taken as a phallus substitute, then the unjustified terror inspired by a manacled Caesar suggests that the price paid for unqualified repression of sexual impulses is fear and anxiety, and the more violent the repression, the greater the fear and anxiety.[13] The continuing threat to Louisa's psyche, in spite of her outward resolution of the conflict, can be perceived in the diction of the closing paragraph. For all its tranquility and dreaminess of mood, the paragraph, especially its conclusion, is studded with sensuous words and phrases that can easily fit into an erotic context: "the taste . . . was so delicious," "her sole satisfaction," "days strung together like pearls," "smooth and flawless and innocent," "fervid summer afternoon," "sweet calls, and long hummings." Moreover, the "smooth," "flawless," "innocent," undifferentiated days are, indeed, too tranquil. In their inert, monotonous, endless sameness they suggest death itself.

Emerson had written, in 1836, that "At present, man applies to nature but half his force," and in *Nature* he tried to point the way toward the reintegration of soul that would enable man once more to apply all of his force to nature. But throughout the nineteenth century, Emerson notwithstanding, the split in man's psyche continued to grow more acute. In her penetrating, artful analysis of Louisa Ellis' divided self, published fifty-one years after *Nature,* Mary Wilkins Freeman transcends the limitations of "local color"; by investing the minutest and most ordinary details with deeper psychic significance she achieved that "poetry of the commonplace" so urgently called for by William Dean Howells.[14]

Notes

1. *A New England Nun, and Other Stories* (New York and London, 1920), p. 6. Subsequent references in my text are to this edition.

2. Theron Alexander, *Psychotherapy in Our Society* (Englewood Cliffs, 1963), p. 18

3. Babette Levy, "Mutations in New England Local Color," *New England Quarterly* XIX (1946), 340.

4. An interesting discussion of Sarah Orne Jewett as a writer in the pastoral tradition is Robin Magowan, "Pastoral and the Art of Landscape in *The Country of the Pointed Firs,*" *New England Quarterly* XXXVI (1963), 229–40. An excellent analysis of Miss Jewett's deeper vision, and of symbolic qualities in her fiction is Hyatt H. Waggoner, "The Unity of *The Country of the Pointed Firs,*" *Twentieth Century Literature* V (July, 1959), 67–73.

5. I do not mean to give the impression that Mrs. Freeman has been entirely overlooked. Carlos Baker, writing in the *LHUS*, asserts that "at the top of her form, she was a finer artist than any of her contemporaries except Miss Jewett, and there was a sharpness of line and

directness of purpose about her first two collections which even Miss Jewett could not match" (New York, 1950), p. 847. Claude Simpson writes that with Mary E. Wilkins Freeman ". . . the short story achieved a degree of artistry and controlled form seldom found in her nineteenth-century contemporaries. . . . Her stories show a finish as well as a solidity of conception that entitles them to high rank, not alone among local colorists, but wherever the short story is appreciated" (*The Local Colorists*, New York, 1960, pp. 64–65). Edward Foster has done the only full-length biography, *Mary Wilkins Freeman* (New York, 1957).

6. *Essays on English and American Literature* (Princeton, 1962), pp. 51–66. Professor Spitzer focuses especially on the connection between Poe's use of the word *atmosphere* and the concept of "environment." Analyzing "The Bride Comes to Yellow Sky," George Montiero shows Stephen Crane using the order-disorder conflict to much the same effect. *Approaches to the Short Story*, Neil D. Isaccs & Louis H. Leiter, eds. (San Francisco, 1963), pp. 221–37.

7. Mrs. Freeman may have learned of the connections among Perseus, St. George, and a sun-god from S. Baring-Gould, *Curious Myths of the Middle Ages* (London, Oxford, and Cambridge, 1869), pp. 226–316.

8. (Princeton, 1957), p. 137.

9. *Symbols of Transformation* (New York, 1962), pp. 214–15.

10. Ibid., pp. 369–72.

11. Jung discusses the bull as fertility symbol on p. 103 of the work cited.

12. *Mimesis* (Garden City, 1957), p. 427.

13. Jung, pp. 173–74.

14. Howells, I must reluctantly report, only half perceived the depth of Mrs. Freeman's achievement. Reviewing *A New England Nun and Other Stories* in *Harper's New Monthly Magazine* of June, 1891, Howells writes: "We have a lurking fear at moments that Miss Wilkins would like to write entirely romantic stories about these honest people of hers, but her own love of truth and her perfect knowledge of such life as theirs forbid her actually to do this. There is apparently a conflict of purposes in her sketches which gives her art an undecided effect, or a divided effect. . . . In the interest of her art, which is so perfectly satisfying in the service of reality, it could almost be wished that she might once write a thoroughly romantic story, and wreak in it all the impulses she has in that direction. Then perhaps she might return to the right exercise of a gift which is one of the most precious in fiction" (LXXXII, 156).

Item, One Empty House

SYLVIA TOWNSEND WARNER

Even when afternoon tea is unlikely—and, though I had only met my hostess twice or thrice before, I felt pretty sure I should not find her among cups and saucers—it is almost impossible for an English visitor not to arrive about teatime. I was about to do so. It was a foggy January afternoon, and though I kept on rubbing peepholes in the Pullman window and peering out for my first impressions of Connecticut, these did not get beyond the admission that a coating of weathered snow seen in a disadvantageous light looks like a coating of mutton fat and that the contours under the mutton fat were not so rugged as I expected. But no doubt they would soon begin to be rugged. A few nights earlier I had sat next to a man of letters at a dinner party—a dinner party of such magnificence that we drank claret (for all this was taking place in the era of prohibition)—and, learning that he was a Bostonian, had said to him, "Tell me about New England. I am going to spend a night there." Sparing to be particular, since my outlook was so patently general, he told me that New England was reverting to the wild; that the farming population had moved westward and snakes were beginning to come down from the mountains. "Rattlesnakes," said I, knowingly. Looking kindly at me through his pince-nez, the cleanest I have ever seen astride a mortal nose, he said that rattlesnakes were among them, though I should not meet any at this time of year since rattlesnakes hate getting cold; and that he was glad I had read "Elsie Venner." I told him I had also read about New England in the stories of Mary Wilkins. He replied with an Indeed; and reinforced the effect of withdrawal by adding that she wasn't thought much of now.

Dusk fell on the mutton fat. The contours continued to be calm. Still, here I was in my English tweed suit, getting out at a station in unknown Connecticut as isolated as any pioneer and instantly and astonishingly being recognized by a perfect stranger and driven off in a car along roads where a sledge would have seemed more natural. At this point my memory wavers. But what came next was a large room, full of people, none of whom was wearing a tweed suit and all of whom were talking, and where several kind persons noticed I wasn't drinking and offered me whiskey.

Reprinted by permission; © 1966 Sylvia Townsend Warner. Originally in *New Yorker* 42 (26 March 1966): 131–38

Before I left London I promised various loving friends that during my trip I would on no account drink spirits and go blind (the sequel was considered inevitably part of the deed); and for a couple of days in New York City I was faithful to my vow. Then a loving American friend explained that I mustn't go on like this, since to refuse spirits was tantamount to casting aspersions on one's host's bootlegger—a most uncivil thing to do. As I always listen to the friend that's nearest, I took the plunge and drank whatever was offered me: spirits in ordinary homes, wine in grand ones, and once—so overwhelmingly grand was the home, and able to employ fleets of bootleggers—beer. My eyesight was none the worse for it, and my moral fibre must have been enormously strengthened because of drinking so much whiskey. I loathe whiskey; the only way I could deal with it was to toss it down neat and think of the poor large men in temperance hostels who hadn't got any.

The party in Connecticut was one of those artistic parties drawn from some international Land of Cockayne. I began to slink into corners, to examine the pictures (views of Cockayne), even to wish I could find some reposeful bore. There was nothing to remind me I was exploring Connecticut. I might as well have been in California with those rowdy forty-niners. Finally the outside guests drove away, and the houseparty began to go to bed. My spirits rose: I had been looking forward to my bedroom. It was in the L of the house, with five tall windows distributed among its outer walls. My hostess came in to ask if I needed anything and to read me one or two of her poems. When she had gone I waited a little longer in case someone else should come in with a few woodcuts or a trilogy. But no one else wanted my opinion; I was left in possession of my handsome bedroom, and went from one window to the next, drawing back the curtains. Outside there were trees. When I switched off the light, the room was flooded with the piercing moonlight of snow and the pattern of branches lay on the floor, so that I seemed to be stepping through a net. Till then I had not rightly felt I was in Connecticut. Now, because of the austerity of the moonlight and the pattern of elm branches on the wooden floor, I did. And I began to think about Mary Wilkins and to reflect that perhaps at the moment I was the only person in New England to be doing so.

I had known her for some time.

After I had been taught to read I was left to read on unassisted. If a title looked promising I tried the book (and thus for years and years never opened Gogol's "Dead Souls," being convinced it was a work of piety). One day I pulled out a volume called "A New England Nun." There were two convents in our town, and a nun was a regular feature at the fishmonger's—but nuns in fiction led more animated lives; though my notions about New England were of the vaguest kind and Mary E. Wilkins not a compelling name, the title, I thought, warranted a try. There was no word of a nun; but from the moment when Louisa Ellis tied on a green apron and went out with a little blue crockery bowl to pick some currants for her tea I lost all wish for nuns and animated lives. I had found something nearer the bone. Though I could not have defined what I had found, I knew it was what I wanted. It was something I had already found in nature and in certain teapots—something akin to the precision with which the green ruff fits the white strawberry blossom, or to the airy spacing of a Worcester sprig. But, scampering between balderdash and masterpiece, I had not so far noticed it could happen in writing too.

Having found it, this mysterious charm, I read on how Louisa, after she had finished her tea and washed up the tea things, took off her green apron, disclosing a pink-and-white apron beneath it, which was her sewing apron. This in turn she took off when she heard a man's steps coming up the walk. Beneath the pink-and-white apron was her company apron, of white linen. The man came into the room; he was her suitor, and his entrance, as usual, frightened the canary. He was honest and good and had wooed her faithfully, but in the upshot she dismissed him and remained alone among the currant bushes; and that was the end of the story.

She must have been about contemporary with Maupassant, I thought: the Maupassant of New England, telling her spinster stories as he told his bachelor ones. . . . But one cannot ramble about in a strange house at three in the morning, not even in a bohemian house—indeed, particularly not in a bohemian house—looking for a Dictionary of American Biography and saying through bedroom doors to persons rousing within, "It's all right, it's only me. I don't suppose you happen to remember what year Mary Wilkins was born?"

Besides, it would be a waste of breath. She wasn't thought much of now. The spinster and the bachelor . . . He would have thought her a quaint character and put her into one of his stories. She would have surmised him to be a bad character and kept him out of any story of hers. For she had the defect of her thrifty virtues; she wrote within her means, which is why one feels a sameness in her stories—a sameness of effort. Keeping within her means, she chose characters who would not lead her into extravagance, situations that remain within the limits of the foreseeable, never essaying the grandeur of the inevitable. But her control of detail gives these stay-at-home stories a riveting authenticity. The details have the flatness of items in an inventory. Item, one green-handled knife. Item, one strip of matting, worn. They don't express, or symbolize; they exist by being there; they have position, not magnitude. And their infallible, irrefutable placing had fastened so many north-facing rooms, hemlocks, oil lamps, meetinghouses, pork barrels, burial grounds, new tin pails, icicles, and dusty roads into my mind that if I had had the courage of my convictions downstairs, when everyone was talking about Joyce and Pound and melting pots, I would have said, "Why don't you think more of Mary Wilkins?"

I didn't. Perhaps this was as well. For one thing, one should not draw attention to oneself. For another, there might have been someone present who had thought enough about Mary Wilkins to cross-examine my admiration. And then I should have been forced to admit that she couldn't get to grips with a man unless he was old, eccentric, a solitary, henpecked, psychologically aproned in some way or other; that she never hazarded herself; that she was a poor love hand; that lettuce juice too often flowed through the veins of her characters instead of blood. Though in one respect I would have fought hard for her carnality; she wrote admirably about food, about hunger, privation, starvation even. There was that story—which, alas, I did not completely remember because I had read it in a spare room and not had the presence of mind to steal the book—about starving on a wintry mountainside. . . .

That bedroom was in Cambridge, England. The biscuit box had gingerbread nuts in it; the presence of my host's top hat in its leather hermitage made me feel I was one of the family; there must have been at least a thousand books on the shelves that occupied one wall—books of the utmost miscellaneity (I had taken Mary Wilkins from between a Bohn Tacitus and "Marvels of Pond Life"); there was a magnifying glass, a bottle of ink, and a bootjack; and at intervals I heard chiming bells conversing in amiable voices about the passage of time. But as I was now in Connecticut and did not wish to grow uncivilly homesick, the best thing I could do would be to fall asleep.

When I woke it was broad day. I dressed and went downstairs, reflecting that if I was late for breakfast, this was not an establishment where it would be held against me. It was not I who was late. There was no sound of life, there were no intimations of breakfast. Perhaps this was a house where breakfast was unlikely. In the large room that had been so noisy the night before there were plates and tumblers and bottles and ashtrays; but the curtains had been drawn back, so someone must be about. After a while a young woman came in. She was small and swarthy, and obviously I was a surprise to her. At first she pretended not to see me, and when I said, "Good morning," she clattered her trayful of glasses and did not hear me. I said I was down too early, and realized that she found me difficult to understand, for, smiling anxiously, she waved her hand toward the window and said, "Nice!" and then burst into a speech I couldn't understand at all. But we communicated in the language of the heart, for, beckoning me through the swing door, she took me into the kitchen, where we drank coffee and ate some leftover canapés.

The sun had come out, so I decided I would go for a walk. I followed the road through some woods and on into a landscape of lifeless snow-covered fields. I knew I was not enjoying myself and had decided to turn back when I caught sight of a house about a quarter of a mile farther on. A house standing alone calls to the imagination. I walked on. However trite it might be—and it looked trite—it was a house I had not seen before and would never see again. I began to walk slower—because if you change pace when you come close to a dwelling the people inside will think that you are prying or canvassing. As I approached, I felt certain the house was empty. It was smaller than I thought—a frame house of two stories, lean and high-shouldered, standing a little back from the roadside. It had an air of obstinately asserting its verticality against the indifferent, snow-covered horizontality all around. A fence guarded its own small portion of snow.

I drew level with it, and saw how very empty it was and how forsaken. The gray paint was scaling off it, streaks of damp ran down from its guttering, the windows were bleared with dust and their glass tarnished. They were too large for the house, and this emphasized the disproportion of the door, which was too narrow. A single trail of footprints led from the gate to the door. They were recent, but not new. They might have been made a week ago, three weeks ago. A week ago or three weeks ago someone had gone into the house and not come out again. I stood for a while registering this in my memory—so well that I can see it to this day. Then I turned back, walking briskly because I had grown cold. I did not speculate at all. This was no business of mine. I had come on a story by Mary Wilkins—a story she did not finish.

Defiant Light:
A Positive View of
Mary Wilkins Freeman

SUSAN ALLEN TOTH

When Hamlin Garland awarded Mary Wilkins Freeman the Howells Medal for Fiction in 1926, he praised her work as providing "unfaltering portraits of lorn widowhood, crabbed age and wistful youth . . . cheerful drudgery, patient poverty."[1] For forty years, literary historians have persisted in this view of Freeman as a pessimistic recorder of New England's decline. Larzer Ziff sees in her tales "the piercing northern night which had descended on a land now barren,"[2] Jay Martin sweepingly enfolds her characters into one general type, "the humorless, vacant, mindless, narrow New Englander,"[3] and Austin Warren has clinically classified her morbid cases of New England conscience.[4] After concluding that most critics since 1900 have treated Freeman as "a historian of New England rural life and as an anatomist of the Puritan will in its final stages of disintegration,"[5] Perry Westbrook himself stresses Freeman's sociological value as "our most truthful recorder in fiction of New England village life," a life drawing to an isolated and impoverished conclusion by the 1880's and 1890's.[6]

Although these judgments have sound basis, their cultural and historical focus on gloom, misery, decay, and extinction has obscured the real dramatic conflict at the heart of Freeman's best short stories. It is a conflict whose positive aspects need to be recognized. Many of her characters suffer, but they also fight their way to significant victories. Living in drab poverty, they still struggle with courageous spirit towards self-expression and independence. This vital struggle is far from being dated as a past or purely local condition that existed only in New England in the decades following the Civil War.

Freeman has a surprisingly modern and complex sense of the constant mutual adjustment necessary between individual and community, between need for independence and social insistence on conformity, between private fulfillment and social duties. Her men and women must assert themselves in ingenious ways to maintain their integrity in the face of community pressures, and Freeman records their varying successes with a wry but sympathetic spirit.

Reprinted from *New England Quarterly* 46 (March 1973): 82–93.

Despite their strikingly modern themes, many of these stories have never received adequate critical attention. Some, like "A Village Singer," have been often anthologized but seldom discussed. Some, like "A Church Mouse," have been praised only in passing, and then mainly for their bitter irony or pathos. Others, like "Arethusa" and "A Slip of the Leash," have long been hidden from notice and out of print. It is time to release Freeman's best fiction from its restrictive label as morbid cultural documentation and to read these powerful and relevant short stories on their own carefully developed and detailed terms.

Individual and community clash intensely in Freeman's world because organized society is inherently hostile to the needs and demands of its constituents. Life is a constant battleground for all. The sense of this underlying hostility sets Freeman's New England stories far apart in tone from those of her contemporaries. Unlike the idealized communities of Deephaven or Dunnet Landing in Sarah Orne Jewett's fiction, unlike Alice Brown's placid Tiverton, or even Harriet Beecher Stowe's earlier pictures of bustling Oldtown, Freeman's isolated villages are far from harmonious social groups. No long-established, mutual reservoir of good will provides sustenance for the business of day-to-day living. In Freeman's villages, each individual must battle the community in order to define his rights and responsibilities.

This problem of definition is often raised by the very old. While in Jewett's fiction the aged are valued as guardians of tradition and as wise advisers to the younger generation, in Freeman's stories the old must fight for their survival with all their strength, a strength fortunately dependent on character rather than on physical heartiness. The old, rather than the younger generation, institute rebellion and demand social justice. Their voices may be weak or cracked, but they insist on being heard.

"A Village Singer" is one of Freeman's best dramatizations of this problem. A deceptively quiet opening places the story in the beginning of spring, when new life is whispering in the village: "The trees were in full leaf, a heavy south wind was blowing, and there was a loud murmur among the new leaves. The people noticed it, for it was the first time that year that the trees had so murmured in the wind. The spring had come with a rush during the last few days. The murmur of the trees sounded loud in the village church, where the people sat waiting for the service to begin. The windows were open; it was a very warm Sunday for May."[7] When the new leading soprano rises to sing her solo in the church, we learn that Candace Withcomb, "the old one, who had sung in the choir for forty years," has been dismissed because the congregation feels her voice has become cracked and uncertain. The subtle relationship between the inevitable arrival of spring and the abrupt dismissal of the aged woman gives the congregation's action an unfeeling harshness, like an indifferent act of nature.

Suddenly, in the midst of the new singer's solo, Candace's strong, angry voice rises into the church; she is sitting at her nearby window and playing her small organ to drown out her rival. Everyone is shocked, and later that evening, after Candace has interrupted the second service, the rather timorous minister calls on her to remonstrate. Candace's reply, full of indignant justice, asserts the demands of her humanity and indicts the callous congregation:

"I know what you're a-goin' to say, Mr. Pollard, an' now I'm goin' to have my say; I'm a-goin' to speak. I want to know what you think of folks that pretend to be Christians treatin' anybody the way they've treated me? Here I've sung in those singin'-seats forty year. I 'ain't never missed a Sunday, except when I've been sick, an' I've gone an' sung a good many times when I'd better been in bed, an' now I'm turned out without a word of warnin'. . . . I'd like to know if it wouldn't be more to the credit of folks in a church to keep an old singer an' an old minister, if they didn't sing an' hold forth quite so smart as they used to, ruther than turn 'em off an' hurt their feelin's. . . . Salvation don't hang on anybody's hittin' a high note, that I ever heard of."[8]

This outpouring of direct, forceful prose shows Freeman's vernacular dialogue at its best, running freely and clearly but with individual speech rhythms and idiomatic speech forms, and ending in a sharp moral aphorism. Candace has clearly refused to be swept aside in the rubbish heap of spring.

Candace then informs the minister that the choir had paid her a surprise visit, given her a party, and left her a present of a photograph album. When they had gone, she opened the album and found there a note of dismissal. Now Candace is taking the only revenge she can, both by singing at her window and by using the choir's gift, the album, as a footstool. This album shows Freeman's skillful and selective use of detail. It is not described at length; it is just "a large red-plush photograph album"; but it is plainly a symbol of false friendship and community betrayal. When the minister sees Candace swing aside her skirts to show him her feet resting on the album, we experience a sudden visual shock at her pitiful revenge. Candace's defiant comment to the minister is both just and ingenious: "I'd sent that photograph album back quick's I could pack it, but I didn't know who started it, so I've used it for a footstool. It's all it's good for, 'cordin' to my way of thinkin.' An' I ain't been particular to get the dust off my shoes before I used it neither."[9]

Candace's anger against the congregation who have turned her off after a lifetime of service has transformed her into what Freeman explicitly calls a Napoleonic figure. Freeman's respect for the old woman's refusal to give in to dismissal and despair is evident in this picture of Candace as she prepares once more to interrupt the service: "She arranged a singing-book before her, and sat still, waiting. Her thin, colorless neck and temples were full of beating pulses; her black eyes were bright and eager; she leaned stiffly over toward the music-rack, to hear better. When the church organ sounded out she straightened herself; her long skinny fingers pressed her own organ-keys with nervous energy. She worked the pedals with all her strength: all her slender body was in motion. . . . Straining her throat with jealous fury, her notes were still for the main part true. Her voice filled the whole room. . . ."10

This stark description conveys the energy and nervous force that transforms a homely, even repellent old woman into a fiery and admirable figure. Candace is not merely a "humorless, vacant, mindless, narrow New Englander" as she sits at her organ and pours all her strength into a defiant song. She is a genuine heroine.

The story ends with a quiet return to the opening picture of approaching spring. Worn out by her defiant vigils and by her self-assertion, Candace becomes rapidly ill and dies. As the fever begins to affect her, she stands at her doorway and sees a forest fire raging in the distance: "She watched with a dull interest the flames roll up, withering and destroying the tender green foilage."11 This image of her own destruction is carried subtly to the final paragraph of the story, when Candace as a gesture of forgiveness has asked the new soprano to sing for her. After the song, Candace looks up at the young girl and delivers a final thrust, revealing "the old shape of a forest tree through the smoke and flame of the transfiguring fire the instant before it falls: 'You flatted a little on—soul,' said Candace."12

Taking a petty incident, the replacement of an old singer with a younger one, Freeman has turned it into a challenge to selfish community spirit, an individual's refusal to be denied humanity and justice, and a sometimes humorous, occasionally pathetic but never maudlin character study of a remarkable old woman. Without wasting space on superfluous description, from the New England early spring to the red-plush photograph album, Freeman uses setting and detail for their maximum effect. Dialogue is sharply to the point, and Candace's monologues provide most of the necessary exposition in terse, clear, idiomatic prose. Even the hint of symbolism is subtle and unobtrusive. "A Village Singer" is typical of Mary Wilkins Freeman at her best.

"A Village Singer" is only one of several fine stories that pit old and no longer fully productive members of a community against its attempt to dispose of them. One such story, low-keyed and little-known, is "A Church Mouse," a parable of the feminine will to survive even in the harshest of male worlds. Hetty, the heroine, is a woman who has grown old in household service and now has no place to go, not even a poorhouse, since her village has not built one. Deciding to apply for the job of tending the local church, she moves without permission, stove, bedstead and all, into the chimney-corner of the church gallery. Hetty survives there for a while, since she keeps the church spotless, but one Sunday morning the congregation can smell the faint odor of yesterday's turnips, Hetty's meager meal. They are outraged, not because the old woman has had no assistance or charity, but because she has defiled the meetinghouse. When they try to oust her, however, Hetty locks herself inside the church. As all the men in the community assemble to evict her forcibly, Hetty's fate looks bleak. "Hetty, small and trembling and helpless before them, looked vicious. She was like a little animal driven from its cover, for whom there is nothing left but desperate warfare and death."[13] But Hetty's courage and resourcefulness have aroused the support of other women in the community. Realizing Hetty's plight, the deacon's wife arrives with the voice of chiding conscience to silence the men and to assure Hetty she can remain in the church. The men are routed, and Hetty wakes next morning joyously to ring the Christmas bell.

Hetty has won her right to home and independence, by asserting her rights and accepting responsibility in return, as she also expects the community to do. Like Candace in "A Village Singer," she refuses to accept the status of an unprofitable figure in village accounts. Even though she may appear to be only "a little animal driven from its cover," she demands recognition of her humanity from those who do not want to be reminded of it. For her as well as for Candace, Freeman has admiration and respect.

The old are not the only members of Freeman's communities who must struggle to maintain their independence, their rights or their plain individuality. Young as well as old must protect themselves against the constant intrusion of village demands. These demands may take the form of an insatiable curiosity that threatens individual privacy at every turn. In the background of Freeman's stories the village gossips are always scurrying, waiting to carry news—preferably disastrous—to their neighbors. These stories are filled with the sounds of eager footsteps entering rooms unannounced; doors flung open into dining rooms, parlors, and even bedrooms; low voices exchanging confidences about someone who has just crossed the threshold.

Against this background of whispers and opened doors, the characters of Freeman's world try to live according to their own consciences. Their determination to be true to themselves in face of community demands provides dramatic conflict in several of Freeman's best stories. Some, like Esther Gay in "An Independent Thinker," wish to be free to follow their own conclusions about religion. Esther, who is very deaf, decides to remain home from "meeting," and knits all Sunday instead, since she cannot hear a word of the services. Although she quietly gives the proceeds of her knitting to the poor, she is heavily ostracized for breaking the Sabbath. When her adored granddaughter cannot marry the man she loves because of his mother's disapproval of Esther, the independent old woman must find a way to remain true to her beliefs but win community approval. She finally does this by taking to live with her an aged, poor woman whose bedridden condition needs constant attendance. Now she can hedge, "Of course I couldn't go to meetin' if I wanted to. I couldn't leave Laviny."[14] She has carried her point with ingenuity and integrity.

Like the picture of Candace Whitcomb at her window singing at the top of her outraged voice, the picture of Esther Gay that opens "An Independent Thinker" is a triumph of economy: "Esther sat at the uncurtained window, and knitted. She perked her thin, pale nose up in the air, her pointed chin tilted upward too; she held her knitting high, and the needles clicked loud, and shone in the sun. The bell was ringing for church, and a good many people were passing. They could look in on her, and see very plainly what she was doing. Every time a group went by she pursed her thin old lips tighter, and pointed up her nose higher, and knitted more fiercely."[15] With a few strokes, Freeman sketches the silhouette at the window to emphasize the sharp, determined features that reveal Esther's personality. As the needles click in the sun, Esther's knitting becomes a symbolic gesture of defiance that sets the tone for the story that follows. Like Candace and Hetty, Esther is an unusual but genuine heroine.

Some of Freemans' independent thinkers have been singled out for praise by critics. Ziff, for example, selects the story of a village agnostic, "Life Everlastin'," as one of her best; and Foster finds "A Tardy Thanksgiving," the story of a woman who refuses to celebrate Thanksgiving when she has nothing for which to rejoice, as the "freshest and most satisfying" of the whole collection in *A Humble Romance.*[16] Praise for these stories, however, sometimes obscures their real meaning. Freeman's characters are often cited for "going against the grain of the community," as though their defiant gestures are merely attempts at rebellion against the village code.[17] But Freeman puts much more emphasis on the positive drive towards fulfillment that motivates her strong characters, a fulfillment of what they believe to be their own true selves. They do not fight simply for their ideas but for their independence; they demand, quite simply, a measure of individual freedom. This is not a petty goal, nor is their struggle a futile one.

Among the least noticed of Freeman's stories are those that explore this urge towards self-fulfillment and that insist upon an individual's inviolable right to his own personality. "Arethusa," a story never thoroughly discussed by any critic of Freeman,[18] is one expression of this theme. Although it lacks the finished terseness and dramatic finality of some of her earlier stories, it has a charm of its own. Appearing in the volume *Understudies* (1901), which explores symbolic resemblances between twelve animals and flowers and corresponding human beings, "Arethusa" describes a girl who is wild, secret, and blooming only to herself. Lucy is a strange girl, who takes little interest in ordinary domestic life, and who prefers to roam the fields, particularly the green marshes where the arethusa and other flowers grow. Always in motion, she is barely tied to earth: "Everything about the girl except her hair seemed fluttering and blowing. She wore ruffled garments of thin fabrics, and she walked swiftly with a curious movement of her delicate shoulder-blades, almost as if they were propelling her like wings."[19] Uninterested in men, Lucy alarms her stolid mother, a farmer's wife "who had been insensibly trained by all her circumstances of life to regard a husband like rain in its season, or war, or a full harvest, or an epidemic, something to be accepted without question if offered, whether good or bad, as sent by the will of the Lord."[20] Worried about Lucy's future, her mother finally manages to persuade her to accept Edson Abbott, a young man who is strong, firm, but diplomatic in his wooing. Her acceptance is hardly a joyful assent: "It was full moonlight, and he could see her face quite plainly when she reached him and paused. It expressed the utmost gentleness and docile assent; only her body, which still shrank away from him, and her little hands, which she kept behind her like a child who will not yield up some sweet, betrayed anything of her old alarm. 'I will,' she said, tremulously; 'I will, Edson. Mother says I ought to, and I will.' "[21]

This brief but vivid glimpse of Lucy's nature, with its revelation of sexual repression that might have been recorded by D. H. Lawrence, should have prepared Edson for what happens on their wedding day. She keeps him and the guests waiting while she flees to the swamp to see if the arethusa, her special flower, has broken into bloom. Edson finds her, and she does indeed marry him, but their story does not end so simply. She cannot give up her independence completely. Every spring she goes by herself down to the swamp to see her arethusa, not even allowing her children to follow her. Freeman ends "Arethusa" with an ironic thrust at Lucy's self-satisfied husband: "In his full tide of triumphant possession he was as far from the realization of the truth as was Alpheus, the fabled river god, after he had overtaken the nymph Arethusa, whom, changed into a fountain to elude his pursuit, he had followed under the sea, and never knew that, while forever his, even in his embrace, she was forever her own."[22] Even though Lucy's strange character may seem peculiarly unbalanced to modern readers, Freeman's vision of an inviolable personality is strongly presented. Freeman has sympathy for any character who wants to be "forever her own," whether one's integrity requires holding fast to a particular opinion or to one's whole emotional nature.

Men as well as women need to "be one's own," as Freeman makes plain in one of her interesting failures, "The Slip of the Leash." Published in *Harper's* in 1904, this story is one of her few never collected in a hard-cover volume and it remains almost unknown today. Set "in one of the far Western states," it lacks the sharp-edged specificity and clear focus of her New England stories, but it does have a haunting premise. Perhaps modeled on Hawthorne's "Wakefield," it tells of Adam Anderson, over forty years old with a wife and four children, who leaves his small world because he fears he is losing a sense of his own soul. He loves his family, but he still feels "exultation that he had broken away from that love and its terrible monotony of demand."[23] Freeman is not very sure at describing unleashed wildness, volcanic forces, and deep passions as they manifest themselves outside the tight restraints of a New England village; still she manages to imbue Adam with a kind of weird reality. After some random adventures, he returns as a sort of wild man to live like a hermit in the wood near his old home and to watch his family struggle with their farm. Eventually, as his family becomes poorer and more desperate, Adam returns to them and to his old life. He has found he cannot ignore his ties and responsibilities, but at least he has gained "an infinite preciousness of renewed individuality."[24]

Through Freeman's stories march a procession of characters like Adam, Lucy of "Arethusa," Candace Whitcomb of "A Village Singer," and others like them. They assert their right to individuality, even if they must affront village society to do so. Although their circumstances may be small and confining, their characters are strong and courageous. Jay Martin believes that Freeman's people "have no purpose worthy of commitment," and that therefore "noble in being, they are foolish in action.[25] But surely Van Wyck Brooks is closer to the spirit of these stories when he sees in them "people who were filled with a passion for life."[26] Brooks recognizes the right to remain oneself as a fight to remain truly alive: "Was the Yankee soul at bay? At least, its lights were burning,—this was the fact at the heart of Miss Wilkins's tales."[27]

This defiant light may throw some gloomy shadows, but it illuminates a group of characters whose integrity, strength, and initiative go far to redeem the barren settings in which they are placed. These characters, and the stories in which they live, deserve to be better known. Far from being only the gloomiest of realists or the sternest of social historians, Mary Wilkins Freeman is also a writer of vital and complex short stories whose positive force is vastly underestimated. The struggles she depicts of individual and community glow with an intense and modern light.

Notes

1. Hamlin Garland, *Afternoon Neighbors: Further Excerpts from a Literary Log* (New York, 1934), 319–320.

2. Larzer Ziff, *The American 1890s: Life and Times of a Lost Generation* (New York, 1966), 292.

3. Jay Martin, *Harvests of Change: American Literature, 1865–1914* (Englewood Cliffs, NJ, 1967), 148.

4. Austin Warren, *The New England Conscience* (Ann Arbor: University of Michigan Press, 1966), 157–70.

5. Perry Westbrook, "Mary E. Wilkins Freeman," *American Literary Realism* 2, 139–40 (Summer, 1969).

6. Perry Westbrook, *Mary Wilkins Freeman* (New York, 1967), 15.

7. Mary Wilkins Freeman, "A Village Singer," reprinted in *A New England Nun and Other Stories* (New York, 1891), 18.

8. Freeman, "A Village Singer," 25–26.

9. Freeman, "A Village Singer," 27.

10. Freeman, "A Village Singer," 29–30.

11. Freeman, "A Village Singer," 33.

12. Freeman, "A Village Singer," 36.

13. Freeman, "A Church Mouse," reprinted in *A New England Nun*, 419.

14. Freeman, "An Independent Thinker," reprinted in *A Humble Romance and Other Stories* (New York, 1887), 313.

15. Freeman, "An Independent Thinker," 296.

16. See Ziff, *The American 1890s*, 294; and Edward Foster, *Mary E. Wilkins Freeman* (New York, 1956), 79.

17. See, for example, Ziff, *The American 1890s*, 292.

18. Westbrook gives this story three sentences in his survey of Freeman's work published in the Twayne United States Authors Series in 1967. I have been able to find no other published discussion of "Arethusa." See Westbrook, *Mary Wilkins Freeman*, 153.

19. Freeman, "Arethusa," reprinted in *Understudies* (New York and London, 1901), 148.

20. Freeman, "Arethusa," 153.

21. Freeman, "Arethusa," 158.

22. Freeman, "Arethusa," 169.

23. Freeman, "A Slip of the Leash," *Harper's* CVIX, 669 (Oct. 1904).

24. Freeman, "A Slip of the Leash," 669.

25. Martin, *Harvests of Change*, 151.

26. Van Wyck Brooks, *New England: Indian Summer* (New York: World Publishing, 1940), 472.

27. Brooks, *New England: Indian Summer*, 465.

The Artistry of
Mary E. Wilkins Freeman's
"The Revolt"

JOSEPH R. MCELRATH, JR.

Mary E. Wilkins Freeman's "The Revolt of Mother" is a short story which is now receiving a good deal of attention because of its relevance to the history of American feminism. The mother in revolt is one of those tough-minded, self-aware, and determined females that began to appear at the close of the nineteenth century when the so-called "New Woman" was assuming clear definition. And there's no need to quibble over feminists' characteristic distortions and general hobby-horse riding: Sarah Penn *is* the real thing, a female who successfully revolts against and liberates herself from a familial situation of pernicious male dominance. There is, however, a more important reason for modern readers to focus upon this particular Freeman tale. It is one of her best. Artistically, it transcends the many, many similar pieces that Freeman produced for the American magazine and book reading public of the 1880s and '90s.

It should be stressed here that "The Revolt of Mother" is magazine fiction, first published in *Harper's Monthly* (1890) and then reprinted (with few, and no truly significant, textual alterations) in *A New England Nun* (1891). The reason for this emphasis is that in a collection of Freeman's stories—and this applies to all of them—the quality of individual stories is frequently overlooked or blurred as one finishes a tale and then quickly moves on to the next. In the collections there is a quality of sameness which cannot be denied. Freeman worked with regional types, and by the time one finishes a collection of ten tales he usually knows all he wants to, thank you, about the New England spinster, the New England widow, the New England old folks, and the New England schoolmistress. Freeman's contemporaneous popularity and claim to attention in literary history cannot be fully understood until one forces himself to read her works as they first appeared. Freeman initially drew attention to herself as the author of individual tales which were published in individual issues of magazines. They were originally designed to be read in this manner, and they appear at their best when considered thus.

Reprinted, with permission, from *Studies in Short Fiction* 17 (Summer 1980): 255–61.

Magazine fiction, of then and now, must create certain immediate effects upon its reader which are not so sternly required in book publications. The cash investment in a book—versus the usually forgotten cost of a magazine subscription—insures a degree of patience on the part of the book reader. The magazine reader, on the other hand, may pick up an issue to pass a few idle moments, unmindful of his cash investment of several months previous. He is a bit more fickle, more easily distracted; if he is to be engaged the writer must stimulate his interest within the first few sentences—and thus the snappy-opener gimmicks now commonly associated with "pulp fiction." Once initial interest is stimulated, the magazine storyteller must continue to manipulate his readership so as to counter the distractions of the family parlor which vie with the writer's own demand upon the reader. Moreover, it does not hurt if the writer provides an unexpected "kick" or "twist" at the conclusion of the story, so as to leave the reader in a state of delighted surprise. (There's always that subsequent issue in which the writer will want to round-up his audience once again.)

Poe cannily understood the situation earlier in the century. In tales such as "The Pit and the Pendulum" and "The Tell-Tale Heart" he began in the most sensational fashion and structured from that with a series of crescendo effects. Freeman employs the same technique in "The Revolt of Mother": she abruptly seduces the reader into her fictional world and deliberately arranges her tensely emotional material in a series of crises, each of which seems to momentarily function as a climactic conclusion. With a rapid pace she seems to resolve the central conflict of the story, only to renew the same conflict. Then sne quickly moves to another apparent resolution, whereupon that "resolution" complicates matters further. When the actual conclusion finally does occur—providing the most surprising and unexpectedly emotional resolution of all—the sympathetic reader who delights in complication piled upon complication receives a rich reward: a happy ending totally unanticipated by the crisis-ridden and foreboding events that led up to it. If masterful artistry involves the writer's ability to manipulate the reader's mind and emotions to the point of self-forgetfulness and total immersion in the workings of a tale, "The Revolt of Mother" is a masterwork. At the least, it is a classic example of the artful use of anticlimax as a deliberate narrative device.

Forewarned of a revolt because of the title, the reader begins the story with the expectation of a crisis which will soon develop. If one thought through his expectations before actually commencing the tale, he would hazard the guess that Freeman will fashion her materials toward the mid-story crisis/climax typical to the narrative structure of the conventional short story. Freeman, however, seems to second-guess her readership, aiming at the provision of a unique reading event for an experienced and possibly jaded magazine audience. Without even the "exposition of background data" one expects to find attending the introduction of the principal characters, Freeman immediately proceeds to dramatize the story's emotional conflict and to build toward the first (apparent) resolution.

"The Revolt" begins *in media res*, with the two main characters assuming definition through their actions and the imagery assigned by Freeman to them:[1]

> "Father!"
> "What is it?"
> "What are them men diggin' over there in the field for?"
> There was a sudden dropping and enlarging of the lower part of the old man's face, as if some heavy weight had settled therein; he shut his mouth tight, and went on harnessing the great bay mare. He hustled the collar on to her neck with a jerk.
> "Father!"
> The old man slapped the saddle upon the mare's back (pp. 180–181).

Freeman's technique looks forward to the similar exposition of character through the silent and controlled violence of Ab Snopes in "Barn Burning." Father—Adoniram Penn—is thus introduced as the unsavory villain of the piece, a defiant man who will have his way and who will brook no opposition to his plans. He finally replies, roughly telling Mother to go into the house and mind her own affairs. "He ran his words together, and his speech was almost as inarticulate as a growl" (p. 181).

The sensationality of the opening is enhanced when the reader is allowed a view of the personality questioning Adoniram. It seems as though the sparks will fly, for she does not immediately go into the house; and Freeman provides the first indication of the fiercely independent person with whom Adoniram was to deal. Mother appears the "meek housewife"; but "her eyes, fixed upon the old man, looked as if the meekness had been the result of her own will, never the will of another." As we glance again at her, we are made to see someone who looks "as immovable . . . as one of the rocks in [Adoniram's] pastureland, bound to the earth with generations of blackberry vines" (p. 181). At this point, Adoniram is compelled by her presence of character to reveal to Mother that he is building a barn.

It is Adoniram who then retreats, although he does not change his mind about the barn. He temporarily defuses the situation by his withdrawal; and Freeman then turns to the Mother, explaining through dialogue that Adoniram has conspired to build the barn without her consent and against her known desires. By the time son Sammy reveals to Mother that Father also intends to buy four more cows, the first "act" of the story with its crisis/climax is complete. A stiff-necked Adoniram and equally willful Mother have completed their initial confrontation, and Adoniram has won the contest. Mother does silently return to her kitchen, where we soon discover that she is in no way as sinister as her husband seems and that, while she is strong-willed, she is clearly a sympathetically conceived victim of her husband's obstinate nature.

This constitutes the first resolution of conflict in "The Revolt of Mother," and hence the usefulness of a dramatic term such as "act" in explaining the short story. The first section of the story functions as a one-act play: a conflict was introduced; it moved toward a muted but real climax; and the conflict was resolved by the withdrawal of Adoniram and the capitulation of Mother.[2]

But, the story, and the conflict, as it turns out, have only begun. The second act opens with Mother, saying "nothing more," entering her pantry. As Adoniram expressed his emotionality by roughly handling the mare, Mother likewise employs the means at hand: "a clatter of dishes" is heard. She attempts to resign herself to the situation in dutiful, housewifely fashion. But as she begins washing dishes with her daughter Nanny, the attempt seems to be failing. Her behavior bristles with suppressed rage. Mother "plunged her hands vigorously into the water" as Nanny identifies the cause of the conflict initiated in act one: " 'don't you think it's too bad father's going to build that barn, much as we need a decent house to live in?' " That this is the root of resentment is confirmed by Mother who then "scrubbed a dish fiercely." Her anger is finally articulated: " 'You ain't found out yet we're women-folks, Nanny Penn' " (p. 183).

Nanny goes on to lament the fact that her impending wedding will take place in their ill-decorated "box of a house." She is not exaggerating about the house. We may recall that in act one we were off-handedly told something about their dwelling. The details now assume a larger significance: "The house, standing at right angles with the great barn and a long reach of sheds and out-buildings, was infinitesimal compared to them. It was scarcely as commodious for people as the little boxes under the barn eaves were for doves" (p. 182). Nanny is upset; Mother is upset. But then Mother goes on to display the nobility of character which makes her such a positively fashioned heroine in the eyes of the reader and which, by way of contrast, makes Adoniram seem an even blacker villain. For forty years Adoniram has promised a decent house but has built only the structures he felt he needed for his business. Mother has just passed through the most recent and greatest betrayal of that promise. Yet she has strength of character enough not to exact revenge by turning Nanny against her father. She attempts to appreciate the finer points of her situation, reminding Nanny that "a good many girls don't have as good a place as this" (p. 184). Then she notes what a blessing it is that Adoniram built a cooking shed for them so that they would not have to bake in the house during hot weather.

A few hours later, with both of the children out of the way, a second crisis is initiated by Mother. She calls Adoniram from his work, sits him down, reminds him that she has never complained before, and begins to complain at length about his placing barns and cows above familial obligations. She delivers a brilliantly passionate monologue, clearly vindicating her claim that she and her children have been wronged. "Mrs. Penn's face was burning; her mild eyes gleamed. She had pleaded her little cause like a Webster," hearing in response only Adoniram's blunt reply, " 'I ain't got nothin' to say' " (p. 187). That resolves the crisis. Adoniram shuffles out; Mother goes to the bedroom, and later comes back to the kitchen with reddened eyes. Renewed conflict—crisis—resolution.

A third act begins with Nanny returning to the kitchen miffed, sarcastically suggesting that her wedding might better be held in the new barn which will undoubtedly be nicer than the house. Nanny notes her mother's peculiar expression when she completes this pettish suggestion. It will become clear to the reader several hundred words later that this constitutes actual "crisis" moment of the narrative structure (determining the outcome of the tale): it is here that Mother decides to make the barn their new home should the opportunity afford itself. At present, though, Freeman withholds this information and runs the risk of maintaining reader interest with a peculiar kind of suspense. The questions that comes to mind at this point is, where can the story possibly be going? In view of the many paragraphs remaining, *something* is certainly about to happen. But it is simply unthinkable, given the information Freeman has fed the reader, that Adoniram will change his mind.

The story leaps ahead through the spring months during which the barn is being constructed, and Freeman relates that Mother no longer speaks of the matter. We are duped into thinking that Mother has, indeed, resigned herself to the egotism of her husband—that the conflict of acts one and two has been truly resolved. Freeman now elaborates upon Adoniram's villainy, once again confirming the belief that Mother's situation is a hopeless one. While he claims he cannot afford to build the promised house and is insensitive to Nanny's having to be married in an old "box," he makes plans to go to Vermont to buy "jest the kind of a horse" (p. 189) he has long wanted. As he departs on the buying-trip, a hiss is the audience response that has been engineered by Freeman.

A maxim occurs to Mother after Adoniram's departure: " 'Unsolicited opportunities are the guide-posts of the Lord to the new roads of life.' " To Mother, the opportunity "looks like providence" (p. 190). She forthwith gives directions to the help: move all of the household belongings to the barn. The event is a grandly liberating and heroic one, even if it does seem destined to produce an unhappy outcome. "During the next few hours a feat was performed by this simple, pious New England mother which was equal in its way to Wolfe's storming of the Heights of Abraham" (p. 192), Freeman tells us. But, we should recall that General Wolfe was mortally wounded during that conflict.

Most of the fourth act is given to the rising action leading to the true "climax" of the narrative structure and its rapidly executed denouement and conclusion. What *will* Adoniram do when he returns? We know only the most negative things about his character: he has seemed violent; he has acted in the most egotistical and pig-headed ways; he has been curt with Mother beyond the point of simple rudeness; and he expects no one to cross him, least of all Mother. We are free to imagine only dire consequences.

Reader interest is heightened through more suspense. The local characters begin ruminating over the probable outcome of this revolt; they loiter about the neighborhood on the day of Adoniram's return to see what will happen. We know that Mother is not going to back down. When the local minister comes to reason with her, she is shelling peas "as if they were bullets," and when she looks at him there is in her eyes "the spirit that her meek front had covered for a lifetime" (p. 193). Suspense is further increased when Sammy excitedly announces Adoniram's arrival and Nanny finds "a hysterical sob in her throat" (p. 194). The reader is thus prepared for a stormy conclusion, possibly of blood and thunder.

What the reader does not expect after all that has occurred is a comic reversal. But Freeman does end this tale of impending tragedy with a startling turn to a tragicomic resolution. And the truly amazing thing is that she turns the tables on the reader as convincingly as she does. Adoniram shows none of the anger that seemed to be so great a part of his nature at the story's beginning. Adoniram shows no anger at all. Rather, he is totally bewildered, able only to say " 'Why, mother!' " again and again as he tried to grasp the change that has taken place. What are the cows doing in the house, and why is the house in the new barn? Mother leads him to the supper table and they eat in silence. Afterward, Mother touches his shoulder, breaking into his state of distraction, and he begins—weeping. He totally capitulates, promising to finish the new barn as a house. There is no resentment. Instead there is the first show of his love for Mother in the whole tale: " 'Why, mother,' he said, hoarsely, 'I hadn't no idee you was so set on't as all this comes to' " (p. 196). He is telling the truth, oddly enough. Freeman had withheld the fact that Adoniram's could be, and was, a sensitive and loving nature—albeit an extraordinarily dense one. It is one of the most complicated trick-endings in all of nineteenth-century American short fiction. Freeman did all that she could to suppress suspicion that such an ending could be even remotely possible. Her mastery is especially made manifest when we think back over the story and note how she developed the scenes to obscure positive personality traits in Adoniram which were actually there all the time.

It should therefore appear as no mystery that William Dean Howells celebrated Freeman's technique and vision of life. When Howells reviewed *Main Travelled Roads,* he chided Hamlin Garland for his preoccupation with the grimmer, darker aspects of life. Howells suggested that in every field there were roses as well as thistles and that a truly representative picture of American life should note the beautiful as well as the ugly. The reassuring testimony to the admixture of good and evil in human nature with which

Freeman startles the reader at the conclusion of "The Revolt" is vintage Howellsian realism at its enduring best. "The Revolt" is also, to speak more plainly, literary gimmickry at its best. It is so well executed that, while some readers may resent the withholding of *the* fact about Adoniram that changes everything, the rest of us can enjoy the notion that love can sometimes conquer all, in 1890 and even in the 1980s.

Notes

1. Quotations are derived from the text of "The Revolt" now most in use: see *American Literature Survey: Nation and Region,* 1860–1900, ed. Milton R. Stern and Seymour L. Gross (New York: The Viking Press, 1975), pp. 180–196. Page references within parentheses are to this text.
2. In this essay the major crisis/climax situations are considered. But the reader will want to note the many additional minor crises through which Mother passes as she privately struggles with her plight. Throughout the first half of the story she is almost constantly vacillating between resignation and revolt.

An Uncloistered
"New England Nun"

MARJORIE PRYSE

In his biography of Mary Wilkins Freeman, Edward Foster writes that " 'A New England Nun' . . . has been considered Miss Wilkins' definitive study of the New England spinster."[1] Yet because the spinster has traditionally carried such negative connotations, critics and historians have either phrased their praise of Freeman as apologies for her "local" or "narrow" subject matter, or deemed her depiction of Louisa Ellis in "A New England Nun" as ironic. Jay Martin views her as "an affectionately pathetic but heroic symbol of the rage for passivity." He judges that protagonists like her "have no purpose worthy of commitment. . . . Lacking a heroic society, Mary Wilkins' heroes are debased; noble in being, they are foolish in action."[2] Foster concludes that "it is precisely the absence of desire and striving which is the story's grimly ironic point."[3] Pathetic, passive, debased, foolish, lacking in desire or ambition: such a portrait, they imply, invites the reader to shun Louisa Ellis. Definitive study though she may be, we are not to admire or emulate her.

When Louisa Ellis reconsiders marriage to Joe Dagget, she aligns herself against the values he represents. Her resulting unconventionality makes it understandably difficult for historians, themselves the intellectual and emotional products of a society which has long enshrined these values, to view her either perceptively or sympathetically. For Louisa Ellis rejects the concept of manifest destiny and her own mission within it; she establishes her own home as the limits of her world, embracing rather than fleeing domesticity, discovering in the process that she can retain her autonomy; and she expands her vision by preserving her virginity, an action which can only appear if not "foolish" at least threatening to her biographers and critics, most of whom have been men.

In analyzing "A New England Nun" without bias against solitary women, the reader discovers that within the world Louisa inhabits, she becomes heroic, active, wise, ambitious, and even transcendent, hardly the woman Freeman's critics and biographers have depicted. In choosing solitude, Louisa creates an alternative pattern of living for a woman who pos-

Reprinted, with permission, from *Studies in Short Fiction* 20 (Fall 1983): 289–95.

sesses, like her, "the enthusiasm of an artist" (p. 9).[4] If she must sacrifice heterosexual fulfillment (a concept current in our own century rather than in hers) she does so with full recognition that she joins what William Taylor and Christopher Lasch have termed "a sisterhood of sensibility."[5] For all of her apparent sexual repression, her "sublimated fears of defloration,"[6] she discoveres that in a world in which sexuality and sensibility mutually exclude each other for women, becoming a hermit like her dog Caesar is the price she must pay for vision. "A New England Nun" dramatizes change in Louisa Ellis. A situation she has long accepted now becomes one she rejects. The story focuses on what she stands to lose, and on what she gains by her rejection.

Although Louisa's emotion when Joe Dagget comes home is "consternation," she does not at first admit it to herself. "Fifteen years ago she had been in love with him—at least she considered herself to be. Just at that time, gently acquiescing with and falling into the natural drift of girlhood, she had seen marriage ahead as a reasonable feature and a probable desirability of life. She had listened with calm docility to her mother's views upon the subject. . . . She talked wisely to her daughter when Joe Dagget presented himself, and Louisa accepted him with no hesitation" (p. 7). Wilkins implies in this passage that the "natural drift of girlhood" involving eventual marriage does require gentle acquiescence as well as wise talk from her mother, and that in taking Joe Dagget as her lover, Louisa has demonstrated "calm docility"—as if she has agreed to accept a condition beyond her control. When Joe Dagget announces his determination to seek his fortune in Australia before returning to marry Louisa, she assents "with the sweet serenity which never failed her" (p. 6); and during the fourteen years of his absence, "she had never dreamed of the possibility of marrying any one else." Even though "she had never felt discontented nor impatient over her lover's absence, still she had always looked forward to his return and their marriage as the inevitable conclusion of things" (p. 7). Conventional in her expectations as in her acquiescence to inevitability, however, she has yet placed eventual marriage "so far in the future that it was almost equal to placing it over the boundaries of another life " (pp. 7–8). Therefore when Joe Dagget returns unexpectedly, she is "as much surprised and taken aback as if she had never thought of it" (p. 8).

Given the nature of Joe Dagget's departure, and that of other men of the region after the Civil War who went west or moved to the cities, individually enacting the male population's sense of manifest destiny, Louisa Ellis chose a positive course of action in making her solitude a source of happiness. For Joe Dagget would have stayed in Australia until he made his fortune. "He would have stayed fifty years if it had taken so long, and come home feeble and tottering, or never come home at all, to marry Louisa." Her place in such an engagement, in which "they had seldom exchanged letters" (p. 6), was to wait and to change as little as possible. Joe Dagget might return or he might not; and either way, Louisa must not regret the passing of years. Within such a narrow prescription for socially acceptable behavior, "much had happened" even though Joe Dagget, when he returns, finds Louisa "changed but little" (p. 8). "Greatest happening of all—a subtle happening which both were too simple to understand—Louisa's feet had turned into a path, smooth maybe under a calm, serene sky, but so straight and unswerving that it could only meet a check at her grave, so narrow that there was no room for any one at her side" (p. 7). In appearing to accept her long wait, she has actually made a turn away from the "old winds of romance" which had "never more than murmured" for her anyway (p. 8). Now, when she sews wedding clothes, she listens with "half-wistful attention" to the stillness which she must soon leave behind.

For she has no doubt that she will lose, not gain, in marrying Joe Dagget. She knows, first, that she must lose her own house. "Joe could not desert his mother, who refused to leave her old home. . . . Every morning, rising and going about among her neat maidenly possessions, she felt as one looking her last upon the faces of dear friends. It was true that in a measure she could take them with her, but, robbed of their old environments, they would appear in such new guises that they would almost cease to be themselves" (p. 8). Marriage will force her to relinquish "some peculiar features of her happy solitary life." She knows that "there would be a large house to care for; there would be company to entertain; there would be Joe's rigorous and feeble old mother to wait upon" (p. 9). Forced to leave her house, she will symbolically have to yield her world as well as her ability to exert control within it.

She will also lose the freedom to express herself in her own art. She possesses a still with which she extracts "the sweet and aromatic essences from roses and peppermint and spearmint. By-and-by her still must be laid away" (p. 9). In Perry Westbrook's view, this still symbolizes "what her passivity has done to her." In distilling essences "for no foreseeable use," she "has done no less than permit herself to become unfitted for life."[7] Such an interpretation misses the artistic value, for Louisa, of her achievement in managing to extract the very "essences" from life itself—not unlike her fellow regionalist's apple-picker ("Essence of winter sleep is on the night / The scent of apples . . ."). Her art expresses itself in various way: "Louisa dearly loved to sew a linen seam, not always for use, but for the simple, mild pleasure which she took in it" (p. 9). Even in her table-setting, she achieves artistic perfection. Unlike her neighbors, Louisa uses her best china instead of "common crockery" every day—not as a mark of ostentation, but as an action which enables her to live "with as much grace as if she had been a veritable guest to her own self" (p. 2). Yet she knows that Joe's mother and Joe himself will "laugh and frown down all these pretty but senseless old maiden ways" (p. 9).

She seems to fear that the loss of her art will make her dangerous, just as she retains "great faith" in the ferocity of her dog Caesar, who has "lived at the end of a chain, all alone in a little hut, for fourteen years" (p. 10) because he once bit a neighbor. Louisa keeps him chained because "she pictured to herself Caesar on the rampage . . . she saw innocent children bleeding in his path . . ." (p. 12). In spite of the fact that he looks docile, and Joe Dagget claims " 'There ain't a better-natured dog in town' " (p. 11), Louisa believes in his "youthful spirits," just as she continues to believe in her own. Louisa fears that Joe Dagget will unchain Caesar—" 'Some day I'm going to take him out' " (p. 11), he asserts. Should he do so, Louisa fears losing her vision rather than her virginity. Caesar, to Louisa, is a dog with a vision which, as long as he is chained, he retains, at least in his reputation: "Caesar at large might have seemed a very ordinary dog, and excited no comment whatsoever; chained, his reputation overshadowed him, so that he lost his own proper outlines and looked darkly vague and enormous" (p. 11). Only Louisa senses that setting the dog free would turn him into a "very ordinary dog," just as emerging from her own "hut" after fourteen years and marrying Joe Dagget would transform her, as well, into a "very ordinary" woman—yet a woman whose inner life would be in danger. Louisa "looked at the old dog munching his simple fare, and thought of her approaching marriage and trembled" (p. 12).

In addition, because the name Caesar evokes an historical period in which men dominated women, in keeping Caesar chained Louisa exerts her own control over masculine forces which threaten her autonomy. David Hirsch reads "A New England Nun" as Louisa's "suppression of the Dionysian" in herself, a Jungian conflict between order and disorder, sterility and fertility. He concludes that Caesar's continuing imprisonment "can be viewed as a symbolic castration," apparently of Louisa herself.[8] To a point, the story appears to justify Hirsch's assertions, for Caesar's first entrance in the story visually evokes phallic power: "There was a little rush, and the clank of a chain, and a large yellow-and-white dog appeared at the door of his tiny hut, which was half hidden among the tall grasses and flowers" (p. 2). Yet Caesar emerges from his hut because Louisa has brought him food. If the image involves castration, it portrays Louisa intact and only masculine dominance in jeopardy.

Ambiguous images of sexuality abound in this story, sedate as Louisa's life appears to be. When she finishes feeding Caesar and returns inside her house, she removes a "green gingham apron, disclosing a shorter one of pink and white print." Shortly she hears Joe Dagget on the front walk, removes the pink and white apron, and "under that was still another—white linen with a little cambric edging on the bottom" (p. 3). She wears not one but three aprons, each one suggesting symbolic if not actual defense of her own virginity. When Dagget visits, "he felt as if surrounded by a hedge of lace. He was afraid to stir lest he should put a clumsy foot or hand through the fairy web, and he had always the consciousness that Louisa was watching fearfully lest he should" (p. 6). The visual image of clumsy hand breaking the "fairy web" of lace like the cambric edging on Louisa's company apron suggests once again that Louisa's real fear is Joe's dominance rather than her own sexuality. Joe, when he leaves, "felt much as an innocent and perfectly well-intentioned bear might after his exit from a china shop." Louisa "felt much as the kind-hearted, long-suffering owner of the china shop might have done after the exit of the bear" (p. 5). In Joe's absence she replaces the additional two aprons, as if to protect herself from his disturbing presence, and sweeps up the dust he has tracked in. When she imagines marrying Joe, she has visions of "coarse masculine belongings strewn about in endless litter; of dust and disorder arising necessarily from a coarse masculine presence in the midst of all this delicate harmony" (p. 10).

Taylor and Lasch discuss the nineteenth-century myth of the purity of women in a way which explains some of Louisa's rejection of Joe Dagget and marriage itself. "The myth itself was yet another product of social disintegration, of the disintegration of the family in particular. It represented a desperate effort to find in the sanctity of women, the sanctity of motherhood and the Home, the principle which would hold not only the family but society together." When Louisa waits patiently during fourteen years for a man who may or may not even return, she is outwardly acceding to the principle by which women in New England provided their society with a semblance of integration. However, as Taylor and Lasch continue,

> the cult of women and the Home contained contradictions that tended to undermine the very things they were supposed to safeguard. Implicit in the myth was a repudiation not only of heterosexuality but of domesticity itself. It was her purity, contrasted with the coarseness of men, that made woman the head of the Home (although not of the family) and the guardian of public morality. But that same purity made intercourse between men and women at last almost literally impossible and drove women to retreat almost exclusively into the society of their own sex, to abandon the very Home which it was their appointed mission to preserve.[9]

Louisa Ellis certainly repudiates masculine coarseness along with domesticity—for while within her own home she maintains order with the "enthusiasm of an artist," in Joe Dagget's house, supervised by a mother-in-law, she would find "sterner tasks" than her own "graceful but half-needless ones" (p. 9). In rejecting Joe Dagget, then, in the phrasing of Taylor and Lasch, she abandons her appointed mission.

Freeman goes farther than Taylor and Lasch, however, in demonstrating that Louisa Ellis also has a tangible sense of personal loss in anticipating her marriage. One evening about a week before her wedding, Louisa takes a walk under the full moon and sits down on a wall. "Tall shrubs of blueberry vines and meadow-sweet, all woven together and tangled with blackberry vines and horsebriers, shut her in on either side. She had a little clear space between them. Opposite her, on the other side of the road, was a spreading tree; the moon shone between its boughs, and the leaves twinkled like silver. The road was bespread with a beautiful shifting dapple of silver and shadow; the air was full of mysterious sweetness" (pp. 12–13). As she sits on the wall "shut in" by the tangle of sweet shrubs mixed with vines and briers, with her own "little clear space between them," she herself becomes an image of inviolate female sexuality. However, what she looks at "with mildly sorrowful reflectiveness" is not physical but imaginative mystery. Within the protection of the woven briers, Louisa's ability to transform perception into vision remains intact. What might be described as embattled virginity from a masculine point of view becomes Louisa's expression of her autonomous sensibility.

Therefore when she overhears Joe Dagget talking with Lily Dyer, "a girl full of a calm rustic strength and bloom, with a masterful way which might have beseemed a princess" (p. 13), and realizes that they are infatuated with each other, she feels free at last to break off her engagement, "like a queen who, after fearing lest her domain be wrested away from her, sees it firmly insured in her possession" (p. 16). Freeman writes, "If Louisa Ellis had sold her birthright she did not know it, the taste of the pottage was so delicious, and had been her sole satisfaction for so long" (p. 17). In rejecting marriage to Joe Dagget, Louisa feels "fairly steeped in peace" (p. 16). She gains a transcendent selfhood, an identity which earns her membership in a "sisterhood of sensibility."

In the story's final moment, she sees "a long reach of future days strung together like pearls in a rosary, . . . and her heart went up in thankfulness." Like Caesar on his chain, she remains on her own, as the rosary's "long reach" becomes an apotheosis of the dog's leash. Outside her window, the summer air is "filled with the sounds of the busy harvest of men and birds and bees" from which she has apparently cut herself off; yet inside, "Louisa sat, prayfully numbering her days, like an uncloistered nun" (p. 17). Freeman's choice of concluding image—that Louisa is both nun-like in her solitude yet "uncloistered" by her decision not to marry Joe Dagget—documents the author's perception that in marriage Louisa would have sacrificed more than she would have gained. If the ending of "A New England Nun" is ironic, it is only so in the sense that Louisa, in choosing to keep herself chained to her hut, has thrown off society's fetters. The enthusiasm with which Louisa has transformed "graceful" if "half-needless" activity into vision and with which she now "numbers" her days—with an aural pun on poetic meter by which Freeman metaphorically expands Louisa's art—would have been proscribed for her after her marriage. Such vision is more than compensatory for Louisa's celibacy. Louisa's choice of solitude, her new "long reach," leaves her ironically "uncloistered"—and imaginatively freer, in her society, than she would otherwise have been.

In looking exclusively to masculine themes like manifest destiny or the flight from domesticity of our literature's Rip Van Winkle, Natty Bumppo, and Huckleberry Finn, literary critics and historians have overlooked alternative paradigms for American experience. The very chaos which the challenge of the frontier for American men brought to the lives of American women also paradoxically led these women, in nineteenth-century New England, to make their own worlds and to find them in many ways, as Louisa Ellis does, better than the one the men had left. The world Louisa found herself inhabiting, after the departure of Joe Dagget for Australia, allowed her to develop a vision stripped of its masculine point of view which goes unnoticed—both in her own world, where Joe returns to find her "little changed," and in literary history, which too quickly terms her and her contemporaries sterile spinsters. Yet Louisa Ellis achieves the visionary stature of a "New England nun," a woman who defends her power to ward off chaos just as strongly as nineteenth-century men defended their own desires to "light out for the territories." The "New England nun," together with her counterpart in another Freeman story, "The Revolt of 'Mother,' " establishes a paradigm for American experience which makes the lives of nineteenth-century women finally just as manifest as those of the men whose conquests fill the pages of our literary history.

Notes

1. Edward Foster, *Mary E. Wilkins Freeman* (New York: Hendricks House, 1956), p. 105.

2. Jay Martin, *Harvests of Change: American Literature, 1865–1914* (Englewood Cliffs, N.J.: Prentice-Hall, 1967), pp. 150–51.

3. Foster, p. 106.

4. Mary Wilkins Freeman, "A New England Nun," in *A New England Nun and Other Stories* (New York: Harper & Bros., 1891). Page numbers are included in parentheses in the text.

5. William R. Taylor and Christopher Lasch, "Two 'Kindred Spirits': Sorority and Family in New England, 1839–1846," *New England Quarterly*, 36 (1963), 34.

6. David H. Hirsch, "Subdued Meaning in 'A New England Nun,' " *Studies in Short Fiction*, 2 (1965) 131.

7. Perry Westbrook, *Mary Wilkins Freeman* (New York: Twayne Publishers, 1967), pp. 58–59.

8. Hirsch, pp. 133, 131.

9. Taylor and Lasch, p. 35.

"Unusual" People in a "Usual Place": "The Balking of Christopher" by Mary Wilkins Freeman

Beth Wynne Fisken

Published in the 1914 volume of short stories by Mary Wilkins Freeman entitled *The Copy-Cat & Other Stories,* "The Balking of Christopher" successfully combines two forms, the extended parable and the realistic sketch.[1] Freeman expresses the heightened spiritual insights of her main character in the everyday laconic and understated dialogue of rural New England. The people in her story are presented both as full and complex characters and as representations of certain stages of spiritual enlightenment, as Freeman's artistry renders her characters convincing on both the realistic and symbolic levels. The subtle balance maintained between humor and intensity, narration and inspiration, depiction and instruction, makes "The Balking of Christopher" one of Freeman's most technically impressive as well as emotionally compelling stories.

The title, itself, exemplifies the two dominant modes of the story, in particular, the two interpretations offered for the startling behavior of Christopher, the main character. According to the narrow pragmatism of the community, the Christopher who refuses to plow and work has simply "balked" like a stubborn mule at an obstacle. His name, however, with its sacred meaning, "bearing Christ," reflects the point of view of Reverend Stephen Wheaton in the story, who enters sympathetically into Christopher's quest, his solitary communion with nature on the mountain, and his search for answers to his questions about the purpose behind his existence.

Christopher's unconventional behavior is first presented to the reader indirectly from the point of view of others, as we are permitted to eavesdrop on the good-humored gossip of his mother and sister. Then we are asked to share his rebellious doubts as he reveals them in an anguished confession to Wheaton. Finally, we interpret Christopher through the bewildered loyalty of his wife, Myrtle, and Wheaton's enthusiastic identification with Christopher's retreat to Silver Mountain. These successive versions of Christopher emphasize how difficult it is to know and understand another person. Indeed, the highest praise that can be given is that one "can see with the eyes of

Reprinted, with permission, from *Colby Library Quarterly* 21 (June 1985): 99–103.

other people,"[2] as Christopher says about Wheaton at the end of the story. The imaginative intelligence required for such empathy is rare, however, and most of us are likely to find ourselves groping in the dark when presented with the anomalous behavior of those close to us. It would be enough, perhaps, if we could simply "understand not understanding" (284), a faculty for which Christopher praises his wife. Such an understanding is as genuine an act of love as total comprehension and far more likely to occur in the relationships between men and women, not only in the rural New England world of Freeman's fiction, but in our own world as well.

The affectionate grumblings of Christopher's mother and sister that begin the story serve two purposes. First, they recall the mundane and trivial considerations that generally occupy our minds, repressing the deeper questions that torture Christopher, but second, they anchor the story in the real world, seasoning the intensity of Christopher's spiritual quest with the salt of everyday conversation, the affectionate teasing that keeps us from forgetting that we are human. According to his mother and sister, Christopher, because of his uncommon sensitivity and intelligence, was spoiled by his father and allowed to have his way too much. It is obvious that his mother's criticism arises from a secret pride in his special qualities, a pride that can only find expression in criticism, perhaps as a way of warding off bad fortune or conforming with the expectations of the community. It is also equally obvious that Christopher's sister, Abby, criticizes him to his wife, Myrtle, so she can condescend to her and justify the advantages of her own unmarried state. With skillful economy, Freeman suggests the politics of the family underlying their casual conversation, revealing the snares we lay for those close to us, either in the name of our own anxieties or in the interests of our own self-esteem.

Christopher, in his ensuing confession to Reverend Stephen Wheaton, seems to agree with the consensus of the family that because he is different he is spoiled, as he punctuates his observations with defensive apologies for their unconventionality: "I don't mean to blaspheme, Mr. Wheaton, but it is the truth" (275); "I know I ain't talking in exactly what you might call an orthodox strain" (275). This story is a tribute to what Freeman calls "unusual" people in a "usual place" (281), and she emphasizes how each of her four major characters does not conform to stereotyped expectations. In addition to Christopher's unorthodox rebellion "against the greatest odds on earth and in all creation—the odds of fate itself" (274), there are rebellions on a smaller scale staged by the three others against their roles in life. Myrtle, in her quiet dignity, refuses to condemn what she does not understand; she will not be the nagging wife urged by Christopher's mother and sister at the beginning of the story. Stephen Wheaton is an unexpected clergyman; he is a hot-tempered man of athletic build "with an extraordinary width of shoulders and a strong-featured and ugly face, still indicative of goodness and a strange power of sympathy" (274). He agrees that "I have heard men swear when it did not seem blasphemy to me" (274), and follows Christopher's quest sympathetically in his imagination with such an eagerness that it is as if his own salvation were at stake. Finally, Christopher's favorite niece, Ellen, who takes over the management of Christopher's farm while he is on retreat in the mountains, is an uncommon woman: "a tall girl, shaped like a boy, with a fearless face of great beauty crowned with compact gold braids and lit by unswerving blue eyes" (287). She seems a living embodiment of the meaning of her name—a torch.

After learning of the hardships of Christopher's past life during his confession to Stephen, we can only conclude that these characters define "spoiled" differently than we do. Yet there were hidden advantages in some of those hardships, of which Christopher himself is unaware, but which become clear during the course of the story. His niece, whom he cared for and loved like a daughter, returns to take up his burden on the farm—his past love and kindness bear him delayed but compounded interest. Although he married Myrtle out of compassion rather than love, we soon realize (and Christopher comes to appreciate) that although he did not get the wife he thought he wanted, he got the wife he needed. No ordinary woman would have supported his decision to drop his obligations on the farm in order to physic his soul on the mountain, nor would she have done so with the quiet dignity and generosity of spirit shown by Myrtle. As Christopher later praises her, "She wouldn't think anybody ought to go just her way to have it the right way" (289). There is one other blessing that Christopher does not realize he has, and that is the disguised blessing of hardship itself. As Myrtle wisely observes, "His bad luck may turn out the best thing for him in the end" (282). If Christopher's farm had been successful, he would have been as much a slave to dull routine and work as he had been in failure, but far less likely to rebel or to search for a deeper spiritual dimension to his life. The possibility of salvation is rooted in his dissatisfaction and frustration.

What Christopher searches for on the mountain is an answer to that fundamental question: "Why did I have to come into the world without any choice?" He describes himself as a "slave of life," and when Stephen adds "so are we all" agrees that we are a "whole world of slaves" (275). Echoing the essence of Christ's message in the Sermon on the Mount, he exclaims: "I have never been able to think of work as anything but a way to get money. . . . I have never in my life had enough of the bread of life to keep my soul nourished. I have tried to do my duties, but I believe sometimes duties act on the soul like weeds on a flower. They crowd it out. I am going up on Silver Mountain to get once, on this earth, my fill of the breath of life" (278, 280). What Christopher wants, simply, is a "chance" at the beauty of the spring and the summer.

When Christopher follows the teachings of Christ, divests himself of material responsibilities, and foregoes the elusive and stultifying goal of security to climb that mountain and seek the answers to his questions, he gains, ironically, the very things he neglects, as Ellen and Stephen take up his burden on the farm. Christ's paradox comes true: "But seek first His kingdom and His righteousness, and all these things shall be yours as well,"[3] a miracle that is rendered natural and believable in the world Freeman creates in her story. What Christopher finds on the mountain is a type of transcendental communion with nature which reveals the bounty of the Lord. The beauty of the flowering spring discloses to Christopher the possibility of a joy surpassing the common lot of man: "Lord! Mr. Wheaton, smell the trees, and there are blooms hidden somewhere that smell sweet. Think of having the common food of man sweetened this way! First time I fully sensed I was something more than just a man" (284). Rather than wishing he had never been born, Christopher learns to give thanks for each new day and learns with the trees the secret of "how to grow young every spring" (289) in his own childlike delight in their blossoming. He begins to identify with the trees: ". . . the trees shall keep their sugar this season. This week is the first time I've had a chance to get acquainted with them and sort of enter into their feelings" (288–89). And out of this identification emerges a growing ability to read the language of nature as symbolic of spiritual stages: "I have found that all the good things and all the bad things that come to a man who tries to do right are just to prove to him that he is on the right path. They are just the flowers and sunbeams, and the rocks and snakes, too, that mark the way" (291). He has discovered for himself what Emerson asserts, that "Nature is the symbol of spirit,"[4] a "discipline" in which "every property of matter is a school for the understanding" (36–37). Ultimately, "It is the organ through which the universal spirit speaks to the individual and strives to lead back the individual to it" (49). Christopher is newly reconciled to his lot, newly awakened to the beauty, promise, and love all around him, reflecting God's will working through the ordinary stuff of life.

At the end of the story, when Christopher comes down off the mountain, his face shines like that of Moses after he talked with God and received the Ten Commandments (Exodus xxxiv. 29). Then he sees his niece, Ellen, for the first time, who seems transfigured in the moonlight. We are at first encouraged to believe with him that she is an "angel of the Lord, come to take up the burden I had dropped while I went to learn of Him" (290); yet immediately we are reminded that these are mere mortals, not angels and prophets, by the bewildered reaction of Myrtle, who assures herself that her husband's odd talk is to be expected "simply because he . . . [is] a man" (290). The gossip between Christopher's mother and sister at the beginning of the story, and Myrtle's comment to herself at the end, punctuate the solemnity of Christopher's quest with ironic brackets. Freeman is careful to bring her readers, as well as Christopher, back down from that mountain. No epiphany is authentic unless it can be translated back into the ordinary human terms of affection and endeavor and obligation, the everyday routine of life that Christopher rejects at the beginning of the story. What Christopher has learned is that it was not the circumstances of his life that enslaved him but rather his own circumscribed vision of that life, his inability to perceive the astonishing beauty of the world surrounding him.

This story moves us so deeply because Mary Wilkins Freeman anchors the spiritual message of her parable in the ordinary and possible events of real life. Her characters are fully realized human beings, although they are uncommon people, who, at times, shine with an inner light reflecting a higher spiritual plane. The story begins with the casual gossip of women and ends with the announcement of the impending marriage between Ellen and Stephen, a deliberately conventional ending to an unconventional pilgrimage. This is a wise story according to Emerson's definition of wisdom as the ability "to see the miraculous in the common" (55). In her skillful blending of realistic narration and rich character development with the symbolic elements of the parable, Mary Wilkins Freeman enacts stylistically the moral of her story as voiced by Christopher at the end: "I have found that the only way to heaven for the children of men is through the earth" (291).

Notes

1. This beautifully crafted, poignant story has been unaccountably neglected by scholars and readers of Freeman's work, perhaps because it was written relatively late in her career and was included in a collection which focused on children's stories. Perry D. Westbrook alludes to it in *Mary Wilkins Freeman* (New York: Twayne, 1967), pp. 169–70, and briefly summarizes its main theme: "Christopher's revolt has turned into acquiescence . . . won through a grappling with problems—not in blindly, doggedly forcing oneself into duty, simply because it is the will of God" (p. 70). My essay is the first extended analysis of the technical artistry of "The Balking of Christopher," noting its confident movement between realism and allegory and smooth shifts in point of view, and it is the first discussion of the Emersonian echoes in this story.

2. Mary Wilkins Freeman, "The Balking of Christopher," in *The Copy-Cat, and Other Stories* (New York: Harper, 1914), p. 290. All other references to this story will be to this edition and will be indicated by page numbers in parentheses in the text.

3. The Holy Bible: Revised Standard Version, Matt. vi. 33.

4. Ralph Waldo Emerson, "Nature," in *Selections from Ralph Waldo Emerson,* ed. Stephen E. Whicher (Boston: Houghton Mifflin, 1960), p. 31. All other references to Emerson will come from "Nature" in this edition and will be indicated by page numbers in parentheses in the text. Mary Wilkins Freeman first read Emerson when a girl in Brattleboro, Vermont. Her youthful, philosophical discussions with her best friend, Evie Sawyer, on Emerson and Thoreau evidently sparked a lifelong interest in transcendentalism, as is seen also in her collections *Understudies* (New York: Harper, 1901), and *Six Trees* (New York: Harper, 1903), which are based on the spiritual correspondences between her protagonists and natural prototypes. In 1913, in an article in *Harper's Bazar,* she advised aspiring writers to internalize the precepts of "Self-Reliance." See Edward Foster, *Mary E. Wilkins Freeman* (New York: Hendricks House, 1956), pp. 33–34, 52 and 163.

Silence or Capitulation:
Prepatriarchal "Mother's Gardens"
in Jewett and Freeman

JOSEPHINE DONOVAN

The decades surrounding the turn of the nineteenth century were a period of extraordinary change for white, middle-class American women. Arguably, these years entailed the greatest changes that had ever occurred in any women's lives. For the first time women were allowed into universities; for the first time, into professions such as medicine. For the first time women had a genuine opportunity to leave the world of the traditional woman—the home—and the traditional roles of wife and mother. And, finally, for the first time women were learning, discovering or being told that they had sexual natures that needed expression.

The generation gap between mothers and daughters was, therefore, in this period one of the most acute in history. As seen in the fiction of Sarah Orne Jewett and Mary E. Wilkins Freeman, the mothers held to the traditional roles; remained in the domestic sphere and upheld what was in effect a separatist community of women that adhered to a separate women's value system and a separate women's culture.[1] The daughters, on the other hand, were being lured out of this traditional feminine sanctuary, which was typically associated in Jewett's and Freeman's fiction with nature and with rural life. The daughters were attracted by promises of expanded horizons, new forms of knowledge, entrance into the patriarchal world of the public sphere, and toward an experience of male-dominated heterosexuality (that condoned by the sexologists), abandoning thereby the "female world of love and ritual" that characterized women's nineteenth-century relationships with one another.[2]

Sarah Orne Jewett's "A White Heron" (1886) and Mary E. Wilkins Freeman's "Evelina's Garden" (1896) symbolize significant aspects of this extraordinary transition.[3] Sylvia in "A White Heron" is a representative of the "daughters" generation; a woodland girl, she lives in the essentially preliterate world of the mothers. She is attracted by an urban ornithologist who comes to her rural home seeking a rare white heron. The girl is intrigued by his scientific knowledge, his urban sophistication, and to a lesser extent

Reprinted, with permission of the author, from *Studies in Short Fiction* 23 (Winter 1986): 43–48.

his sexuality. He, on the other hand, represents patriarchal civilization: the world of literacy, scientific (as opposed to holistic, intuitive, non-analytic) knowledge, industrialism and imperialistic militarism. He is interested in the young girl only for exploitative reasons: he wants to use her knowledge of the woods to find the bird in order to kill it and stuff it for his collection; his intent is to colonize nature and ultimately the female sanctuary where Sylvia flourishes.

It has been pointed out that "A White Heron" is a kind of reverse fairy tale in which "Cinderella" rejects the handsome prince in order to preserve her woodland sanctuary.[4] Significantly, in Grimm's version of the legend, with which Jewett would have been familiar, the Cinderella figure had planted twigs on her mother's grave out of which, "nourished by her tears of lamentation," grew a tree from which emerged a "white bird that [was] her mother's spirit."[5] The heron in Jewett's story is a similar representation. That the ornithologist wishes to kill it, to colonize it, is a symbolic expression of the confrontation that is occurring during this historical period between patriarchal civilization and the preliterate world of the "mothers" generation.

The confrontation is further illuminated when regarded through the perspective provided by the new French feminists who follow French Freudian theorist Jacques Lacan. Lacan reinterpreted Freud's stages of childhood development, in particular the transition from the preoedipal to the oedipal state, as a "fall" from a blissful state of oneness with the Mother—an intransitive state of preliterate silence—into the transitive state of patriarchal language, what he calls "the Symbolic."[6] Hélène Cixous, one of the French feminists influenced by Lacan, notes, "As soon as we exist, we are born into language and language speaks (to) us, dictates its law, a law of death. . . ."[7]

Women in this perspective are faced with a dilemma: either they may remain in the prepatriarchal world of the Mother (the world of nature), which means they remain silent, or they enter the patriarchal world of language (culture) and are forced to submit to its misogynist exigencies. As Xavière Gauthier explains, women can "find 'their' place within the linear, grammatical, linguistic system that orders the symbolic, the superego, the law . . . a system based entirely upon one fundamental signifier: the phallus." Or, they can refuse to engage in the realm of the Symbolic, of the patriarchal systems. That means, however, they remain silent. And, "as long as women remain silent, they will be outside the historical process. But, if they begin to speak and write *as men do,* they will enter history subdued and alienated. . . ."[8]

At no point in women's history was this dilemma more acute than at the turn of the century, because, as indicated above, it was then that women had for the first time the option of entering patriarchal civilization, the realm of the Symbolic. Sylvia in "A White Heron" faces this dilemma. Either she can remain in a realm of preoedipal silence and preserve her matriarchal sanctuary, or she can speak, reveal the bird's whereabouts to the ornithologist, and thereby end its life. To save the bird's life (symbolically the "mother's" life) means to sacrifice a friendship with the ornithologist. But such a friendship has already been presented in the story as one of submission. When Sylvia and the stranger search the woods for the bird, ". . . she did not lead the guest, she only followed, and there was no such thing as speaking first" (167). The price of patriarchal knowledge is submission to male direction. That Sylvia learns implicitly. In the end Sylvia remains silent: "No, she must keep silence! What is it that suddenly forbids her and makes her dumb? . . . The murmur of the pine's green branches is in her ears, she remembers how the white heron came flying through the golden air and how they watched the sea and the morning together, and Sylvia cannot speak; she cannot tell the heron's secret and give its life away" (171). Sylvia prefers to remain in the prelapsarian, preliterate, preoedipal world of the mothers. She chooses feminine nature over patriarchal culture.[9]

Another story which symbolically reflects this historical dilemma is Freeman's "Evelina's Garden." Here, however, a different choice is made. The central woman character is impelled to destroy the prepatriarchal "female-identified" Eden of the "mothers" in order to go over to the side of patriarchy. This story, therefore, signifies the triumph of "male-identified" culture over feminine nature.

"Evelina's Garden" concerns two women of different generations: the older Evelina Adams is a variation of the New England spinster but represents the "mothers" generation. In the wake of a failed proto-romance with a man (she exchanged glances with him in church once), Evelina decided to live a separatist, reclusive life, similar in fact to Louisa Ellis in Freeman's classic, "A New England Nun" (1887). She devotes her life to cultivating her garden and lives "in a perfect semblance of peace, if it were not peace" (115). Here, as in "A New England Nun," Freeman views the preservation of the separatist prepatriarchal realm less positively than Jewett. Freeman, reflecting herself perhaps something of the "daughters' " impatience with the narrowness of the traditional sphere, sees that the price women pay for staying in the female sanctuary may be confinement, illiteracy and ignorance.

On the other hand, Evelina, by having a place of her own that is free from patriarchal intrusion, is able to create an extraordinarily beautiful garden. We may see Evelina's garden as her art, following Alice Walker's perception in "In Search of Our Mothers' Gardens."[10] (Similarly we may see Louisa Ellis's obsession with her household rituals as a form of art. Freeman notes, she "had almost the enthusiasm of an artist over the mere order and cleanliness of her solitary home.")[11] The implication of these stories is that women's art may be created only in the preoedipal, prepatriarchal, "maleless" sphere of the Mothers, a thesis that has in fact been proposed by the French feminists.

The other woman in "Evelina's Garden" is also named Evelina (Leonard). She is the older woman's younger cousin, who comes to live with her in her declining years. The younger Evelina learns to tend the older woman's garden;

and the story can be seen to symbolize the generational transition. The younger woman falls in love, however, with Thomas Merriam, the son of the man with whom the older Evelina had had her brief encounter. This love is kept secret from the older woman for fear of engendering her disapproval.

When the old woman dies, her will in fact stipulates that the young Evelina will receive nearly all the older woman's considerable estate, but on two conditions: one, that she never marry; and two, that she continue to care for the garden. The older woman—the "mother"—is therefore attempting to keep the young woman—the "daughter"—within the female sanctuary, to prevent her from engaging in patriarchal systems such as marriage and to encourage—indeed force—her to maintain her "mother's" garden.

The young Evelina is determined to marry, to enter the patriarchal world and to leave the prelapsarian realm of the feminine. She claims she will reject the inheritance and marry Thomas nevertheless. Thomas, however, feels he cannot ask her to live beneath her accustomed socio-economic status, and therefore as a matter of pride refuses to wed. Evelina realizes that she must break the terms of the will otherwise, which means that she must destroy the garden.

One night Evelina therefore secretly enters the garden and tears each plant up root by root. The stronger shrubs "she had striven to kill with boiling water and salt" (179). All the time she engages in this violent act of destruction she weeps and moans, " 'Poor Cousin Evelina! poor Cousin Evelina! Oh, forgive me, poor Cousin Evelina!' " (179). With the terms of the will broken and the inheritance rejected for reasons independent of him, Thomas agrees to marry.

Thus, the younger Evelina makes the opposite choice to that taken by Sylvia. She elects to enter the patriarchal realm, but the price is the destruction of the feminine realm and the roots of women's culture. The scorched-earth character of the destruction signals the painful annihilation that is going on historically in women's lives at the end of the nineteenth century. The female-identified world of the mother's generation is in the process of being destroyed. In its ashes is emerging patriarchal domination.

Freeman addressed this transition in a number of other stories. In some cases, for example "Old Woman Magoun" (1905) and "The Long Arm" (1895), the "mothers" resort to violence to keep the "daughters" within the feminine sanctuary and to keep patriarchal intruders at bay. In "A Poetess," however, the woman's art, her poetry, is destroyed by the woman herself when she learns that it does not measure up to patriarchal standards. She burns all her poems, places the ashes in a jar, which she asks to have buried with her.

Women writers of this generation perhaps more than any other found themselves between the land of their mothers' gardens, on the one hand, and on the other, the realm of patriarchal language and publication—the realm of Lacan's "Symbolic." Jewett's masterpiece, *The Country of the Pointed Firs*

(1896), may be seen, on one level, to reflect this dilemma. The narrator of the work is a woman author, an apparent Jewett persona. She returns one summer to the world of the mothers for reinspiration, to reconnect with its ancient feminine rituals, enacted by herbalist-witch Almira Todd. But the author only visits the preliterate prepatriarchal rural area of Mrs. Todd. She cannot stay. She no longer belongs there. She can only attempt to give voice to its culture. Jewett herself was able to do so successfully. The next generation of women writers—Edith Wharton, Willa Cather, Ellen Glasgow—was much more ambivalent toward their mothers' gardens, and their art must be read with this understanding.[12]

Through a feminist decoding of the subtext of paradigmatic stories like "A White Heron" and "Evelina's Garden," we come to see their deeper meaning (or to put it another way, their "gynocritical" significance);[13] we come to identify them in the context of their historical moment in women's history; at the same time we see that they give voice to the deep-seated psychological events that are occurring in women's lives as a result of these historical transitions. In this way, literature is seen not as a simple *mimesis* but as a mediated reflection of historically-induced psychological events.

Notes

1. For a more extensive discussion of this thesis, see Josephine Donovan, *New England Local Color Literature, A Women's Tradition* (New York: Ungar, 1983), pp. 99–138.

2. See Carroll Smith-Rosenberg, "The Female World of Love and Ritual: Relations between Women in Nineteenth-Century America," *Signs*, 1 (Autumn 1975), 1–29. Also useful on this transitional period are: Lillian Faderman, *Surpassing the Love of Men: Friendship and Romantic Love Between Women from the Renaissance to the Present* (New York: Morrow, 1981), pp. 239–53; Nancy Sahli, "Smashing: Women's Relationships before the Fall," *Chrysalis*, 8 (Summer 1979), 17–27; and Estelle Freedman, "Separatism as Strategy: Female Institution Building and American Feminism, 1870–1930," *Feminist Studies*, 5 (Fall 1979), 512–29.

3. "A White Heron" appeared originally in *A White Heron and Other Stories* (Boston: Houghton, Mifflin, 1886) and is reprinted in *The Country of the Pointed Firs and Other Stories* (Garden City, N.J.: Anchor, 1956). References in the text are to this edition. "Evelina's Garden" appeared in *Harper's Magazine*, 93 (June 1896), 76–98, and is reprinted in Mary E. Wilkins [Freeman], *Silence and Other Stories* (New York: Harper, 1898). References are to this edition.

4. See Annis Pratt, "Women and Nature in Modern Fiction," *Contemporary Literature*, 13 (Autumn 1972), 476–90. Also note her discussion of the "green-world archetype" in Annis Pratt, *Archetypal Patterns in Women's Fiction* (Bloomington: Indiana University Press, 1981).

5. Louise Bernikow, *Among Women* (New York: Harmony, 1980), p. 30.

6. A useful introduction is Jacques Lacan, *The Language of the Self: The Function of Language in Psychoanalysis*, trans., with a commentary by Anthony Wilden (Baltimore: Johns Hopkins, 1968).

7. Hélène Cixous, "Castration or Decapitation?" *Signs*, 7 (Autumn 1981), 45.

8. Xavière Gauthier, "Is There Such a Thing as Women's Writing?" *New French Feminisms: An Anthology*, ed. Elaine Marks and Isabelle de Courtivron (New York: Schocken, 1980), pp. 163–64.

9. Ann Romines sees the nature/culture clash evident in Freeman's "A Poetess." See Romines, "A Place for 'A Poetess,' " *The Markham Review,* 12 (Summer 1983), 64.

10. Alice Walker, "In Search of Our Mothers' Gardens," *Ms.* 2, no. 11 (May 1974).

11. Mary E. Wilkins [Freeman], *A New England Nun and Other Stories* (New York: Harper, 1891), p. 9. The story originally appeared in *Harper's Bazar,* 20 (7 May 1887), 333–34. See Marjorie Pryse, "An Uncloistered 'New England Nun,' " *Studies in Short Fiction,* 20 (Fall 1983), 289–95, for a similar interpretation. An interesting work that examines women's household chores as religious rituals is Kathryn Allen Rabuzzi, *The Sacred and the Feminine: Toward a Theology of Housework* (New York: Seabury, 1982).

12. See Josephine Donovan, *After the Fall: The Demeter-Persephone Myth in Wharton, Cather, and Glasgow* (University Park, Pa.: Penn State University Press, 1989). Portions of this article appear in Chapter One.

13. On "gynocriticism" see Elaine Showalter, "Feminist Criticism in the Wilderness," *Writing and Sexual Difference,* ed. Elizabeth Abel (Chicago: University of Chicago Press, 1982), pp. 9–35.

Signs of Undecidability:
Reconsidering the Stories of
Mary Wilkins Freeman

ELIZABETH MEESE

It is not, in the final analysis, what you don't know that can or cannot hurt you. It is what you don't *know* you don't know that spins out and entangles "that perpetual error we call life."
　　　　　　　　　　　　—Barbara Johnson, *The Critical Difference*

Ourself behind ourself, concealed—
should startle most—
　　　　　—Emily Dickinson, "One need not be a Chamber. . . ."

The most fortunate circumstance of women's writing in the western world has been that its production—though ignored, devalued, suppressed, or misrepresented—could never be completely extinguished. Women could be denied education, publication, and critical recognition, but as Woolf keenly observed, ink and paper were the cheapest, most readily available tools for the practice of one's trade. She immediately detected this essential feature of the "profession of literature": "There is no head of the profession; no Lord Chancellor . . . no official body with the power to lay down rules and enforce them. We cannot debar women from the use of libraries; or forbid them to buy ink and paper; or rule that metaphors shall only be used by one sex, as the male only in art schools was allowed to study from the nude; or rule that rhyme shall be used by one sex only as the male only in Academies of music was allowed to play in orchestras."[1] Women could not be programmed or policed thoroughly enough to stop their literary activity. We have been saved by the very nature of the craft: the act of writing is solitary, accessible to almost anyone who is literate (still a fact of its elitism), and as such the institution of literature admits its own subversion.

　　Recent developments in critical strategies for approaching texts and

Reprinted, with permission, from *Crossing the Double-Cross: The Practice of Feminist Criticism*, by Elizabeth Meese. © 1986 The University of North Carolina Press.

new understandings of how the patriarchal regime of truth plays within criticism equip us for the defensive, resistant re-reading of women's writing that critics like Annette Kolodny and Judith Fetterley urge us to undertake. By exposing the masculinist misreadings upon which criticism has relied, we can begin to understand more specifically what it means for women writers to become feminist writers. The case of the New England local colorist Mary Wilkins Freeman, who published from 1881 to 1918, illustrates a transitional phase when the interplay of feminism and antifeminism are textually inscribed, and responses to her work demonstrate how this struggle is both suppressed and simplified through misreading.

Although she was one of the women writers who managed to "ascend" to the novel, Freeman's twelve volumes of short stories are of particular interest because they present works that typify the writing done by women during the reign of the local color tradition in the late nineteenth and early twentieth centuries. Just as certain genres are undervalued, so are some literary historical periods—perhaps, in the case of the local color tradition, because of the predominance of the short story genre, or even because so many women wrote and published at the time. One of the many local colorists whose works have been undervalued and even misrepresented, Freeman gives us more than most critics after William Dean Howells have led us to believe. Few writers of equivalent, albeit modest, stature have elicited so many erroneous, personal attacks masquerading as literary criticism. She deserves renewed and careful consideration.

Whether through malice or narrowness of view, traditional (masculinist) critics have interpreted Freeman's work as though she structured a determinate and decidedly negative view of her characters, their relationships, and settings. They feel the need to pass judgment on these obscure women struggling with their relationships to the social institutions that attempt to command their loyalties. I would like to propose another view of Freeman's response to the content of her work: her own experience of sexual politics led her to represent the interplay of forces through undecidable or purposefully "unreadable" images that both affirm and negate, sometimes alternately and at other times simultaneously, but always resisting a determination of the text's meanings. A strong argument can be made for Freeman's strategic approach to these complexities and for her persistent refusal to inscribe within her fiction the simple or singular judgment of her female characters that her role as a writer within her sociohistorical context might have dictated and that later critics seem to want. These signs of undecidability, then, can be read as demonstrations of how the author reflects the conscious and unconscious experiences of her personal inner life and her perception of the public expectations for women in society; their differential treatment, privilege, and status, as presented in the external world; and the differences between the social codes for women and for writers. These discrepancies form the site of more or less conscious tension, alienation, and dissonance, creating a break within an otherwise self-perpetuating, self-conforming system.

It is easy to take my point to mean "ambivalence" on Freeman's part, and doubtless some psycho-social dynamic informs the author's unsettling production. If readers sum up and settle her position again, even in the self-contradictory term "ambivalence," they attempt to close the textual gaps, thereby denying the ambiguities of language and reducing the infinite play of signification, by substituting another form of consistent (insistent) narrative authority. With respect to such discursive conflicts as we find in Freeman, Paul de Man notes: "No contradiction or dialectical movement could develop because a fundamental difference in the level of explicitness prevented both statements from meeting on a common level of discourse; the one always lays hidden within the other as the seen lies hidden within a shadow, or truth within error."[2] In the record of language proceeding from conflicting codes (cultural and literary, personal and social, private and public), Freeman allows us to represent the problematics of gender in its complexity rather than through a reductive, controlling simplicity.

Freeman's undecidable or unreadable texts demand that we read and re-read or "write" as we produce her texts and ours. Explaining Barthes' distinction between the readerly and writerly text, Barbara Johnson remarks: "The readerly is defined as a product consumed by the reader; the writerly is a process of production in which the reader becomes a producer; it is 'ourselves writing." The readerly is constrained by considerations of representation: it is irreversible, 'natural,' decidable, continuous, totalizable, and unified into a coherent whole based on the signified. The writerly is infinitely plural and open to the free play of signifiers and of difference, unconstrained by representative considerations, and transgressive of any desire for decidable, unified totalized meaning."[3] Read from this perspective, Freeman's writerly texts contain the strongest arguments against the positions they attempt to take. The same can be said of the texts her critics make.

In view of her own departure from conventional role expectations and of the changing cultural norms for women, Freeman creates a more than "realistic" scene by producing irreconcilable and unresolvable oscillations between the positive and negative features of women's lives in the New England villages of the period. By means of this effect, she presents the impossibility of fixing the text's meaning according to prescribed gender role and gives us an allegory for reading new possibilities for women. In other words, she simultaneously undermines and develops, (dis)articulating the roles of the period. Thus, Freeman's questioning of her milieu's representation of women's sexual decidability offers us a bridge between women's writing of the past and feminist texts today.

As is often the case, a review of the major critical appraisals Freeman has received demonstrates the course of significant misunderstandings. There are at present two book-length critical works on Freeman—Edward Foster's

Mary E. Wilkins Freeman and Perry D. Westbrook's *Mary Wilkins Freeman*—
and a number of commentaries and articles, the most important among them
by Ann Douglas Wood, Susan Toth, Alice Brand, Leah Blatt Glasser, and
Josephine Donovan.[4] Both Foster and Westbrook assume a conventional view
of the local color genre and Freeman's preoccupations as a writer working in
that mode. Foster's overview of the author's relationship to place and time
situates her between the Puritan village as it survived in Randolph, with its
rigid, decaying environment, and the idealistic milieu issuing from the
Concord community. As the first to construct a major bio-critical work,
Foster confronts significant difficulties that shape his interpretation and the
readings of many critics after him.

In his determination to produce a chronicle of the relationship between
Freeman's life and works, Foster relies on the comments of friends, neighbors, and only a few scraps of concrete written evidence in the form of letters
and essays. The absence of concrete evidence is a common problem for
biographers of women writers, including those writing of major as well as
minor figures. The manuscript material Foster cites is of considerable value,
as is the basic biographical chronology that he manages to reconstruct. Still,
the skeletal nature of this outline frequently requires his inventiveness,
through which he constructs his subject according to his image of Freeman-
as-woman. The problem of Freeman's late marriage at forty-eight plagues
him from the outset. When Freeman returned from Mount Holyoke at
nineteen, Foster explains that family finances necessitated that she marry
soon: "It was not that Miss Wilkins disliked young men in general; she
thought and dreamed in a normally romantic way. It was that she could not
imagine herself falling in love with any of the boys who came her way in
Brattleboro; they seemed to her dull, clumsy, self-conscious, and appallingly
young. It was fun for her to sit demurely and let them babble while she
peered beneath the youthful swagger; she could not take them seriously."[5]
And a variation on the theme later in Freeman's life: "She was devoted to her
friend [Mary John Wales], but was she quite ready to put aside all thought of
marriage? That must have been the question she was asking, for by this time
she was forty-five."[6] More serious problems issue from the way Foster reads
Freeman's characters through his construction of the author's attitudes. De-
picting Freeman, perhaps correctly, as a woman who was fiercely uncertain in
her judgment of the characters in her stories, the villages where the stories
are set, and the relationships between female and male characters, Foster
broaches the essential question: Was she or wasn't she ambivalent about her
subjects? But in his eagerness to advance his answer, he betrays the writer
and her works.

Perhaps the most damaging refrain in Foster's book, anticipating
Marder's view of Woolf's *Three Guineas,* is his characterization of Freeman as
a neurotic woman: "She was at once within and outside the spirit of the
culture from which she drew her themes and characters; she loved—and

almost hated the people of whom she wrote. Out of this partially neurotic ambivalence comes much of her intensity and her deepest insight into her characters."[7] In this description, it is Freemans' feminism, her double-edged view of sexual politics, combined with Foster's own judgment of her characters that earns her the label of "neurotic." Foster's misreading stems from the conflicting codes inscribed in her texts and his desire to fix Freeman's position on the basis of gender-biased judgments concerning her life and relationships as elaborated in the biographical fiction he creates in order to situate and control his subject. Suffering not so much from neurotic ambivalence as multiplicity of view, Freeman sees a complex realism in the village's prescribed conventions and alternative possibilities that are not without cause or consequence. Foster's position creates a lasting critical problem, reinforced by his easy identification of Freeman herself with the first-person narrative voice in "The Shrew," an unpublished manuscript fragment. The unfinished work opens as follows: " 'I am a rebel and what is worse a rebel against the Over-government of all creation. . . . I even dare to think that, infinitesimal as I am. . . . I, through my rebellion, have power. All negation has power. I, Jane Lenox, spinster, as they would have designated me a century ago, living quietly, and apparently harmlessly in the old Lennox homestead in Baywater, am a power.' "[8] Foster calls the fragment a "story," but echoing the narrator's words, he ends his discussion by asking: "Was Miss Wilkins indeed a 'monster'?"[9] In the absence of substantial autobiographical evidence, Foster's general propensity for seeing Freeman's fiction as "lightly disguised" autobiography, read as a "man" reads a "woman," creates especial problems for later critics. For example, Wood, spinning her own fiction, refers to this same fragment which seems to her "almost like a witch's confession. . . . Witches were popularly supposed to have the power to blight life, and this power, Freeman, who had lost a lover, a sister, a mother and a father within a short space of time in her young womanhood, must surely have felt was hers."[10] Witches also have other power; they are power—a truth hidden in the shadow of Wood's text which suggests itself as her text tries to deny it. Wood's interpretation suggests how Foster's view, when combined with the attendant misreadings of some of the texts, fixes Freeman's place as one of New England's large cast of "striving neurotics."[11] Through his approach to the undecidability inherent in Freeman's texts, Foster poses lasting critical problems that create a tradition of (mis)interpretation that later feminist critics seek to supplant but, in their own singlemindedness, also tend to perpetuate.

While critics after Foster contribute to our understanding of Freeman's works, the unquestioned allegiance some hold to a particular view of the author herself or to their own understanding of women's roles (feminist and nonfeminist) determine their readings of her work. Deriving his biographical perspective from Foster, Westbrook frequently compares Freeman to the "old maids" and "spinsters" of her fiction. Wood characterizes the local colorists as displaying "what seems to a modern observer a nearly neurotic fixation on one or both of their parents"; although she lists Freeman among these, she cites neither example nor source for her assertion. [12] Wood depicts local color writers as reflecting "attenuation, even impoverishment" in their lives, careers, and fiction. [13] (I prefer to see some of them in Willa Cather's terms: "Miss Jewett wrote of the people who grew out of the soil and the life of the country near her heart, not about exceptional individuals at war with their environment. This was not a creed with her, but an instinctive preference. She once laughingly told me that her head was full of dear old houses and dear old women, and that when an old house and an old woman came together in her brain with a click, she knew that a story was under way." [14])

An examination of Foster's interpretation of "A New England Nun," a reading that remains largely unqualified or uncontested, will illustrate my point. Foster characterizes Louisa Ellis's existence as a "nearly sterile design for living" and describes the story as "Miss Wilkins' definitive study of the New England spinster." [15] He refuses in this case, however, to equate the author with her character whom he believes, out of his own predilection, she "roundly condemned," concluding, rather, that "in 'A New England Nun,' she exorcised an image of atrophy which may have been deeply disturbing." [16] All of the critics writing after Foster—with the exception of Susan Toth, who doesn't cite his work at all, and Michele Clark and Josephine Donovan, who make reference to it but employ an exclusively feminist optic—rely on his basic characterization of Freeman's life and values. Larzer Ziff, in *The American 1890s,* also mentions "A New England Nun," advancing the view that Freeman "clearly presents the single state as a frustrated existence, since in it a woman is deprived of what Mrs. Freeman considers to be her birthright—a man." [17]

Freeman's own staunch indeterminacy of view creates these interpretive problems. In *Blindness and Insight,* Paul de Man explains how the text, any text, stages "the necessity of its own misreading": "It knows and asserts that it will be misunderstood. It tells the story, the allegory of its misunderstanding: the necessary degradation of melody into harmony, of language into painting, of the language of passion into the language of need, of metaphor into literal meaning. In accordance with its own language, it can only tell this story as a fiction, knowing full well that the fiction will be taken for fact and the fact for fiction; such is the necessarily ambivalent nature of literary language." [18] Taking Freeman's best known story, "A New England Nun," as a case in point, I want to illustrate the author's refusal to center her work in the value system of her contemporaries, electing instead to display the shadows of her own doubt, foreshadowings of feminist deconstructions of the sexual politic, through the imagery she employs and the characters she draws. Her refusal to judge—women, the aged, the poor, and the culture of New England villages—renders her meaning "unreadable." In the case of Louisa Ellis, Freeman constructs the reflection of possibility in women's roles as a result of indeterminacy or the impossibility of determining an appropriate role or meaning for women's experience (and hence, the meaning of her own fiction).

Critics, feminist and nonfeminist alike, who make the choice the author refuses to make by determining the indeterminate, limit the richness of the text and its value to later readers. Only Leah Glasser and Josephine Donovan, through their feminist views, resist this arbitrarily delimiting move. It is as though most critics fear the possibilities embedded in the text's complexity, in its contrariness that, when pushed to the extreme, challenges the phallocentric economy in which the story and its readers are situated. The kind of reading or interpretation one gives to the text depends ultimately upon which imagistic strain the reader takes most seriously. In effect, the meaning is created by the reader as much or more than it is by the writer or the text. "Such unreadability," Jonathan Culler argues, "does not result simply from a central ambiguity or choice but from the way in which the system of values in the text both urges choice and prevents that choice from being made."[19] Furthermore, if Freeman passes judgment on her characters, she simultaneously judges herself: by refusing their choices, she risks restricting her own.

Our knowledge of Louisa Ellis begins with the story's title, in which the author calls her "A New England Nun," but the significance of that superficially pejorative designation remains to be shown in the working out of the fiction itself. Louisa is suspended between states: solitude and marriage, control and chaos, harmony and disorder. We enter the story following Louisa's fourteen-year separation from her betrothed, Joe Daggett, and just before their subsequently resumed courtship. When she is alone, Louisa's internal and external worlds are in harmony: "There seemed to be a gentle stir arising over everything for the mere sake of subsidence—a very premonition of rest and hush and night."[20] This stir is also the stirring action of the narrative, a premonition of peace that evokes the possibility of its disturbance.

Louisa's life and house are in order. The house doesn't seem to be the "rocklike prison" or "claustrophobic trap" of Wood's description; perhaps it is, in this case, "a frail refuge from a world more frightening than any prison."[21] Freeman shows us something more like Jewett's idea of a house in the solitary, but pleasant and colorful, surroundings of her character's daily activities. The author's description is not without its negative associations: Louisa looks older than she is, her motions are slow and deliberate, her routines have no apparent meaning or value, except to the character herself. Freeman tells several stories and leaves the ultimate interpretation to her readers. When Joe enters, he brings disorder to the house, to the canary in its cage (doubtless an analogue to Louisa), and to Louisa. He has "heavy feet" and an "uneasiness" about him, but despite the comic disarray he occasions, one suspects Joe's natural ease in his disdain for rigidity, especially when we encounter him later in another context. In Louisa's presence, however, "he was afraid to stir lest he should put a clumsy foot or hand through the fairy web, and he had always the consciousness that Louisa was watching fearfully lest he should" (p. 84). Through the juxtaposition of Louisa and Joe, Freeman thematizes difference, rematerializing the story's opening in another register: "It was late in the afternoon, and the light was waning. There was a difference in the look of the tree shadows out in the yard" (p. 79).

The reader soon learns that Louisa set out on this unlikely course toward marriage through "falling into the natural drift of girlhood," from which perspective she regarded marriage "as a reasonable feature and a probable desirability of life" (p. 86). With gentle encouragement from her mother, Louisa unhesitatingly fulfills her socially prescribed role by accepting Joe's proposal of engagement and marriage. Although Joe leaves for fourteen years in order to secure his fortune, Louisa has always envisioned marriage as the "inevitable conclusion of things." Freeman, however, refuses to subscribe to any such inevitability. As Louisa projects her marriage "so far in the future that it was almost equal to placing it over the boundaries of another life" (p. 86), Freeman, in fact, projects it beyond the boundaries of her story, thereby subverting the socially desired outcome and the power of marriage as a social institution.

During Joe's absence, Louisa becomes a woman, free from the control of her own mother. She determines an alternative course. Her "feet had turned into a path, smooth maybe under a calm, serene sky, but so straight and unswerving that it could only meet a check at her grave, and so narrow that there was no room for any one at her side" (pp. 85–86). The author preserves her character's way of life, forestalling Louisa's need to leave "her neat maidenly possessons" in order to merge her home with her betrothed's old family homestead. On the brink of consigning Louisa to life with Joe and his aged mother, a "domineering, shrewd old matron" (p. 88), Freeman stages a break from tradition and extends Louisa's alternative course. She saves both of her characters from the mutually disturbing fate of making a future with one another. Taking a moonlight stroll one night, Louisa overhears Joe's declaration of love to another woman, Lily Dyer, and his simultaneous vow to honor his commitment to Louisa. When, through Louisa's agency, each liberates the other from the determined course, they discover more tenderness for each other than they had experienced before. Freed from the arbitrariness of social prescription, they achieve a new authenticity of affection. That night, Louisa "wept a little" (p. 96); whether these are tears of sorrow or relief, Freeman refuses to disclose. In the morning, the character awakens feeling "like a queen," reigning undisturbed over her peaceful domain with no apparent regrets.

In her concluding passages, Freeman offers the following summary: "If Louisa Ellis had sold her birthright she did not know it, the taste of the pottage was so delicious, and had been her sole satisfaction for so long. Serenity and placid narrowness had become to her as the birthright itself" (pp. 96–97). Confronting the assertion of what Louisa did not know, readers must wonder what they themselves in fact know. Did the character sell her birthright to marriage and a man? Meaning pivots on the initial word: "If. . . ." There is not enough, or perhaps there is too much here to know. In the story's final sentences, Freeman fuses the imagistic and symbolic strains—the rosary of the nun and the harmony of the external world set "right" again, that is, under Louisa's control: "She gazed ahead through a long reach of future days strung together like pearls in a rosary, every one like the others, and all smooth and flawless and innocent, and her heart went up in thankfulness. Outside was the fervid summer afternoon; the air filled with the sounds of the busy harvest of men and birds and bees; there were halloos, metallic clatterings, sweet calls, and long hummings. Louisa sat, prayerfully numbering her days, like an uncloistered nun" (p. 97). The ending satisfies us; it is neat, like Louisa's life. But what judgment is Freeman making? What story is she telling? Is it that classic indictment of the New England spinster for which the author is best known? I don't believe it is so simple.

An examination of the text itself reveals the sense in which all readers are only partially attentive and fundamentally misled if they choose to read the story as a tale of either the "profound disillusionment and hostility" in the "counterfeit" and "self-mutilative" lives of Freeman's characters like Louisa,[22] or "the positive drive towards . . . fulfillment of what they believe to be their own true selves . . . a measure of individual freedom."[23] Westbrook sees a mitigating aspect to Louisa's gesture, but cannot resist invoking the old categories: "But Louisa, realistically assessing the ingredients of her own and the others' happiness, emerges as the strongest of the trio, pitiable though the barrenness of her own existence may be. Louisa has allowed her life to slip into paralysis over a period of fifteen years; for this she is culpable and for this she pays. As things now are, she will be happier, or less miserable, single than married. . . ."[24] Clark takes a more judicious course by focusing on Freeman's ability "to empathize with" and "to understand how a woman's character adapted to being without a man, because *she* was learning to adapt."[25] And Donovan reads Freeman's ambivalence in the price Louisa pays for order and control: "eternal restriction to a limited sphere."[26]

Indirectly, Freeman discloses her level of empathy with Louisa in a letter written to Marian Allen in 1907. Having spent the summer supervising the construction of her new house, Freeman says: "Sometimes I wish I could have a little toy house, in which I could do just as I pleased, cook a meal if I wanted to, and fuss around generally. . . . If I had my little toy house nobody could say anything, and if I get what I may for this serial [*The Shoulders of Atlas*] I don't know but I shall have it."[27] The resemblance between Freeman's toy house and Louisa's (as well as Edna's in *The Awakening*) is provocative, the resonances of desire and value deep enough— inhabiting Foster's own text—to unsettle his one-dimensional view of the author's story. Is she presenting an image of ordered meaninglessness, sterility, and sublimation? Is she creating a version of woman's assertion of control, independence, and autonomy? Is there something in both views, or in the difference between or within them?

By expanding my consideration to include other critics and stories, I would like to explore additional ways in which Freeman's texts stage the drama of critical (mis)readings. I have chosen to focus on three other stories, from among many, which call into question Freeman's attitudes toward female characters confronting social expectations. Alice Glarden Brand selects "A Conflict Ended" to illustrate her thesis concerning Freeman's misanthropy: "Freeman's stories were . . . an exposé of contempt for men's impotence, incompetence, and aggression and for women's passivity, dependence, and rage."[28] Susan Toth uses "Arethusa" to demonstrate that many of Freeman's critically neglected stories explore the "urge toward self-fulfillment and . . . insist upon an individual's inviolable right to his [sic] own personality."[29] And, finally, I choose "The Revolt of 'Mother,' " instructive because its reception caused Freeman later to deny her defiance and her text's artistic integrity.

In "A Conflict Ended," Freeman creates at least three stories—two parallel, interactive tales that explore the difference between men and women, and a third story (or is it the only one?) that contains the interplay of the two. One strand follows Esther Barney and Marcus Woodman, lovers whose relationship is never consummated because it remains frozen in a contest of will between the two of them and between Marcus and the new minister; both standoffs are further circumscribed in a shadowy projection of the townspeople's attitude. The second strand explores the relationship between younger lovers, George and Margy, who are similarly arrested by the demand that George's mother be housed with them. These two stories lead us to ask whether or not Margy and George are simply enacting an inevitable recapitulation of the older lovers' earlier fate. Through these two narrative strands, Freeman poses the dilemma of relationships between men and women by exposing the difference between relationships and locating it within individuals in relationship.

Brand needs to claim that the men Freeman creates are impotent and the women passive. Marcus, who is more fully characterized than George, is paralyzed by the force of his will. An old feud concerning the selection of a new minister with a different approach to doctrine results in Marcus's decision never to set foot in the church. He has spent ten years on the front steps as a gesture of his own rigid determination. While his is a religious dispute dignified by New England history, Marcus's behavior finally entraps him; resistance becomes a way of life, perpetuating itself beyond the point of sense and affection. Marcus resigns his prospective bride, personal happiness, and community standing as long as he allows his will to determine his behavior. Esther also refuses compromise—she is afraid to wed the town's laughing stock. In the other pair, Margy, determined not to live with George's old, domineering mother, resigns her own lover rather than compromise. George, similarly, remains singlemindedly committed to inflicting his mother on his prospective bride (though his position is the most highly sanctioned social responsibility in the story).

Through her interpretation, Brand simplifies these contests, defusing their moral value by undoing the tensions inherent within and between them. Without rationale, she represents Marcus's principled stand as "consummate mulishness" and describes his character as one of "stubborn blandness or ignorant indignation," while she views Margy's ultimate capitulation to her lover's desire as an outrageous compromise "in order to see the young heroine achieve the exalted state of matrimony." She describes marriage for Marcus as "the ultimate punishment for his impotence." Esther, whom Brand characterizes as calculating and full of guile, is motivated exclusively by her "nagging sense of the social premium on marriage."[30] Freeman provides Esther with a more complex decision, which Brand might have seen paralleled in a different reading of Louisa's circumstance: "She was more fixed in the peace and pride of her old-maidenhood than she had realized, and was more shy of disturbing it. Her comfortable meals, her tidy housekeeping, and her prosperous work had become such sources of satisfaction to her that she was almost wedded to them, and jealous of any interference."[31] Exploring the tensions between autonomy and compromise, Freeman places a certain value on these acts of will; without them life and character would be bland, unprincipled.

Like all of us, Brand is blind to the inconsistency inhabiting her own judgment: Marcus cannot be condemned for adhering to his willfulness and Margy castigated for abandoning hers. Freeman plays off these parallels to force the larger, more complex issue of the relationship between individual will and human affection. The older characters represent the extreme fate of those who confuse what they think they have to do, and what others expect them to do, with what they really want. Esther's description of Marcus illustrates this view: " 'No, he ain't crazy; he's got too much will for his common sense, that's all, and the will teeters the sense a little too far into the air. I see all through it from the beginning. I could read Marcus Woodman jest like a book' " (p. 326). The reader too reads Marcus like a book, though his contrariness makes the reading difficult.

As we have seen in "A New England Nun," Freeman has no compulsion to resolve conflicts or to valorize marriage. Each of her characters in "A Conflict Ended" sees marriage for love as a prerequisite for personal happiness but loses sight of its importance when it is complicated by an act of will. Margy's ability to weigh what she really wants against everything else undoes the conflict between herself and George, and ultimately frees Esther and Marcus as well. Freeman gives Margy her reward—George's mother goes to live with his brother—the author's way of suggesting that Margy has done what was needed to construct a positive relationship.

The writer frees the past from its paralysis and projects a future, not without conflict since tensions recapitulate themselves, but with the capacity for human resolution. Thus, she grants Marcus "the grand mien of a conqueror" as he mounts the steps to enter the church: "He trembled so that the bystanders noticed it. He actually leaned over toward his old seat as if wire ropes were pulling him down upon it. Then he stood up straight, like a man, and walked through the church door with his wife" (pp. 334–35). Here the tensions in content and form snap as Freeman resolves her narrative in a few closing sentences. A reading such as this, which attributes some integrity to the characters' actions, calls into question Brand's conclusions concerning Freeman's misanthropy and cynicism. It is no longer possible to view the women as "lemmings, invariably committing some form of suicide at the hands of men," or as people without "life-affirming experiences . . . inexorably drawn to stasis within predatory or parasitic relationships."[32] The characters are characters in a book, whose life stories play out fictional struggles for us to interpret as we can, reading their drama within ours.

To extend the scope of my discussion, I want to supplement Brand's view with Susan Toth's antithetical position, which she presents through the little discussed "Arethusa." Freeman bases this tale on the mythic story of the river god Alpheus and his beloved, the nymph Arethusa, whose name was taken for the rare, spring-blooming wild orchid. Freeman writes at the outset: "But it is seldom that any man sees the flower arethusa, for she comes rarely to secluded places, and blooms to herself. . . . She is the maiden."[33] Against this backdrop, Freeman draws obvious parallels between the etiology of arethusa provided in the tale of the nymph and water god and the story of the shy country maiden Lucy Greenleaf and her suitor Edson Abbot.

Lucy's character presents no model of strength for emulation. The small, delicate Lucy is as ethereal as the flower and the mythic prototype to which the author links her: "Everything about the girl except her hair seemed fluttering and blowing. She wore ruffled garments of thin fabrics, and she walked swiftly with a curious movement of her delicate shoulder-blades, almost as if they were propelling her like wings" (p. 148). Lucy has almost no corporeality. An ephemeral, gauze-like presence, with a spiritual rather than a physical reality—if she has any reality at all—Lucy spends most of the story in flight: "She half amused, half terrified herself with the sound of imaginary footsteps behind her. When she reached the green marsh, she felt safe, both from real and imaginary pursuers" (p. 150). She acquiesces to others and to life itself, with no more interest in the realities of daily life than the marsh orchid. She insists correctly that the flower should not be picked, for it would die. The reader cannot escape the fear that someone will inadvertently "pick" Lucy, reaping analogous mortal consequences because of the identification between character and flower (recalling the dying women of Hawthorne's allegorical tales). The feeling is reinforced by the belief that marriage is as inappropriate for Lucy as it was for Artemis' follower Arethusa.

Freeman draws Lucy in strict contrast to her mother, "a farmer's widow, carrying on a great farm with a staff of hired men and a farmer. She was shrewd and emulative, with a steady eye and ready elbow for her place in the ranks" (p. 149). Mrs. Greenleaf's love for her daughter creates a fragile bridge between these very different women and forms Lucy's fundamental link to reality—a less subtle version of the relationships Hurston examines in *Their Eyes Were Watching God* or Marilynne Robinson constructs in *Housekeeping*. In Freeman's story, the mother's principle task is to transfer her protective function to a husband. Mrs. Greenleaf's view of marriage, which she shares with Sarah Penn, is precisely what we might expect of someone in her situation: "This woman . . . had been insensibly trained by all her circumstances of life to regard a husband like rain in its season, or war, or a full harvest, or an epidemic, something to be accepted without question if offered, whether good or bad, as sent by the will of the Lord, and who had herself promptly accepted a man with whom she was not in love, without the least hesitation, and lived as happily as it was in her nature to live ever after" (p. 153). However, her limitations are tempered by the pragmatic anxiety that a caretaker must be found for her unworldly daughter.

What makes this story work is not so much the elusive, unchanging Lucy—who doesn't like men, wishes to live with her mother forever, and believes God will take care of her—but the genuine affection of Mrs. Greenleaf and the sensitive perseverance of Edson Abbot, who represents Freeman's ideal male. Mrs. Greenleaf is not one of the mothers Donovan describes, who "are trying to keep their daughters 'home,' in a female world."[34] Edson sees Lucy as a challenge, abandoned by other men in the village because of her strangeness, and he assumes the role played by Margy in the previous story. He is flexible, understanding, and certain in his knowledge of what it is he wants for himself. He pursues his goal of marriage with diplomacy, courting Lucy as one would a wild, timid animal, humoring her despite her peculiarities. Exercising complete restraint, "he could always keep a straight course on the road to his own desires" (p. 159).

To disturb the reading of "Arethusa" as a heterosexist tale, in which the man is motivated by his desire to bring the "wild," free female into his sphere of control, to civilize her, Freeman reinforces the positive aspect of Lucy's betrothal and impending marriage. In this, the author grants more value to compromise than Toth can afford to admit. Lucy benefits from her relationship with Edson, becoming more clever and functional: "She seemed to take a certain pleasure in her new tasks, and she thrived under them. She grew stouter; her cheeks had a more fixed color" (p. 163). The results are unquestionably felicitous. Her character is not transformed substantially, however, as Lucy precipitates a crisis by choosing the moment of her wedding to search the swamp for arethusa. Gestures such as this in Freeman's fiction challenge Donovan's general observation that "Mary E. Wilkins seems to have imbibed a moral atmosphere which assumes the male prerogative."[35] Rather, the author offers a resolution that, by retaining its own complexity, appears to compromise no one. Edson gets his bride, Mrs. Greenleaf provides for her daughter's future, and Lucy still pays solitary annual visits to arethusa. And in a gesture of authorial resistance to this perfect patriarchal arrangement, Freeman carefully undercuts Edson's power over Lucy: "In his full tide of triumphant possession he was as far from the realization of the truth as was Alpheus, the fabled river god, after he had overtaken the nymph Arethusa, whom, changed into a fountain to elude his pursuit, he had followed under the sea, and never knew that, while forever his, even in his embrace, she was forever her own" (p. 169).

But Freeman does not end the story here "with an ironic thrust at Lucy's self-satisfied husband,"[36] as Toth argues. The author makes it clear that Edson differentiates himself from other men by indulging what he unwittingly regards as his wife's "harmless idiosyncrasy" (pp. 168–69), despite his blindness to the spiritual substructure of Lucy's attachment. Although provided for in life, Lucy remains true to her own nature as exemplified in the orchid, "clad in her green leaf": "This soul, bound fast to life with fleshly bonds, yet forever maiden, anomalous and rare among her kind, greeted the rare and anomalous flower with unending comfort and delight. It was to her as if she had come upon a fair rhyme to her little halting verse of life" (p. 169). These final lines underscore what Toth perceives as "Freeman's vision of an inviolable personality,"[37] but her interpretation is limited in that she never applies this consideration to Edson in order to extend her interpretation of "Arethusa." By seizing one side of the dilemma of identity and desire, the critic diminishes the story's power.

Similarly misunderstood, Freeman's "The Revolt of 'Mother' " is a story the author was asked to comment on frequently during her lifetime. Her renunciation of the defiance she created inevitably confuses the feminist reader. I believe that in fiction Freeman assumes an authentic position (that is, she "authorizes" the conflicting codes) and in nonfiction she constructs a duplicitous story concerning her view of Mother's action and herself as a writer. The work and its circumstances epitomize the ways in which Freeman stages our (mis)readings. The story begins with a man's intention to construct another barn on a site where he had promised forty years ago to build his family a new house. He conceives of and begins to execute his plan without informing his wife and daughter. The ensuing conflict results in another contest of wills between the men and women of Freeman's world. "Mother," or Sarah Penn, is a small, benevolent woman whom Freeman likens to "one of the New Testament saints."[38] She nonetheless perceives the unmistakable inequity in her husband's housing of his animals in contrast with his family. The daughter recognizes this too, but Sarah, upholding the mother's role, defends Father (Adoniram Penn) as a good provider, albeit one who sees the world differently from the women. Freeman is not kind to Father, whom she presents through animal imagery. A man of action, Adoniram "ran his words together, and his speech was almost as inarticulate as a growl" (p. 116). His identity manifests itself in his barns and livestock and is perpetuated in his inarticulate son Sammy.

The feminist critic's interest in this story, the reason it was chosen as the title piece for the recent Feminist Press collection of Freeman's selected stories, derives from the phenomenal act of defiance at its center. For the first time in forty years of marriage, Sarah Penn oversteps the bounds of her role as silent companion and domestic servant to her husband. Her first transgression is " 'to talk real plain' " to him (p. 124). . . . Comparing the Penn house with the larger ones of less prosperous neighbors, Mother presents the final charge that their daughter Nanny, too weak to perform all of the household tasks, will have to go somewhere else when she marries. Time after time, Father reiterates his refrain—" 'I ain't got nothin' to say' "—and the narrator concludes that in spite of Mother's impressive performance, "her opponent employed that obstinate silence which makes eloquence futile with mocking echoes" (p. 126). (Adoniram plays the resistant critic to Mother's feminist interpretation of her text.) Freeman backs Father into a corner. Having refused to reconsider his plan, he expects his wife to accept it, but the story that Freeman chooses to tell requires Mother's rejection of the plan—a notion that has never occurred to Adoniram. In response to Nanny's gently mocking suggestion that her wedding be held in the new barn, Sarah Penn conceives a plan of her own.

For a woman in one of Freeman's New England villages, and for some women today, the only thing worse than objecting to her husband's decision is acting to oppose it. Sarah Penn allows a maxim to form in her mind: " 'Unsolicited opportunities are the guide-posts of the Lord to the new roads of life' " (p. 130). Just as the new barn is finished, providence assists her by calling Adoniram away on business. Then Sarah Penn moves out of her house and into the new barn—dishes, stove and all. Her children are awe-struck: "There is a certain uncanny and superhuman quality about all such purely original undertakings as their mother's was to them" (p. 133).

As with any feminist resistance to patriarchal authority, Sarah Penn's action receives complete disapproval from the town chorus. Freeman well knew the interpretations that would be offered: "Some held her to be insane; some, of lawless and rebellious spirit" (p. 134). The minister comes to invoke the moral force of institutionalized religion, only to elicit the following, incontrovertible response: " 'I've got my own mind an' my own feet, an' I'm goin' to think my own thoughts an' go my own ways, an' nobody but the Lord is goin' to dictate to me unless I've a mind to have him' " (p. 135). Upon his return, Adoniram is shocked into amazed and even more inarticulate bewilderment. Through action, Sarah's meaning makes itself plain to him, and he finally understands what the new house means to her. Both are overcome by this reversal—Adoniram weeps and Sarah covers her face with her apron. Accentuating the effect, Freeman summarizes the attack: "Adoniram was like a fortress whose walls had no active resistance, and went down the instant the right besieging tools were used" (p. 139).

Though the surface of the story seems far from ambiguous, some critics still manage to delimit the narrative's power. Foster's basic approach to the story as a "comic folk tale" seems completely misdirected. He observes: "We are amused by the battle of the sexes—anywhere; and we cheer when any worm turns."[39] I can't agree with his assumption that "we" are amused. While Westbrook admits a truth beyond probability of event and locates it in the fiercely individualistic New England character, he undercuts his position and Freeman's story with the following assertion: "The greatest disservice done to this story was President Theodore Roosevelt's comment in a speech that American women would do well to emulate the independence of Sarah Penn. From then on, the story was removed from the category of comic fantasy where it belongs and placed before the public as a serious tract on women's rights, which it surely is not."[40] The masculinist critics deny Freeman's imaginary defiance of sex roles by relegating it to comic fantasy, another way of saying that Sarah Penn's revolt need not be taken seriously; it is fun, and we should enjoy it.

Westbrook's comment points to the notoriety and discomfort "The Revolt of 'Mother' " brought its author. In 1917, near the end of her writing career, Freeman wrote of the story: "In the first place all fiction ought to be true and "The Revolt of Mother" is not true. . . . There never was in New England a woman like Mother. If there had been she certainly would not have moved into the palatial barn. . . . She simply would have lacked the nerve. She would also have lacked the imagination. New England women of the period coincided with their husbands in thinking that the sources of wealth should be better housed than the consumers. . . . I sacrificed truth when I wrote that story, and at this day I do not know exactly what my price was. I am inclined to think coin of the realm."[41] This passage is often quoted, puzzled over, and qualified by critics. None of them offers the qualifying vision of Blanche Colton Williams, who cites two other passages from the same article in *Saturday Evening Post* (8 December 1917).[42] One shows how Freeman situated the disclaimer by first voicing her frustration that "people go right on with almost Prussian dogmatism, insisting that the Revolt of Mother is my one and only work. It is most emphatically not. Were I not truthful, having been born so near Plymouth Rock, I would deny I ever wrote that story. I would foist it upon somebody else."[43] The story's disproportionate fame, resulting from its treatment as a tract, reduces Freeman's entire project. When she is called upon publicly to pass judgment on Sarah Penn, a gesture she refuses within her fictions, she protects her right to create the possible by denying the probability of Sarah's action. Assiduously resisting efforts to limit her story to a treatise on women's rights, Freeman plays the nonfeminist reader who interprets the story according to the period's social realities, the realm of the status quo rather than of defiant possibilities—a position the story itself advances in the view of Sarah's actions as uncanny and "superhuman" (p. 133).

Freeman's renunciation of the ending may be read as the ultimate reclamation of text and author by the dominant, phallocentric discourse. In her statement, Freeman at once denies the truth-value (the desire for defiance) and affirms the fictive quality of Sarah Penn's action. The questioning strikes too close to home, for it was Freeman, after all, who had the imagination, the rebellious capacity, to construct Sarah Penn's revolt. A citizen of the world she chronicles, Freeman takes a position similar to the one Flannery O'Connor adopts later. When her friend Maryat Lee encourages her to see James Baldwin in Georgia, O'Connor refuses: "In New York it would be nice to meet him; here it would not. I observe the traditions of the society I feed on—it's only fair. Might as well expect a mule to fly as me to see James Baldwin in Georgia."[44] By refusing overt declaration, the writer imagines she can protect her position as artist and social critic. Again only Blanche Williams included Freeman's additional comment from the *Post* article that women in New England villages often hold the household reins, and for good reason: "They really can drive better."[45] Once more Freeman expresses a less compromised view and preserves the freedom purchased through her unyielding undecidability. The reader knows from the beginning that Sarah's revolt is a fiction, that the text of the story and the text of the disclaimer are equally true and untrue.

If we are to read Freeman's fiction in the tradition of her best known critics, we substitute our own desire for narrative authority for the author's persistent denials and evasions and for the text's own essential subversiveness. The reader/critic's dilemma is inescapable. No one is to blame. The rhetoric of Freeman's texts places us in what Culler describes as "impossible situations where there is no happy issue but only the possibility of playing out roles dramatized in the text."[46] The beauty of Leah Glasser's article on Freeman rests in her struggle to read the writer as she finds her rather than as Glasser, representative of the contemporary feminist reader, would like her to be. Glasser allows herself to confront the troubling ambiguities of Freeman's " 'slavery' as well as her 'rebellion.' "[47] Roland Barthes' comments on Greek tragedy apply equally well to the task of interpreting Freeman's work; he describes the texts as "being woven from words with double meanings that each character understands unilaterally (this perpetual misunderstanding is exactly the 'tragic'); there is, however, someone who understands each word in its duplicity and who, in addition, hears the very deafness of the characters speaking in front of him [or her]—this someone being precisely the reader (or here, the listener)."[48] It is not easy (or perhaps even possible) to be the reader upon whom nothing is lost. However, we make less rather than more of the fiction when we play the character's part and resolve the tensions inherent in the task of formulating moral judgments during a time of change and possibility—a choice that Freeman's perception of internal and external realities would not permit her to make. Her view demanded both sides of the situation, as opposed to an unqualified depiction of gender roles, aging, poverty, and rural life of the period.

Each strand of meaning requires the existence of the other and is inhabited by its opposite, making it impossible to choose between them or to decide what Freeman really meant for us to understand. The text's meaning does not reside in story "A" or "B"; instead it is "A" and "B" and the combination of the two. The effect of the human compulsion to choose a resolution is to illustrate Culler's point that "texts thematize, with varying degrees of explicitness, interpretive operations and their consequences and thus represent in advance the dramas that will give life to the tradition of their interpretation. Critical disputes about a text can frequently be identified as a displaced reenactment of conflicts dramatized in the text, so that while the text assays the consequences and implications of various forces it contains, critical readings transform this difference within into a difference between mutually exclusive positions."[49]

As Freeman's readers, we follow suit, continuing to play out the text's struggles in our interpretive debates. By reducing the critical drama to a contest between simple oppositions, criticism perpetuates itself. But Freeman, in a necessary strategy, outwits us all. She anticipates us, encouraging and demanding our differences of view by encoding them within her fictions. She constructs us as she did her characters, particularly in her refusal to write an easy solution to the problematics of gender. Through her insistence on this complexity she stages the text's resistance to temporality. But returning for a moment to Barthes' view of the tragic, I cannot deny the relationship between Freeman's renunciation of "The Revolt of 'Mother' " and the characters in a Greek play who limit their understanding of what they hear and say as they stage the text's misunderstandings. In her nonfiction Freeman accepts the role in which woman has been cast (as O'Connor accepts southern racism) when she denies Sarah's rebellion. She retreats from her own feminist moment and plays the "woman," exposing her personal inability to escape temporality. The price of denial is great. . . .

Notes

1. Woolf, *Three Guineas*, 90.

2. De Man, *Blindness and Insight*, 102–3. His chapter on Derrida's reading of Rousseau (pp. 102–41) presents a model for interpretation which proceeds from this analysis.

3. Johnson, *The Critical Difference*, 5–6.

4. There are several other works on Freeman that have secondary significance to this study: Michele Clark's Afterword to Freeman's *The Revolt of Mother and Other Stories*, and Julia

Bader's "The Dissolving Vision." Clark's purpose is to establish a very brief bio-critical context for reading a new collection of Freeman's stories. Bader's study concerns the tension between the narrative design of realism and the blurring dissolution of the local colorists in the works of Jewett, Freeman, and Gilman.

5. Foster, *Mary E. Wilkins Freeman,* 32.

6. Ibid., 141.

7. Ibid., 69–70.

8. Ibid., 142.

9. Ibid., 143.

10. Wood, "The Literature of Impoverishment," 27.

11. Foster, *Mary E. Wilkins Freeman,* 191.

12. Wood, "The Literature of Impoverishment," 14.

13. Ibid., 16.

14. Cather, Preface to *The Country of the Pointed Firs,* 9.

15. Foster, *Mary E. Wilkins Freeman,* 106, 105.

16. Ibid., 108, 109.

17. Ziff, *The American 1890s,* 293.

18. De Man, *Blindness and Insight,* 136.

19. Culler, *On Deconstruction,* 81.

20. Freeman, "A New England Nun," 79. Further references are cited in the text.

21. Wood, "The Literature of Impoverishment," 21.

22. Brand, "Mary Wilkins Freeman," 83, 89.

23. Toth, "Defiant Light," 90.

24. Westbrook, *Mary Wilkins Freeman,* 59.

25. Clark, Afterword to *The Revolt of Mother and Other Stories,* 177.

26. Donovan, *New England Local Color Literature,* 132.

27. Foster, *Mary E. Wilkins Freeman,* 172. This calls into question assertions like Wood's: "I have already spoken of the nearly empty pestiferous old house which dominated the Local Colorists' imaginations and of its iconographical links with the diseased and barren womb" ("The Literature of Impoverishment," 28).

28. Brand, "Mary Wilkins Freeman," 83.

29. Toth, "Defiant Light," 90.

30. Brand, "Mary Wilkins Freeman," 88, 89.

31. Freeman, "A Conflict Ended," 331. Further references are cited in the text.

32. Brand, "Mary Wilkins Freeman," 98.

33. Freeman, "Arethusa," 147. Further references are cited in the text.

34. Donovan, *New England Local Color Literature,* 121.

35. Ibid., 129.

36. Toth, "Defiant Light," 92.

37. Ibid.

38. Freeman, "The Revolt of 'Mother,' " 122. Further references are cited in the text.

39. Foster, *Mary E. Wilkins Freeman,* 93.

40. Westbrook, *Mary Wilkins Freeman,* 64–65.

41. Foster, *Mary E. Wilkins Freeman,* 91–92.

42. Freeman, "Mary E. Wilkins Freeman," 25, 75.

43. Williams, *Our Short Story Writers,* 170.

44. O'Connor, *The Habit of Being,* 329.

45. Williams, *Our Short Story Writers,* 170.

46. Culler, *On Deconstruction,* 81.

47. Glasser, " 'She Is the One You Call Sister,' " 188.

48. Barthes, *Image-Music-Text,* 148.

49. Culler, *On Deconstruction,* 214–15.

Bibliography

Bader, Julia. "The Dissolving Vision: Realism in Jewett, Freeman, and Gilman." In *American Realism: New Essays,* edited by Eric J. Sundquist, 176–98. Baltimore: Johns Hopkins University Press, 1982.

Barthes, Roland. *Image-Music-Text.* Translated by Stephen Heath. New York: Hill and Wang, 1977.

Brand, Alice Glarden. "Mary Wilkins Freeman: Misanthropy as Propaganda." *New England Quarterly* 50 (1977): 83–100.

Cather, Willa. Preface to *The Country of the Pointed Firs and Other Stories,* by Sarah Orne Jewett, 6–11. 1925. Reprint. Garden City, N.Y.: Doubleday and Co., 1956.

Clark, Michele. Afterword to *The Revolt of Mother and Other Stories,* by Mary Wilkins Freeman, 79–97. Old Westbury, N.Y.: Feminist Press, 1974.

Culler, Jonathan. *On Deconstruction: Theory and Criticism after Structuralism.* Ithaca, N.Y.: Cornell University Press, 1982.

DeMan, Paul. *Blindness and Insight: Essays in the Rhetoric of Contemporary Criticism.* New York: Oxford University Press, 1971.

Donovan, Josephine. *New England Local Color Literature: A Woman's Tradition.* New York: Frederick Ungar Publishing Co., 1983.

Foster, Edward. *Mary E. Wilkins Freeman.* New York: Hendricks House, 1956.

Freeman, Mary Wilkins. "Arethusa." In *Understudies: Short Stories,* 147–69. 1901. Reprint. Freeport, N.Y.: Books for Libraries Press, 1969.

———. "A Conflict Ended." In *The Best Stories of Mary E. Wilkins,* selected by Henry Wysham Lanier, 320–35. New York: Harper and Brothers, 1927.

———. "A New England Nun." In *The Revolt of Mother and Other Stories,* 79–97. Old Westbury, N.Y.: Feminist Press, 1974.

———. "The Revolt of 'Mother.'" In *The Revolt of Mother and Other Stories,* 116–39. Old Westbury, N.Y.: Feminist Press, 1974.

Glasser, Leah Blatt. "'She Is One You Call Sister': Discovering Mary Wilkins Freeman." In *Between Women: Biographers, Novelists, Critics, Teachers and Artists Write about Their Work on Women,* edited by Carol Ascher, Louise DeSalvo, and Sarah Ruddick, 186–211. Boston: Beacon Press, 1984.

Johnson, Barbara. *The Critical Difference: Essays in the Contemporary Rhetoric of Reading.* Baltimore: Johns Hopkins University Press, 1980.

O'Connor, Flannery. *The Habit of Being.* Edited by Sally Fitzgerald. New York: Farrar, Straus, Giroux, 1979.

Toth, Susan Allen. "Defiant Light: A Positive View of Mary Wilkins Freeman." *New England Quarterly* 46 (1973): 82–93.

Westbrook, Perry D. *Mary Wilkins Freeman.* New York: Twayne, 1967.

Williams, Blanche Colton. *Our Short Story Writers.* New York: Moffat, Yard, and Co., 1920.

Wood, Ann Douglas. "The Literature of Impoverishment: The Women Local Colorists in America 1865–1914." *Women's Studies* 1 (1973): 3–45.

Woolf, Virginia. *Three Guineas.* New York: Harcourt, Brace and World, 1938.

Ziff, Larzer. *The American 1890s: Life and Times of a Lost Generation.* New York: Viking, 1966.

"Eglantina": Freeman's Revision
of Hawthorne's "The Birth-mark"

John Getz

By the 1890s, Mary Wilkins Freeman's short stories, published chiefly in the Harper's magazines, and her two collections of stories, *A Humble Romance* (1887) and *A New England Nun* (1891), had established her as an important American literary figure, one whom reviewers had to notice. Almost from the beginning, critics compared her to Nathaniel Hawthorne. Many authors would have been flattered to be linked with such an acclaimed predecessor, but Freeman's letters reveal a decidedly cool reaction.

It is easy to see why critics in the 1890s and early 1900s were drawn to the comparison. Besides using New England characters and settings, Freeman had family roots in Salem and in 1893 published a play about the witch trials, *Giles Corey, Yeoman*. The parallels with Hawthorne, while interesting today, must have had special appeal at a time when critics were making the case for the academic study of American literature.[1] Constructing an American literary history was an important part of the project, and the similarities between Freeman and Hawthorne added coherence to a narrative that ran from the Puritans through Hawthorne to the present.

The first critic to develop the Freeman-Hawthorne comparison in depth was Charles Miner Thompson in the *Atlantic Monthly*.[2] Thompson believed that Freeman, like Hawthorne, was descended from a judge at the Salem witch trials, and he suggested that this background shaped her sensibility as it had Hawthorne's: "Without burdening too much the weary back of heredity we may recall her witch-persecuting Puritan ancestors in Salem, and, remembering Hawthorne's similar ancestry, say to ourselves that she was probably a serious, imaginative child, with a faculty for brooding over questions of conduct, who could be expected to feel the pathos in the humorous stories and deeply to relish the grim and tragic ones" (668). Acknowledging Freeman's usual classification as a realist, Thompson also found in her work "the purest vein of romance and ideality, and even a certain touch of mysticism and allegory," reminiscent of Hawthorne. The example Thompson cites from Freeman's novel *Pembroke*—"the physical deformity which seems to

This essay was written specifically for this volume and is published here for the first time with the permission of the author.

accompany Barney Thayer's deformity of character" (675)—certainly recalls Hawthorne's portrayal of Roger Chillingworth.

In 1903 Lawrence Hutton in *Harper's Weekly* reported a comparison of Freeman and Hawthorne that dated back to 1894; shortly after the publication of *Pembroke* that year, Arthur Conan Doyle had called it "the greatest piece of American fiction since *The Scarlet Letter.*" Hutton added, "I have found his opinion shared by other eminent critics since then, and in England especially is her name heard most frequently in connection with Hawthorne's."[3]

Freeman's letters in 1904 and 1919 suggest she was anything but flattered by these comparisons. Perhaps she feared that although the comparisons were generally complimentary, they might eventually lead to her dismissal as a mere imitator of Hawthorne. In 1904 she backed out of an agreement with the *Independent* to write a comparison of her characters and Hawthorne's for the centenary of his birth. Calling her mind "an absolute blank on that particular subject," she offered to substitute a new short story of her own.[4] In 1919 Fred Lewis Pattee, one of the academic crusaders for the study and teaching of American literature, requested biographical information from Freeman for his introductions to a new edition of *A New England Nun, and Other Stories.* In a letter answering him, Freeman made the extraordinary claim that none of her reading influenced her work: "I did, however strange it may seem, stand entirely alone. As a matter of fact, I would read nothing which I thought might influence me."[5]

In another letter to Pattee she claimed not to know whether she was descended from a judge at the Salem witch trials—an ancestry that Pattee, like Thompson, had already reported as fact in his brief treatment of her work in *A History of American Literature since 1870.*[6] Perhaps wishing to emphasize her own creativity, Freeman showed more interest in a family legend of descent from a "famous theoretical inventor." She had not included Bray Wilkins, the man the critics believed to be her ancestor at the witch trials, in *Giles Corey,* although witch-hunting magistrate John Hathorne figures prominently in the play. She responded to Pattee's estimate that she was "in soul more akin to Hawthorne than to anyone else": "I do not know if I am 'akin to Hawthorne.' I do not care for him as I care for Tolstoi, Scheinkewitz [*sic*], and Hardy."[7]

Although the early comparisons of Freeman with Hawthorne do not dismiss her as his imitator, they lay a foundation for later critics to do so. Freeman's resistance to comparison with Hawthorne may also have been based on the realization that these early comparisons sometimes diminished her work even while praising it. Measuring her against Hawthorne, critics sometimes found Freeman limited if only by her subject, which they usually identified as New England in its final phase of decline.

For Thompson, Freeman's New England is "accurate in the particular" but "distorted and untruthful . . . in the general" because she shows only its grim side (670). He finds Freeman doubly limited by her formative years in

Brattleboro, Vermont, when it was not yet fully recovered from decline and by the limited range of experiences open to girls and women:

> The narrow field for the observation of life thus afforded her was still further restricted, of course, by the fact of her sex. Had she been a boy, she would have roamed the fields, gone fishing and hunting, had the privilege of sitting in the country store and listening to the talk of the men of evenings; she would have taken an interest in the local politics, and have learned to look at life as the men look at it, with the larger and more catholic view which is theirs not by virtue of greater insight, but by virtue of the undeniably larger, freer lives they are permitted to live. As she was a girl, her outlook was confined to the household; her sources of information were the tales of gossiping women, which would naturally relate mostly to the family quarrels and dissensions that are the great tragedies of their lives. (667–68)

Although Thompson acknowledges that the differences between men's and women's experience are cultural rather than innate, he clearly makes men's perspectives the norm without recognizing their limits, an example of what Joanna Russ calls "the double standard of content," by which women's writing is judged inferior to men's. For Russ, the claim "She wrote it, but look what she wrote about" is "perhaps the fundamental weapon" that has been used to suppress women's writing.[8] Thompson suggests that Freeman's doubly limited experience prevents her from endowing her characters with the "beauty" and "grandeur" of the old Puritans, who "exercised their stubbornness upon a great issue" (671). While crediting her originality and "great natural gift," Thompson clearly cannot rank her with Hawthorne. In fact, he wishes she would become more like Hawthorne by cultivating the vein of romance or idealism that now "allies her, however distantly, to the literary family of Hawthorne" and allows "at least a hesitating comparison to the author of the most beautiful American romances" (675).

After Freeman declined to write the Hawthorne centennial article for the *Independent,* Paul Elmer More took on the task. His title, "Hawthorne: Looking Before and After," reveals his priorities.[9] For More, Hawthorne was "the one artist who worked in materials thoroughly American and who is worthy to take a place among the great craftsmen of the world." The reason More gives for Hawthorne's eminence is that "he came just when the moral ideas of New England were passing from the conscience to the imagination and just before the slow, withering process of decay set in" (173). In More's scheme, writing about New England during its final phase of decline dooms Freeman to inferior status. Announcing the past and present against which he will set his treatment of Hawthorne, More reveals his condescending attitude toward her: Hawthorne "stands as a connecting link between old Cotton Mather and—*magna cum parvis*—Mary Wilkins Freeman" (174). Apparently she is a "small thing" when compared with Cotton Mather as well as with Hawthorne.

Although More acknowledges Freeman's genius and ends with the hope that a note of "growing humanitarianism" in her work will point the way for a revival of New England and its literature (186–87), much of his essay diminishes her by contrasting her material with Hawthorne's. While praising Hawthorne's universality and linking *The House of the Seven Gables* with Greek tragedy, (181–82), More finds Freeman's tales "thoroughly provincial": "Her stories are not tragic in the ordinary sense of the word; they have no universal meaning and contain no problem of the struggle between human desires and the human will, or between the will and the burden of circumstances. They are, as it were, the echo of a tragedy long ago enacted; they touch the heart with the faint pathos of flowers pressed and withered in a book, which, found by chance, awaken the vague recollection of outlived emotions" (181).

Freeman's short story "Eglantina" is her literary response to Hawthorne and perhaps to critics like Thompson. Published in 1902, "Eglantina" precedes More's essay but follows Thompson's and much of the discussion of Freeman and Hawthorne cited in Lawrence Hutton's *Harper's Weekly* article. Freeman reprinted "Eglantina" in her collection *The Fair Lavinia and Others* in 1907 and turned it into a "romantic parlor play" for the "romance number" of the *Ladies' Home Journal* in 1910, but the story has not been reprinted since.[10] "Eglantina" has attracted almost no attention from critics. Perry D. Westbrook dismisses it, along with almost all the other stories in *Fair Lavinia,* as "pretty much without substance."[11] But "Eglantina" deserves scrutiny. The story can be read as a revision of Hawthorne's "The Birth-mark," a favorite with his audience in Freeman's day. With her "A Humble Romance," "The Birth-mark" was on the list of runners-up in 1897 when *Critic* conducted a public opinion poll to identify the best American short stories.[12]

The central situation in "The Birth-mark" and "Eglantina" is the same: the presence of a birthmark on a woman's face.[13] Both women's birthmarks temporarily disappear when they blush but reappear starkly if emotions cause their cheeks to turn pale. In Hawthorne's story Georgiana's birthmark is shaped like a tiny hand. By making Eglantina's birthmark look like a rose, Freeman recalls the imagery in which Georgiana describes herself shortly before her death: "My earthly senses are closing over my spirit like the leaves round the heart of a rose, at sunset." Moreover, as Georgiana's birthmark fades away near the end of the story, it has "the faintest rose-color" (54–55).

Georgiana's monomaniacal husband Aylmer uses his scientific genius to remove the birthmark, poisoning her in the process. Science also plays a role in "Eglantina," but Freeman's story eliminates Hawthorne's warning against its excesses. In "Eglantina" science heals.

The subject of the operation in Freeman's story is not Eglantina but her stepbrother and fiancé, Roger Proctor, who was blinded as an infant by scarlet fever. The operation restores his sight. By making Roger blind for most of the story, Freeman prevents him from being the kind of physical threat to Eglantina that Aylmer is to Georgiana. In this context Roger Proctor's last name is significant, for Freeman, who had studied the Salem witch trials enough to write *Giles Corey,* knew John Proctor was one of the victims killed in the hysteria. Besides the limits of his physical power, Roger differs sharply from Aylmer in loving Eglantina as she is; Aylmer, in contrast, is so obsessed with perfecting Georgiana that it is difficult to accept the references in the story to his love for her.

With such a different focus, "Eglantina" seems to be a much more benign story, but is it? Realist that she is, Freeman eliminates Hawthorne's sensational plot and shifts the emphasis to character. In the process she also rewrites his tale from a woman's perspective, with some startling results.

First, as her title suggests, Freeman makes Eglantina the central character, in contrast to Hawthorne's focus on Aylmer. This move allows Freeman to develop one of the most surprising and often overlooked aspects of "The Birth-mark": Georgiana's complicity, even active participation in her own death.[14] Like Georgiana, Eglantina demonstrates a lack of self-regard, symbolized by her hatred of roses even though her name refers to the kind of rose that grew over her family's front porch. She even sickens at the scent of roses. It is also significant that when Eglantina looks at her face in the mirror, she sees only her birthmark (388). Hawthorne's story shows a similar scene of warped perception, reducing Georgiana to her birthmark, but here the allegorizer is Aylmer. When he photographs Georgiana, using a process he invented, the resulting picture is "blurred and indefinable; while the minute figure of a hand appeared where the cheek should have been" (45).

Eglantina's lack of self-love leads to self-destructive behavior. Convinced that Roger will be unable to love her when, after the operation, he sees her birthmark, she sends her beautiful cousin Charlotte to him to impersonate her and plans to drop out of his life forever. Characters in many of Freeman's stories make similarly pointless self-sacrifices. It is no accident that most of these characters are women or that Eglantina's standard for judging herself worthless is her appearance. Eglantina's mother also lacked a sense of her own worth when she blamed herself for the birthmark because while she was pregnant she had wished for roses in winter. Freeman's syntax leaves open the possibility that Eglantina's mother may actually have died from grief over her newborn daughter's birthmark: the mother "mourned until she died, not long after, because of her disfigurement, and often kissed, with tears of self-reproach . . . the mark on the little cheek" (388).

Eglantina's ruse involving her cousin does not fool Roger. Disappointed in Charlotte, he rejects her and is reunited with Eglantina in what appears to be a complete shift from Georgiana's death at the end of "The Birth-mark." Roger would seem to be doing what the final lines of "The Birth-mark" recommend and Aylmer failed to do: "Yet, had Aylmer reached a profounder wisdom, he need not thus have flung away the happiness, which would have woven his mortal life of the selfsame texture with the celestial. . . . he failed to look beyond the shadowy scope of Time, and, living once for all in Eternity, to find the perfect Future in the present" (56).

But Freeman's story does not end with the reunion of Eglantina and Roger. The final paragraph passes over the rest of Eglantina's life as quickly as possible before reporting her death: "Eglantina lived and died, and her long grave is in the graveyard of Litchfield Village, and at the head is a marble stone on which are cut the verses beginning—'Eglantina, tall and fair' " (395). This paragraph is a long way from "They lived happily ever after." It is as if Eglantina is simply swallowed up by her union with Roger. We are not even told how she died. It may have been soon after childbirth, like the deaths of her mother and stepmother, since childbearing posed a serious threat to women of Freeman's day. But the author is making a subtler point, one going far beyond Hawthorne's story: for a woman without a strong sense of her own identity and worth, marriage, even to a man who loves her, can become a kind of death. Being "settled" in marriage—the hope of Eglantina's father for his daughter (389)—may not be so different for a woman from being settled in her grave. The outside narrator attributes Roger's mother's death in childbirth to her devotion to her husband: "She was a mild and delicate creature, whose only force of character lay in loving devotion, and that proved too strenuous for her fragile constitution. She died a year after her marriage, and her little daughter died with her" (387).

Against this background the restoration of Roger's sight symbolizes his assumption of the power Eglantina gives him over her life. In effect, he becomes her "proctor." Even Roger's innocent blue eyes cast an appropriating male gaze that reduces her to silence by the end of the story. Roger's first name, after all, is not that of the witch-trial victim; in the Hawthornian context of this story, the name Roger recalls Roger Chillingworth. Of course, Roger Proctor is not capable of the actions of Chillingworth or Aylmer, and he is very devoted to Eglantina. But he has some of their stubborn possessiveness, as Eglantina herself notes: "he is one who, if love go amiss, will come to harm in himself." The narrator adds, "And that was quite true, for Roger Proctor was a man to be made or marred by love" (390). Surprisingly, Roger too sometimes judges women by appearance. He rejects Charlotte not because she lacks Eglantina's character but because he does not find her face as beautiful as he had hoped.

It is not clear whether Roger survives Eglantina, although there is reason to believe he does. The verse on her headstone is the first line of a poem he carved for her on a shutter in the parlor of their house while he was blind. (Both carvings of this verse adorn enclosures.) "Eglantina" begins with the complete poem, giving Roger the first words of the story as well as the last. Silenced in death, Eglantina survives only as a muse of the male poet and the subject of his poem, just as Georgiana lives on only in Aylmer's journal of failed experiments.

When Freeman turned "Eglantina" into a "romantic parlor play" for the

Ladies' Home Journal eight years later, she omitted the somber note of the last paragraph.[15] As befits the "romance number" of the magazine, the play ends with Eglantina and Roger's joyful reunion. We should not, however, overlook the play's own subversive elements, which partially compensate for the lack of the final paragraph, especially the development of Charlotte as Eglantina's alter ego. In the play Charlotte more than once correctly tells Eglantina that her foolish self-sacrifice can actually harm Roger (38). Charlotte also makes it clear that she does not love any man, even the charming Roger, and does not want children (14, 38). Although some of Charlotte's dialogue invites the conventional judgment that she is frivolous and selfish, her presence in the play as a woman who makes choices for herself highlights Eglantina's incompleteness and lends credibility to Aunt Pamela's remark: "Eglantina was always so unselfish, one might think she was underwitted" (14). And Eglantina's own lament near the end of the play picks up a major concern of the story: "I have never been happy, Charlotte; that is, not happy in my own self" (38).

Besides revising Hawthorne's "The Birth-mark" from a realist's and a woman's perspective, Freeman seems to be saying something about the connection critics were beginning to see between her fiction and Hawthorne's. Eglantina's birthmark can represent this connection, real but not limiting. Of course, critics who pair Freeman with Hawthorne may eventually see only the birthmark and allow her to live on only as his creation—another of his texts—just as Eglantina is reduced to Roger's poem. In any case these critics put Freeman under a male gaze that, like Roger's, appears benign but finally can silence and bury her like Eglantina. As early as 1902, Freeman seems to foresee the fall from critical favor that began in her later years and continued after her death in 1930. In 1926, the same year she received the Howells Medal for Fiction and was elected to the National Institute of Arts and Letters, she wrote to an aspiring author, "I have not myself any more pull or influence than you have. I wonder if it will console you a bit if I tell you that after my success and with my measure of international fame, I am none too sure of a market for my own wares." She attributed her plight to changes in literary fashion "since the War and since even the pre-war days for I think the change antedated the War."[16]

But the defeat in "Eglantina" is the title character's, not Freeman's. By protesting the male gaze in marriage and literary criticism, Freeman refuses to be silenced like her main character. Instead she insists on the limits of self-sacrifice and the importance of women's valuing and asserting themselves apart from what men think. She also resists the artistic self-silencing of the title character in her earlier story, "A Poetess": Betsey Dole burns her poems when they seem inferior by male standards. Anything but silenced in "Eglantina," Freeman shows her artistic power by appropriating and transforming one of Hawthorne's most famous stories for her own purposes. In "Eglantina" it is Freeman's voice that is heard, not Hawthorne's. She is the actual author of Roger's poem that begins and ends the story. Thus, she really gives herself the last word. By surviving the critics who buried her, Freeman is having the last word again today with the current revival of interest in her work.

Notes

1. See Gerald Graff, *Professing Literature: An Institutional History* (Chicago: University of Chicago Press, 1987), 211–13.

2. Charles Miner Thompson, "Miss Wilkins: An Idealist in Masquerade," *Atlantic Monthly* 83 (May 1899): 666. Page numbers are given in the text.

3. Lawrence Hutton, "Mary E. Wilkins Freeman," *Harper's Weekly,* 47 (21 November 1903), supplement: 1880.

4. Freeman to Hamilton Holt (10 April 1904), in *The Infant Sphinx: The Collected Letters of Mary E. Wilkins Freeman,* ed. Brent L. Kendrick (Metuchen, N.J.: Scarecrow Press, 1985), 298–99.

5. Freeman to Fred Lewis Pattee (5 September 1919), in *The Infant Sphinx,* ed. Kendrick, 382.

6. Fred Lewis Pattee, *A History of American Literature since 1870* (New York: Century, 1915), 236.

7. Freeman to Fred Lewis Pattee (25 September 1919) in *The Infant Sphinx,* ed. Kendrick, 384–85.

8. Joanna Russ, *How to Suppress Women's Writing* (Austin: University of Texas Press, 1983), 40.

9. Paul Elmer More, "Hawthorne: Looking Before and After," *Independent* 56 (30 June 1904): 1489–94; reprinted in More, *Shelburne Essays: Second Series* (Boston: Houghton Mifflin, 1905), 173. Page references given in the text are to the Shelburne essays.

10. I have not found the story in recent collections.

11. Perry D. Westbrook, *Mary Wilkins Freeman* (New York: Twayne, 1967), 167.

12. Kendrick, ed., *The Infant Sphinx,* 2. In the first rank were Freeman's "The Revolt of Mother" and Hawthorne's "The Snow Image."

13. Nathaniel Hawthorne, "The Birth-mark," in *Mosses from an Old Manse,* vol. 10 of *The Centenary Edition of the Works of Nathaniel Hawthorne* (Columbus: Ohio State University Press, 1974), 37–38; Mary E. Wilkins [Freeman], "Eglantina," *Harper's Monthly Magazine* 105 (August 1902): 388. Further references to "The Birth-mark" and to "Eglantina" are given in the text.

14. For a discussion of Georgiana's complicity, see Judith Fetterley, *The Resisting Reader: A Feminist Approach to American Fiction* (Bloomington: Indiana University Press, 1978), 32–33.

15. Mary E. Wilkins Freeman, "Eglantina: A Romantic Parlor Play in Three Acts," *Ladies' Home Journal,* 27 (July 1910): 38. Page numbers are given in the text.

16. Freeman to Jean O'Brien (27 February 1926) in *The Infant Sphinx,* ed. Kendrick, 401–2.

Going to an Unknown Home:
Redesign in *The Portion of Labor*

MARTHA SATZ

The Portion of Labor, Mary Wilkins Freeman's 1901 novel, lacks an illustrious critical reputation.[1] Edward Foster, Freeman's biographer, terms it her "least successful novel" and berates Ellen, its heroine, as a "tedious bore."[2] Perry Westbrook views Ellen even more harshly, sneeringly calling her a "virago," chiding Freeman for creating what he takes to be an unrealistically strong figure.[3] A social protest novel, *Portion of Labor* contains disquisitions on the value of labor and the inequities of capitalism. The narrative deals with the working and living conditions of laborers in a shoe factory and their relation to the upper middle class, the owners of the factory. The plot concerns the talented, intelligent Ellen Brewster, the daughter of working-class parents, who as a young runaway from home is briefly kept by a rich woman, Cynthia Lennox. Years later, when Ellen graduates from high school, Cynthia, remorseful for her earlier action, offers to send Ellen to Vassar, an offer Ellen must refuse because of her family's severe financial exigencies. Instead, Ellen enters the factory as a menial worker and comes to appreciate the dignity of ordinary labor. While working in the factory, she leads a strike that eventually changes working conditions. Only after she has negotiated changes with the factory owner, Robert Lloyd, Cynthia's nephew, does she allow her romantic relationship with Robert to flourish.

Yet this work, ostensibly a social protest novel dealing with the inequities of the economic and social fabric, functions on a visionary level as well. As such, it characterizes the lives of women in 1901, the time of writing, and imagines them as they may be in an optimistic future. It portrays the elements of women's lives—maternity, sisterhood, passionate friendship, the infatuation of the schoolgirl crush, romantic love between women, meaningful work, power, and egalitarian male-female relationships—and does so without subjugating any of these autonomous elements to the traditional values of heterosexual love, the family, and the patriarchal community. Although it might be said that as an economic and societal reformer Freeman failed in this fiction, she did succeed as a visionary architect of women's lives. *Portion of Labor,* portraying as it does the fulfilled life of a strong woman amid

This essay was written specifically for this volume and is published here for the first time with the permission of the author.

a web of intense, essential relationships among women, can be fruitfully examined within the context of Freeman's other works treating women's relationships and lives.

The visionary quality of *Portion of Labor* suffuses its opening. The narrative begins with the youthful heroine's vision of the trees outside her window marching homeward. Having heard them called Norway spruces early in childhood, Ellen imagines them yearning to return home and undertaking that goal under cover of darkness. She attributes to them an "air of expectancy of progress" (1). The image strikes a poignant chord, linked as it is to Ellen by the narrative voice and the chronology of events, for the expectancy belongs to the child rather than the trees she observes. Thus Ellen is the locus of an exploration of progress.

The narrative forcefully emphasizes the link between the trees and Ellen by explaining that this private vision "was one of the secrets of the soul which created her individuality" (2). Indeed, Ellen's first act is to run away from home, a self-initiated sojourn that provides her with an alternative maternal figure and directs her to another way of life. The image of Ellen and the trees is both heartrending and paradoxical, an image of deeply rooted entities electing in spite of their roots to loose themselves and march home, a home they have never seen but which in Ellen's imagination they cry for. It is an image of longing for an unrealizable home.

Yet the image is not complete, for on the other side of the house is another sort of tree of which Ellen also has an imaginative picture. In her vision, cherry trees once grew in the Garden of Eden and thus are vestiges of the ideal realm in this imperfect world. This novel, ostensibly about economic and working conditions, struggles in its opening pages with notions of the ideal: one that, in spite of its natural affinity, is far away and unreachable; the other, proximate, that gives a glimpse of that part of the ideal which is recoverable.

But the opening image does more than metaphorically preview Ellen's struggle between two ways of life, her rooted working-class background and the world of riches, education, and taste proffered by Cynthia Lennox, the woman who finds and nurtures Ellen when she runs away. The image also establishes an aesthetic realm beyond the prosaic one Ellen inhabits, for she, as the text early makes clear, takes the literal world and transforms it into the aesthetic, metaphorical realm without realizing she is doing so. A striking passage revealing this tendency occurs during Ellen's early retreat from home. At a grocery shop window,

> Ellen looked at the great shelf laid upon with flesh and vegetables and fruits with the careless precision of a kaleidoscope, and did not for one instant connect anything thereon with the ends of physical appetite, though she had not had her supper. . . The turnips affected her imagination like ivory carvings: she did not recognize them for turnips at all. . . . However, all at once

everything was spoiled, for her fairy castle of illusion or a higher reality was demolished . . . by pity and sentiment. . . . All at once she looked up from the dazzling mosaic of the window and saw the dead partridges and grouse. (18–19)

Similarly, when Cynthia Lennox spins tales of the parrot inhabiting her house and then shows Ellen the real one, Ellen rejects the parrot in favor of the story about it, for "a parrot was too fine and fierce a bird for Ellen . . . she preferred Cynthia's story about him better than the gorgeous actuality of the bird himself" (45).

These initial characterizations of Ellen suggest the several levels on which the text of the novel functions. In its prosaic dimension, the novel struggles with economic and social problems, the conditions of the working class, and the meaning of labor—matters in which "sentiment and pity" intervene. Yet the work also functions to weave a story, an aesthetic ideal that, like Cynthia Lennox's story of the parrot, is more pleasing than the real. This narrative portrays the lives of women woven in a tapestry composed of the cherry tree of homely life and the spruce of the envisioned ideal.

The work deals with the intensity of women in their relationships with one another, with passions that are sensual and irrationally unbridled: motherhood, the infatuation of the crush, romantic love. These relations, however, are rendered familiar by being presented within the network of less passionate relationships akin to them, such as sisterhood and deep friendships.

Foremost in this novel is the elemental passion of parenthood, especially maternity. The maternity portrayed does not derive from the family but, rather, supersedes and transcends it and, in its most powerful form, arises completely independently of it. In her home environment Ellen is enfolded by parental figures—her mother, her father, her aunt, her grandmother. They disagree and fight, but what draws them together is their overpowering love for Ellen. Ellen's grandmother, Mrs. Zelotes, hostilely disapproves of her daughter-in-law, Ellen's mother, but at Ellen's birth "it came to pass that the two women met only upon that small neutral ground of love, and upon all other territory were sworn foes" (7). At Ellen's disappearance, the whole community becomes parental, overcome with grief at her absence, obsessed with her whereabouts, and then euphorically triumphant upon her discovery, desiring to do anything to welcome her back and comfort her.

Maternal feeling is, however, essentially embodied in Cynthia Lennox. She is portrayed as someone dominated by a sole passion, the nurturing and love of children. She is almost rhapsodic when she finds Ellen in the street. She brings the child to her home, lavishing gifts, attention, and love on her, desperately trying to divert her as Ellen cries for her mother. The love is physical, passionate, and overpowering: "Cynthia's arms were embracing all her delicate little body with tenderest violence, and kissing her little, blushing cheeks with the lightest and carefulest kisses, as though she were a butterfly which she feared to harm with her adoring touch" (42). Cynthia's whole being is involved in loving the child, embracing and talking to her, and using unfamiliar eloquent language as a means of seduction.

Cynthia is aware that she runs a grave risk by keeping Ellen in her house, for in effect she has kidnapped this child for whom the whole community desperately searches. But her need for the child, or "unassuaged longing," as the narrator terms it, is so great that she is heedless of the danger (23). One child has been wrested from her and her need to keep this one is extreme: after her sister's death, Cynthia had cared for her nephew in his early years, but he had been taken away by his father. Freeman carefully maps the topography of Cynthia's maternal feelings.

Concerned about another infatuation, George Eliot notes in *Middlemarch* that customarily novelists devote themselves to detailing only one passion, that between men and woman, and she accordingly bemoans the fact that the story of love for work is seldom recounted.[4] The same might be said of maternal passion: its chronicle has been neglected. But one of the tasks of Freeman's novel is to detail just this. Lyman Risley, who has courted middle-aged Cynthia Lennox for many years, sees the bent of her character as somewhat perverted, if endearingly so, but her passionate maternity in the context of the novel is not seen as strange. It is echoed by other women in the work. For example, Ellen's first teacher, enchanted by the child, is inhibited in her attempts to reprimand her: "She was as helpless before her as before a lover. She was wild to catch her up and caress her instead of pestering her with questions" (143).

And Ellen reciprocally responds to Cynthia. In the two nights and a day that Ellen stays with Cynthia, they forge a deep bond. Indeed, although Ellen is a small child at the time and is threatened, bribed, and cajoled to say where she has been, she never reveals the secret. Cynthia remains a strongly positive figure for Ellen during the course of the novel and thus her maternal fervor is implicitly underwritten by the narrative.

In the context of Mary Wilkins Freeman's works, Cynthia Lennox stands in the company of other isolated, strong, nurturing women whose dominant passion is to care for unprotected beings. Living on the margins of society, these women provide an alternative feminine nurturing enclave. In "A Gatherer of Simples" a herb woman, Aurelia Flower, lives by gathering the healing plants of the earth to cure others.[5] The narrator suggests she is a woman whose superiority can be judged only by unconventional standards, a jack-in-the-pulpit if one had never seen a rose. Aurelia informally adopts an unwanted two-year-old girl and becomes "actively happy for the first time in her life. . . . The comfort she took with the child . . . was unspeakable" (288). She takes the girl, Myrtle, on her wanderings for healing plants. The narrator paints an idyllic picture of mother and child: "Home they would come in the tender spring twilight, the baby asleep in her carriage, with a great sheaf of flowers beside her, and Aurelia with another over her shoulder" (288).

When a grandmother of the child comes to claim her, Aurelia becomes distraught, protesting, "I can't help thinking that Providence ought to provide for women" (291). Like Cynthia Lennox, Aurelia Flower kidnaps the child. She keeps her when the girl, having run away from her grandmother's house, reappears on Aurelia's doorstep. For Aurelia, however, "Providence does provide": the grandmother dies that very night, much to the satisfaction of the entire community, whose members recognize Aurelia's extraordinary maternal abilities as superior to those of any of the other, more conventional women in the story. As Marjorie Pryse comments, "In 'A Gatherer of Simples,' . . . the idea of mother becomes, for Freeman, significantly associated with unconventionality."[6]

In "Christmas Jenny" another unorthodox woman lives apart from society, establishing a nurturing domain. Christmas Jenny, so called because she derives much of her livelihood from selling evergreen wreaths at the holiday season, is, like Aurelia Flower, initially described as kindred to the plants that surround her, "a sylvan face with features composed of bark-wrinkles and knot-holes."[7] Jenny wholeheartedly concerns herself with the living creatures around her. As she first appears in the narrative, she advises her friend Betsey Carey how to cure her tantrum-prone husband; however, to the community, especially to the men, Jenny's behavior is suspect. The minister and deacon of the town, drawn by tales of strange doings in her home, come to investigate, violating her house in her absence. In her "curious sylvan apartment" they find cages of rabbits and birds and a deaf-and-dumb boy dressed like a girl, all well cared for and happy. None of this, however, is comprehensible to the minister and deacon.

Jenny's friend Betsey Carey comes over snow and ice, "on hands and knees in some places," to defend Jenny, for she knew that the men were coming and that no one was at home "that's got any tongue to speak for her" (170–71). Freeman provides the voice of a woman to defend female nurturance. Betsey tells the men of Jenny's loving care of all the creatures around her, an effort that, Betsey says, speaking in the language of the minister and deacon she is confronting, is as good as that of any missionaries.

The men, faced with the woman's rage and with something beyond their scope, hastily and shamefacedly retreat from their invasion. The story illuminates the existence of a separate female realm, one more loving, more nurturing, and potentially stronger than the brittle harshness produced by patriarchal values. The mute boy in girls' clothing reveals too the possibility of undermining the rigid sexual distinctions and antagonisms that produce conflict and hostility.

The beautifully furnished rooms of Cynthia Lennox seem far indeed from the pastoral lairs of these women of nature, but she is as isolated as they are and as unconventional. Her nurturing of the child Ellen is as intense as that lavished by these healing women. As the years go by, Cynthia's care-taking shifts to an arena different from her former one but more appropriate to the situation of one adult female's nurturing of another. She offers to send Ellen, the extraordinarily intelligent young woman who is nevertheless bereft of opportunities, to Vassar. And within her realm, Cynthia produces androgynous values. As Ellen, the small child, roams around Cynthia Lennox's rooms, she becomes aware of the haunting presence of another child. When Cynthia presents Ellen with an enormous, resplendent doll, the child inquires about the doll's previous mother and the mystery is clarified: Cynthia's nephew had been the "doll's mother." Many years later, a romantic interest arises between her nephew, Robert, and Ellen. The fact that they as children sequentially mothered the same doll underlies their relationship and provides a reservoir of mutuality despite the enormous societal gulf that separates them.

Thus, Cynthia's domain, although it may not be a rustic cottage, is nevertheless the source of loving but unconventional values. And Cynthia, by presenting Ellen with a doll, renders the child symbolically and emulatively a mother, thereby initiating her into the nurturing network of women.

Cynthia Lennox, like Aurelia Flower, Christmas Jenny, and other characters in Freeman's works, embodies and glorifies maternal feeling, one traditional trait of women.[8] The narrative is striking in its unabashed portrayal of maternal passion and in its total failure to diminish or domesticate that trait; it never becomes secondary to men or marriage. Although Cynthia Lennox eventually marries her longtime admirer, Lyman Risley, she does so only after he becomes an invalid and therefore another recipient of her nurturing. As the narrator in "Two Old Lovers" explains about the female member of a long-courting couple, "there was something rather mother-like than lover-like in her affection for him."[9]

Sisterhood, although it does not play a preeminent role in *Portion of Labor,* is nevertheless portrayed as a bedrock element in women's lives. Ellen's aunt, her mother's sister, lives with the family before her marriage, and the sisters constantly bicker and fight. But as Andrew Brewster, Ellen's father, learns when he tries to intervene and take his wife's part, the relationship between the sisters is sacrosanct: "[T]he minute Andrew tried to take sides with his wife and assail Eva in his turn, Fanny turned and defended her. 'I am not going to desert all the sister I have got in the world,' she said. 'If you want me to leave, say so, and I will go, but I shall never turn Eva out of doors' " (9). Later on, after Eva marries and is subsequently left by her husband, she has a severe mental breakdown. The whole family undergoes great sacrifices so that they can keep Eva in a humane mental facility. Ellen's mother, Fanny, occasionally feels guilty about the expense but protests that she would do anything for her sister. Sisters, throughout Freeman's work, undergo extreme sacrifices for each other, sometimes, as in *By the Light of the Soul,* sacrificing the man they love, and other times, as in "Amanda and Love," their own happiness.[10] Often the sister relationship is between an older and a much younger sister, a relationship that echoes the maternal one.

But the relationship of sisterhood also provides a model for strong, indissolu-
ble ties between women, profound loving relationships that are emphatically
not secondary to the relationship between woman and man.[11]
    Female friendship is an intrinsic part of *A Portion of Labor* as well. In her
early school days Ellen forges a deep bond with the very poor and very
forceful Abby Atkins. As they grow to young womanhood, both, conscious
of the importance of the friendship in their lives, are unabashed about
expressing their feelings. Abby, appreciative of Ellen's intellect, warns her
never to marry any working-class man, taking an interest, she says, because
"I think more of you than any man ever will. I don't care who he is" (228).
Ellen responds in kind, and the narrative detail lavished on their feelings
emphasizes passion, physical attraction, and commitment:

> Abby felt Ellen's warm round arm against hers with a throbbing of
> rapture, and glanced at her fair face with adoration. She held her in a sort of
> worship, she loved her so that she was fairly afraid of her. As for Ellen, Abby's
> little, leather-stained, leather-scented figure, strung with a passion like a
> bundle of electric wire, pressing against her, seemed to inform her farthest
> thoughts.
>   "If I live longer than my father and mother, we'll live together, Abby,"
> said she.
>   "And I'll work for you, Ellen," said Abby rapturously. (140)

Friendship such as that between Abby and Ellen is treated seriously in this
work, as it is generally in the fiction of Mary Wilkins Freeman. In "A Moral
Exigency," for example, although the protagonist, Eunice, is happy because
of her engagement to a young man who was originally courting another
woman, Ada, she eventually breaks the engagement because Ada's pleading
evokes a strong sensuous memory of the school-yard love they shared.[12]
    The nurturing, sensual friendship between Ellen and Abby is a relation-
ship akin to one even more intense and passionate, the crush. Ellen's first
passion is directed to her teacher, Miss Mitchell. Her feelings even extend to
the teacher's mother, whose physical appearance does not endear: "Old Mrs.
Mitchell might have earned more money in a museum of freaks than her
daughter in a district school. She was a mountain of rotundity, a conjunction
of palpitating spheres" (140). Nevertheless, Ellen is in love with both Miss
Mitchell and her mother, and the narrator offers an interpretation of the
feeling: "she loved those women of former generations better because they
gave her breathing-scope for her imagination" (141). Through her girlish
love, Ellen is searching for intellectual and spiritual satisfaction, other realms
of experience to explore. The narrative takes pains to examine the wide
prevalence of the girlhood crush. Accordingly, Amabel, Ellen's small cousin,
has a crush on Ellen and once again the narrator accompanies the feeling with
explanation and interpretation: "Ellen was what she herself would be when

she was grown up. Through Ellen her love of self and her ambition budded into blossom" (173–74).

The numerous narrative recountings of the intense feelings of girls for admired older members of the same sex, accompanied as they are by explanations, serve as a prelude to the description of Ellen's love for Cynthia. The narrative interprets its various instances of the female crush as a reimagining of self and a defining of aspirations. It is no surprise, then, that Ellen, as a young woman, should feel intensely about Cynthia, who long ago introduced her to new vistas of experience expressed in unfamiliar language and who now offers to send her to Vassar. Cynthia consistently calls forth the best from Ellen. When Ellen freezes with anxiety as she stands before the audience to deliver her high school valedictory, "Cynthia Lennox, on the farther side of the hall, was gazing full at her with an indescribable gaze of passion and help and command. Her own mother's look could not have influenced her. Ellen raised her valedictory, bowed, and began to read" (141). Indeed, Ellen falls in love with Cynthia just at the moment Cynthia offers to send her to Vassar and thus responds to the older woman's nurturing.

Ellen's fervent love for Cynthia is described as all-encompassing and unique, the love of a young woman for a maternal figure who promises to nurture what Ellen deems best about herself. In no way belittled, the love is portrayed as grandiose, resonating with the experience of a character of another of Freeman's stories, "The Love of Parson Lord." In this story a girl named Love, whose own mother has died, enters her minister father's church, sees the motherly squire's wife, and experiences the maternal with the awe usually reserved for the divine: "That morning Love heard no more of her father's discourse. She was conscious of nothing except that mother presence, which seemed to pervade the whole church. The inexorable fatherhood of God, as set forth in the parson's sermon, was not as evident to the hungry little heart in His sanctuary as the motherhood of the squire's lady. She continued to gaze at her at intervals, with softly furtive eyes of adoration . . . and when she sometimes received a tenderly benignant glance in return, she scarcely knew where her body was, such was the elation of her spirit."[13] The girl's vision in one moment of love metaphorically inverts patriarchal values. Love's harsh minister father and Christianity's judgmental cosmic Father are subordinated to benignant motherhood.

Echoing this moment, the narrative in *Portion of Labor* says of Ellen's love for Cynthia, "She made a sort of divinity of the older woman, and who expects a divinity to step down from her marble heights, and love and caress?" (144). Ellen's love for Cynthia transforms the girl's very self; she imitates her every gesture. Thus, her love acts to shape and define her. It is a distinctively female love, occurring within the context of a strong young women's development.

Critics, both condemnatory and not, both traditional and feminist, have wanted to label the relation between Ellen and Cynthia as homosexual, lesbian. Josephine Donovan, for example, cites a passage in which Ellen expresses her desire to kiss Cynthia as clearly establishing the lesbian nature of the relationship and then proceeds to criticize the plot of the book because Ellen fails to run away with Cynthia.[14] Yet such labeling is reductive and does a disservice both to Freeman's text and to the intricate network of life-supporting connections she portrays. It is vital to remember that Ellen's intense relationship with Cynthia locates itself within a web of essential, passionate relationships among women.

Carroll Smith-Rosenberg argues in her article on the friendships of eighteenth- and nineteenth-century American women that to judge such friendships from the twentieth-century viewpoint is a mistake.[15] To ask whether these women, who were emotionally primary in each others' lives, engaged in or desired to engage in genital sexual relationships is to distort the relationships, to ask the wrong questions. The friendships must be considered on their own terms in the social, cultural context in which they existed. Adrienne Rich in some ways extends this argument, asserting that to make the focal question about women's relationships whether or not they involve genital sexual relations is to impose on women a male standard of evaluation and sexuality.[16] Nancy Sahil and Lillian Faderman, writing about the time period in which Freeman worked, assert that the female crush was a perfectly acceptable and acknowledged relationship and that periodicals as mainstream as *Harper's* and the *Ladies' Home Journal* contained stories dealing with the frustration and eventual satisfaction of women's passion for each other.[17]

Freeman portrays the integrity, passion, and formative and transformative aspects of women's relationships with each other without ever subordinating them to romantic male-female relationships. Ellen indeed will marry, but her relationship with Cynthia will influence her choice, and, as in "The Love of Parson Lord," it will never be altogether clear how strongly the suitor's relationship to the maternal figure has influenced that choice, for Ellen marries Cynthia's nephew and Love in "The Love of Parson Lord" marries the grandson of the squire's wife.

Enmeshed as she is in a variegated web of relationships, Ellen is an autonomous, uncompromisingly strong figure. Indeed, she surprises those around her with her intellect and power. Her high school teacher explains, from his conservative perspective, that her mind has the virtues of the traditionally male and female; she is logical as well as intuitive. Furthermore, Ellen projects strength. When a fellow worker comes to dun her father for borrowed money, she addresses the intruder with dignity and power: " 'Will you please not speak so loud,' said she, in a voice which her father had never heard from her lips before. It was a voice of pure command, and of command which carried with it the consciousness of power to enforce. . . . The man shrank back a little, he had the impression as of someone overtowering him, and yet the girl came scarcely to his shoulder" (326).

Freeman also gives Ellen the gift of oratory, gives her a voice in the public sphere; her speech has the power to move people. Her high school valedictory about the dignity of labor inspires the audience to such a degree that a riot almost ensues. Her words lead the workers to a strike, and when she comes to realize that the strike is producing too much human anguish, she leads the workers back to the factory, an action in which she assumes great control and force.

Ellen's direct power and strength surpass these qualities in other unconventional characters in Freeman's work who evince strength and challenge patriarchal values by assuming nontraditional roles. One thinks, for example, of the characters in "A Village Singer," "A Poetess," and "A Church Mouse."[18] Yet these characters die or suffer apparently because of their very challenge to authoritarian males and their institutions. In contrast, Ellen succeeds in her bold enterprises and wins the admiration of the community.

Ellen also falls in love with a man. Thus an apparently traditional relationship, culminating in marriage, becomes part of her life, a relationship like that of Cinderella, elevating Ellen in class and social standing. But in this avenue, too, tradition metamorphoses into vision. The relationship between Ellen and Robert is undergirded by a sense of equality and commonality that struggles with, and perhaps overrides, the fact that they are woman and man, worker and factory owner. As children, Robert and Ellen loved the same doll and the strongly maternal woman who gave it to them, creating a bond of mutuality. Even here, however, the parenting seems to vary with gender. As a boy, Robert burned the doll with a red-hot poker because, he says, "I always had a notion when I was a child that it was only a question of violence to make her wake up and demonstrate some existence besides that external grin" (216–17). Ellen only loved and kissed the doll, believing that love could make its life manifest. But recognizing the doll sparks Robert into an appreciation of Ellen's strong spirit as he realizes the ferocity with which as a child she protected Cynthia. This spiritual bond is enhanced by his reluctant appreciation of Ellen's intellect. As their relationship grows and they begin to discuss and argue about a variety of matters, Robert reflects, "Decidedly this child can think" (147). But then, "he did not wish to place Ellen Brewster on the same level of argument on which another man might have stood. . . . She seemed more within his reach, and infinitely more for his pleasure, where she was" (147). Yet the evolution of the relationship leads Robert to see Ellen on the same level. Politically, she opposes him, leading a strike against his management, vigorously arguing with him about art, politics, and philosophy. When they finally join together, they come in mutuality, in an equality made possible by the fact that as children they nurtured the same doll and loved the same maternal figure. Cynthia has produced in Robert the possibility of appreciating a woman as an equal. Cynthia's domain, like that of Christmas Jenny, is the source of a new order of values.

In "Good Wits, Pen and Paper" Freeman advises the girl who wishes to write to "write in her own way, with no dependence upon the work of another for aid or suggestion. She should make her own patterns and found her own school."[19] In *The Portion of Labor* Freeman does just that. She normalizes power in women, infatuations and passions between women, equality between women and men, and maternal fervor separate from marriage.

Critics discussing Mary Wilkins Freeman often allude to her reputed self-doubts about her vision, quoting excerpts from a story fragment: "I am a graft on the tree of womanhood. . . . Sometimes I think I am a monster."[20] But she provides another perspective for the vision of *Portion of Labor*. At the end of another of her works, *By the Light of the Soul,* the heroine, Maria, meets a deformed female dwarf. The woman takes Maria to her house and to her bedroom, where everything is curved and diminutive. Maria thinks to herself about her new friend, "Miss Blair had planned for herself a room wherein everything was misformed, and in which she herself was in keeping." The designer of this room remarks, "What a pity I cannot make the whole earth over to suit me. Instead of only this one room!"[21] In *Portion of Labor,* Freeman has indeed made over a room in which strong and unconventional women are now in keeping.

Notes

1. Mary E. Wilkins Freeman, *The Portion of Labor* (New York: Harper's, 1901). All subsequent references are to this edition and cited with page numbers in the text.

2. Edward Foster, *Mary E. Wilkins Freeman* (New York: Hendricks House, 1956), 154, 70.

3. Perry D. Westbrook, *Mary Wilkins Freeman,* (New York: Twayne, 1967), 128.

4. George Eliot, *Middlemarch,* ed. Gordon S. Haight (Boston: Houghton Mifflin, 1968), 107.

5. Mary E. Wilkins Freeman, "A Gatherer of Simples," in *A Humble Romance and Other Stories* (New York: Harper's, 1887), 281. Page numbers are given in the text.

6. Marjorie Pryse, "Afterword," in *Selected Short Stories of Mary E. Wilkins Freeman* (New York: W. W. Norton, 1983), 319.

7. Mary E. Wilkins Freeman, "Christmas Jenny," in *A New England Nun, and Other Stories* (New York: Harper's, 1891), 163. Page numbers are given in the text.

8. For example, Sylvia Whitman in *The Shoulders of Atlas* (New York: Harper's, 1908) is dominated by her maternal passion for a young female relative, and in "A Patient Waiter" (*A Humble Romance,* 399–414) an old woman's passion for her lover becomes transformed into identification with his granddaughter.

9. Freeman, "Two Old Lovers," in *A Humble Romance,* 32.

10. Mary E. Wilkins Freeman, *By the Light of the Soul* (New York: Harper's, 1907); "Amanda and Love," in *A New England Nun,* 288–304.

11. In "A Far-Away Melody" (*A Humble Romance,* 208–18) Freeman movingly describes the relationship between two elderly sisters who have lived their lives together, one longing to follow the other to her death.

12. Freeman, "A Moral Exigency," in *A Humble Romance.*

13. Mary E. Wilkins Freeman, "The Love of Parson Lord," in *The Love of Parson Lord and Other Stories* (New York: Harper's, 1890), 14.

14. See, for example, Josephine Donovan's treatment of this story in *New England and Local Color Literature: A Woman's Tradition* (New York: Frederick Ungar, 1983), 124–25.

15. Carroll Smith-Rosenberg, "The Female World of Love and Ritual: Relations between Women in Nineteenth-Century America," *Signs* 1 (Autumn 1975): 1–29.

16. Adrienne Rich, "Compulsory Heterosexuality and Lesbian Existence," *Signs* 5 (Summer 1980): 631–60.

17. Lillian Faderman, *Surpassing the Love of Men: Romantic Friendship and Love between Women from the Renaissance to the Present* (New York: William Morrow, 1981); Nancy Sahil, "Smashing: Women's Relationships before the Fall," *Chrysalis* 8 (Summer 1979): 17–27.

18. Freeman, "A Village Singer," "A Poetess," and "A Church Mouse," in *A New England Nun*.

19. Mary E. Wilkins Freeman, "Good Wits, Pen and Paper," in *What Women Can Earn: Occupations of Women and Their Compensation,* ed. Grace H. Dodge et al. (New York: Frederick A. Stokes, 1898), 29.

20. Quoted in Foster, 142–43.

21. Freeman, *By the Light of the Soul,* 489.

Rereading Mary Wilkins Freeman: Autonomy and Sexuality in *Pembroke*

DEBORAH G. LAMBERT

Pembroke (1893) is Mary Wilkins Freeman's second novel.[1] Generally considered the best of her longer works, it, like the majority of her short stories, has a New England setting and concerns individuals interacting within a small community.

The plot of *Pembroke* turns on the engagement of Barney Thayer and Charlotte Barnard, an engagement Barney breaks following a political disagreement with Charlotte's father. For 10 years after that night Barney stays away, though first Charlotte and then her father ask for a reconciliation. It is clear that neither of the lovers will marry anyone else. During their long separation, we are introduced to other characters who are in the business of finding mates and marrying. In the center of the novel, between the lovers' quarrel and their reunion 10 years later, is the unhappy story of Barney's mother, Deborah, a domineering woman who alienates herself from two of her children and believes herself responsible for the death of her third child, a sickly boy.

Since it was written by a woman, the quest in this story of marriage, independence, sexuality, and female power occurs within town boundaries and substitutes for a journey west or down the Mississippi, an experience that continues over a decade. Replacing space by time, its economy employs marriages, parties, clothing, illnesses, and births—the common objects of women's lives—as symbolic counters, instead of guns, Indians, bears, compasses, and fishing trips. To read Freeman well requires imagining the complex meaning of everyday things in women's quests and decoding texts we have not been trained to read. In Susan Glaspell's story "A Jury of Her Peers" women "read" an accused woman's kitchen while puzzled men, illiterate in the language of the kitchen, see only empty flour bins and sticky jam pots, unlikely and unmanly symbols.[2] Read as the women in this story read, *Pembroke* offers an analysis of the politics of marriage and an exploration of female power and sexuality that make up an emotionally tangled, even obsessive, story of the limits imposed on women.

Although Freeman left no autobiography and drawing parallels between

This essay was written specifically for this volume and is published here for the first time with the permission of the author.

an author's life and work should be done with caution, the events of her life suggest a struggle between creative needs and a desire for a woman's traditional role. Unconventional in some respects, her life was painfully conformist in others. After the deaths of her parents in 1880 and 1883, she was on her own, with no inheritance, no training, and no skills. Although she is thought to have fallen in love at this time, she apparently never received the expected proposal. Since she had to support herself, writing was a reasonable, respectable choice.[3] She began earning her living writing stories for children. In the New England of the 1880s, however, young women did not live alone. At the age of 30, without family, she moved in with her childhood friend Mary John Wales. Instead of seeking a husband and becoming a wife, as many women in her circumstances might have done, she found a "wife" in Mary Wales. Her old school friend believed in Freeman's talent as a writer and nurtured it, providing Freeman with comfortable private rooms, freedom from the practical problems of living, and the support of affection and admiration. In the sanctuary Wales provided for her, Freeman spent the 18 most productive years of her life.

Despite this apparently ideal arrangement, she seems never to have made peace with her life as a single woman and writer. According to accounts, she seems to have been obsessed with establishing her credentials as a conventionally feminine woman: she continued to talk about her lover and display his photograph; she paid great attention to her clothing, weight, and appearance; and eventually she began to lie about her age. Since she did not marry or spend her energies caring for others but instead became successful while being cared for by Mary Wales, she lived a life more "masculine" than "feminine," and this reversal may have compelled her to display conventional feminine behaviors. As she grew older and more successful, her guilt about rejecting the woman's role seemed to intensify: in an unpublished short story the central character, a "spinster," refers to herself as a "rebel," a "hybrid," a "monster," and "a graft on the tree of human womanhood."[4] In 1893, the year *Pembroke* appeared, she met Dr. Charles Freeman, who was said to resemble her first lover. Four years later they were engaged, and finally, in 1902, when she was 49, they married. Perhaps as her reputation increased, she especially needed to assert her womanliness by marrying. Moreover, she could still grasp the sexual and psychological comforts of marriage without worrying that children would disrupt her life. Still, after meeting Freeman, she took four years to decide and five more years to marry, so that it was nine years in all before she left the Wales's house and moved to New Jersey with Freeman.

In *Pembroke* Mary Wilkins Freeman's analysis of sex, marriage, and power relations is radical. Unlike many of her contemporaries, she pays generous tribute to the force of the sexual instinct and creates bucolic scenes flooded with sexual feeling, without either degrading or censuring passion. A cherry-picking party, the novel's central image, asserts the importance of sexuality. Freeman describes the party scene and its setting in glowing, sensuous language, with the summer ripeness of the natural world echoing the sexual alertness of the young couples. As they play mating games in the open air, "the girls' cheeks flushed deeper, their smooth locks became roughened. The laughter became louder and louder. . . . [I]t became like a bacchanalian rout in a New England field on a summer afternoon, but they did not know it in their simple hearts" (138). Striking throughout this innocent scene is the power of Freeman's evocation of sexual feeling, the love and protection she lavishes on its claims. Absent from the revel are any judgmental hints that sexuality is a lesser or lower human capacity. Living in the time and place where Calvinistic notions lingered—as we see in Deborah and the minister's wife—Freeman creates a narrator who celebrates these innocently licentious festivities. Nor does this narrator suggest that women have less right to sexuality than men.

Yet despite the value Freeman places on the sexual impulse itself, she presents no example of a happy sexual union. In the world of *Pembroke,* although sexual attraction leads to marriage and sex is presented as a splendid instinct, marriage is flawed. Women especially are diminished by it. Society—not nature—has produced an irreconcilable conflict between sexuality, which Freeman renders in almost lyrical terms, and the state of marriage, in which women must sacrifice greatly. But conversely, avoiding this trap and preserving autonomy diminish the individual: in *Pembroke,* a woman's assumption of power is usually destructive. Freeman's view of women's actual possibilities is bleak indeed, despite her liberating treatment of female sexuality.

Emphasizing loss, anxiety, and aversion, all Freeman's imagined possibilities constitute a gloomy politics of marriage, even though the single life, more clearly here than in her well-known story "A New England Nun," impoverishes as well. Through *Pembroke's* four couples she explores various attitudes toward sexuality, but in no case is there a happy solution to the problem of competing desires for sexual gratification and autonomy. The novel's primary couple, Barney and Charlotte, avoid fulfilling their passion, even though their courtship exists mainly in moments of physical contact and is strongly sexual. When Barney visits Charlotte, they hardly speak; they embrace. Theirs is an erotic connection, with a startling absence of other dimensions. Similarly silent, Sylvia and Richard's relationship focuses on Sylvia's yearning for a sign of affection. They, like Charlotte and Barney, postpone marriage for a decade, again reflecting resistance to sexual desire.

These four characters resemble each other in a fundamental psychic way, making pairs of doubles. Not only do Charlotte and Sylvia, niece and aunt, look alike, but Barney is so much like Richard that, in one of the novel's most powerful moments, Sylvia mistakes him for her lover. But Barney's mistake, when he takes Sylvia for Charlotte, precedes hers: "a woman stood there in a dim shaft of candle-light which streamed from the room beyond. He started, for he thought it might be Charlotte; then he saw that it was

Sylvia Crane" (168). Barney's relation to Richard is also explicitly that of a double: "For a moment he [Barney] could not stir; he had a feeling of horror, as if he saw his own double. There was a subtle resemblance which lay deeper than the features between him and Richard Alger. Sylvia saw it, and he saw his own self reflected as Richard Alger in that straining mental vision of hers which exceeded the spiritual one" (171). Richard and Barney, Sylvia and Charlotte, finally make one couple. But this is not a subplot echoing and playing off the main plot, developing its themes in a minor key; rather, it is the same plot—the same couple, the same characters, in one significant, relevant dimension: the failure to marry, the refusal of sexual connection.

Barney, with whom the novel begins, provides the loose thread that unravels the text's symbolic fabric. Barney is sensitive to clothing, to its potential for communicating mood, status, affection, and occasion. In particular, he is preoccupied with clothing Charlotte's body. That he is concerned with keeping it covered appears in his possessive rage when he notices her bare neck at a party: "Suddenly the fierceness of the instinct of possession seized him; he said to himself that it was his wife's neck; no one else should see it. He felt like tearing off his own coat and covering her with rude force" (131). Clothing plays a crucial role in Barney's unspoken emotional life. Through his responses to it, he communicates both his sexual feeling for Charlotte and his need to mask and deny that feeling. He is essentially torn about sexual experience, desiring yet afraid. His conflict, which culminates in his refusal to marry Charlotte, appears in his submerged fascination with clothing her and in his fantasy life as well.

Cloth, clothing, the garments that warm, conceal, decorate, and reveal the human body—these become the counters for expressing sexual feeling. Freeman uses vests, dresses, and yard goods as symbols, couching sexual feeling in language both traditionally female and socially acceptable. Implicit in this symbolic language is a vision of sexuality that is woman-centered. Presenting sexuality from a woman's point of view, talking about it in a specifically female way, Freeman attributes to Barney a sensibility that leads him to speak the female language. Her statement about sexuality, as revolutionary in its way as Kate Chopin's in The Awakening (1899), returns to women the power of naming and defining their own sexuality, instead of yielding to received definition. To the accustomed way of reading male texts and decoding their formulations of sexual matters, Freeman's language implies and adds another way of thinking.[5]

But Freeman alters conventional fictional practice by transforming the symbolic role of clothing. Throughout Pembroke the "language of clothing" suggests an immense preoccupation with sexuality, in clothing observed and touched, sewn and altered, slipped on and off. Like Freeman's own preoccupation with her appearance, this emphasis proclaims sexuality in socially and fictionally acceptable terms and communicates sexual desire respectably. The texture and weight of fabric—the silk of Barney's vest, the soft wool of

Charlotte's shawl—offer *Pembroke*'s readers, as well as its characters, frequent sensuous pleasures. Colors and styles proclaim occasions, as Sylvia's white cap announces her a virgin bride. Clothing worn, bought, and offered communicates goals, intentions, and relationships: Barney's vest is an emblem of his courtship; his plan to buy Charlotte "one new silk every year and two new bonnets" (4) promises husbandly commitment to provide; the blue-figured shawl Charlotte returns measures the limits of intimacy, as does Barney's gift, 10 years later, of yards of "beautiful silk shimmering with lilac and silver-rose color" (303). For the muted characters in *Pembroke* who seek mates, clothing is a way of revealing feeling and desire.

Even more significant about Barney is his tendency to say no to life. He refuses what he calls his happiness. *Pembroke* never explains his extraordinary traits, his awareness of clothing, or the reasons, whether psychological, ethical, or political, for his continuing, irrational refusal. Occurring early in the novel, his exile becomes a given of the text, accepted, like the feud between the Montagues and the Capulets, so that the story can proceed. Only once or twice is there access to Barney's interior life and images that offer a clue to his status in the book and to the hidden reasons for his long evasion, which antedates his quarrel with Charlotte's father.

The quarrel occurs because the idea of marriage to Charlotte has stimulated anxieties that Barney's fantasy of marriage reveals. Stealing moments from his visit to Charlotte, Barney stops at the house he is building for them. As he imagines the life he and his wife will lead together, he becomes fearful. Surveying the site of his married life, he "half sobbed," his brain is "numb," and he starts at "a long black shadow on the floor" (7). This may be the shadow of marriage, as well as a premonition that the dark side of himself is about to emerge; certainly fears rather than hopes surround the image. After this moment, his mind skips past years of marriage, births of children, the intimacies of family life, to death: "I shall marry Charlotte, we shall live here together all our lives and die here. . . . I shall lie in my coffin in the north room, and it will be all over" (7). This is an odd rushing toward death on the eve of marriage (and the image is the same as Ethan Frome's fearful and regressive vision of life with Mattie, his wife's niece).[6] The narrator says that, despite his fears, Barney "stepped out proudly like a soldier in a battalion" (7). Marriage, like battle, seems to threaten him with loss of life.

By developing the imagery that links marriage to death, the narrator highlights the former as a state of immense danger to the self. The fears that lead to Barney's flight from Charlotte concern the losses of identity and autonomy. Either loss diminishes the self. Marriage threatens his sense of separate selfhood and endangers the boundaries separating him from others; it means death to certain of the self's valued aspects. These brief moments early in the novel are among the few that give insight into Barney; paradoxically, they are the only moments when he exists as a character. Freeman drops the question of his psychology after this, leaving Barney static, an allegorical figure of refusal. He exists in the novel passively, at a distance, as the accepted focus of Charlotte's constant love. Their separation maintains a degree of tension, given the (literary) expectation that the story must close with their reconciliation and marriage.

Barney's fear of his self's dissolution in marriage is like a woman's fear. Although men may fear marriage as keenly as women, man's autonomy is not usually felt to be as fragile as woman's, for clearly, as Jo March in Louisa May Alcott's *Little Women* (1869) and Freeman's own Louisa in "A New England Nun" suggest, it is the woman who loses herself in marriage, legally sacrificing many rights and psychologically submerging herself in another. Here again Freeman relies on the strategy of splitting and doubling to portray the self in conflict. As Sylvia and Richard are doubles of Charlotte and Barney, so these two, Barney and Charlotte, reduce to one self in conflict—a woman, desiring love and marriage, yet fearing it, fleeing from it, postponing it.

Less conspicuously, behind a veil of traditional ideology about women's virtue, Charlotte also shields herself from marriage during the 10 years after the estrangement. Courted by the admirable Thomas Payne, she ignores her mother's pleas, the townspeople's conventional wisdom, and her own recognition that Payne is "handsome and stately, full of generous bravery," while Barney is "crouching beneath some awful deformity" (302). Charlotte's determination to remain true to the man who has rejected her is hardly more rational than Barney's fear cloaked as adherence to principle. The motive for Charlotte's extraordinary choice may be the same avoidance Barney manifests so glaringly.

Charlotte Barnard and Barney Thayer (even their names echo) are aspects of a single self, while Barney and Richard are younger and older versions of the self that refuses, that cannot yield to passion. In Barney's unreasoning self-denial, Freeman encodes the even stronger need for the autonomy that makes possible the creative life. *Pembroke* displays woman's dilemma, contrasting and weighing the deepest drives in the psyche: toward union with another and toward the autonomy of a creative life.

Sexual desire exacerbates the dilemma. Although *Pembroke* portrays marriage as a great good, it also makes clear that, given society's rules, sex is costly and women pay the higher price. Freeman is revolutionary in arguing that original sin is in not sex but society and marriage. Her narrator is free from traditional Christian attitudes toward sex and shows them to be the views of certain of her characters: the narrator and the events of the novel condemn marriage and the way female sexuality is understood in patriarchal society. Rebecca Thayer, Barney's sister, who seems to compensate for his denial with her transgression, represents the traditional sexual victim. Unlike the heroine of Susanna Rowson's *Charlotte Temple* (1791), one of her many literary antecedents, Rebecca survives childbirth and remains within her community; eventually her sexuality is partially redeemed by motherhood.[7] Freeman's anatomy of her case is remarkable for demonstrating how a sexual victim is created. The narrator dissects patriarchal attitudes, chiefly expressed through Deborah, that condemn Rebecca for her pregnancy, simultaneously showing that such attitudes are neither necessary nor universal.

Pembroke's male characters, not its female characters or its narrator, express traditional, negative views of female sexuality. The unfortunate Rebecca becomes the symbol of female sexual evil through another instance of Freeman's doubling—her identification with Mrs. Jim Sloane, the town's fallen woman. Living in poverty at the edge of the village, Mrs. Sloane has been judged guilty of unspecified sexual misdeeds: "Everybody spoke slightingly of Mrs. Jim Sloane. The men laughed meaningly. . . . Poor Mrs. Jim Sloane . . . was a byword and a mocking to all the people" (201). In her flight from home Rebecca first collapses in Mrs. Sloane's yard and then assumes her mantle of shame when she accepts Mrs. Sloane's shawl. An old blue plaid wrap, it has been Mrs. Sloane's "uniform" (210). Rebecca marries William Berry in this shawl and wears it as she leaves the house, although her "very identity seemed to be lost" (210) under it. Mrs. Sloane and later Rebecca become the scapegoats who allow Barney and William to project and repudiate sexuality. Barney, a relative of Mrs. Sloane's, has "always felt a loathing for the woman" (202), while for William the trip to Mrs. Sloane's house reveals "the shame and squalor of the soul itself" and makes him feel "transplanted into a veritable hell" (205). In marked contrast to the liberal views of the narrator, these two young men, as well as the defeated Rebecca, are horrified by human sexuality as symbolized by the woman who is openly sexual. The narrator acknowledges the force of traditional attitudes in a male-defined social world but puts these views in perspective for the reader by limiting and circumscribing them.

The narrator's detachment from traditional sexual attitudes appears again in her description of Rose Berry, William's sister and Charlotte's friend, who indulges her sexuality guiltlessly. Interested in "love" but not one man in particular, Rose attempts to seduce Barney in the heat of the cherry-picking party. In his characteristically negative and fearful way, Barney realizes that Rose's look is a sexual invitation, and he contrasts her with Charlotte, who, "during all his courtship had never looked up in his face like that" (131). Though Rose was born "in the heart of New England and bred after the precepts of orthodoxy," she is nevertheless "a pagan and she worshipped 'love' himself" (131–32). Her overt pursuit of sex produces no destructive results except for Barney's predictable rejection and Charlotte's momentary resentment. Although the narrator expresses mild contempt for Rose's lack of deeper qualities of heart and mind, her single-minded pursuit of sex has, quite unconventionally, no dire consequences, even though she finally marries impulsively. Her experience enables us to see how Rebecca is destroyed by traditional sexual values, and in the context of *Pembroke*'s exploration of sexuality, Rose's uninteresting fate—her marriage to Tommy Ray—makes an argument for sublimation, or at least the postponement of gratification.

Emphatic in reclaiming and revaluing sexuality, *Pembroke* simultaneously and powerfully denounces marriage. In this novel marriages occur when women become vulnerable, not when they remain strong. Traditionally representing a heroine's maturity and victory, marriage here indicates and symbolizes the defeat of women. Barney and Richard, who unreasonably resist marrying, finally capitulate when circumstances diminish the women. Richard discovers he can marry Sylvia as she is being moved to the poorhouse. Penniless and half-starved, Sylvia is humiliated and powerless beyond all normal circumstance. Seeing her helplessness, Richard marries her to save her. Barney and Charlotte's reconciliation hinges on an analogous, though less extreme, situation. After he falls ill and Charlotte has nursed him for six weeks, the town begins to talk, and the minister visits to remonstrate. Understanding that Charlotte's reputation is in danger, Barney proposes at last in order to rescue her from disgrace. Her vulnerability seems to reduce his own. In *Pembroke* men choose to marry when their women have suffered a significant loss of power or status.

In Freeman's politics of marriage, weakness in females is a necessary precondition for marriage, whereas money and the ethic of female chastity are the reasons that people marry. As Richard's response to Sylvia's plight demonstrates his economic power, so Barney has social power to redeem Charlotte's honor. Economic probity and social purity: two virtues at the roots of Protestant New England's values. Freeman was one of the few writers advancing such an unsentimental perspective in her day. Unblinking looks at the roots of marriage as an institution appear in the writing of contemporary feminist theorists, but until the current interest in women's texts encouraged rereading of Freeman (and Elizabeth Stuart Phelps, Rose Terry Cooke, Sarah Orne Jewett, and Jane G. Austin, among others), *Pembroke*'s enlightened views were lost.[8]

Freeman's painful exploration of women's possibilities continues with the story of Deborah Thayer, Barney's mother. Deborah's unfortunate relationships with her children occur in the middle of the novel; she rises like a specter in the void between the couples' separations and their reunions. Deborah, whose will has not been broken, rules her family as a biblical matriarch and judge. When her family crumbles, public opinion holds her, the mother, responsible for Barney's refusal to marry, for Rebecca's pregnancy, and for the death of Ephraim, her youngest child. And indeed Deborah responds to the misdeeds of her children by turning them out, when compassion might have prevented greater disaster. This is a revealing study of a powerful woman and her inevitable punishment. Although Charlotte's father, Cephas, abuses his power and injures his family, his tyranny is treated indulgently, even humorously; similarly, the miserliness of Silas Berry, Rose's father, and the humiliation he causes his family receive no serious comment from characters or narrator. Yet Deborah is blamed for the fate of her family. Implicitly, female strength of will inevitably goes astray, becoming the destructive domination of others. Deborah's power transforms her into a freak of nature whose distorted character breeds deranged, illicit behavior in her children and eventually produces illness and death. Her punishment, like Lilith's, is the loss of her children. Although she finally learns that she did not directly cause Ephraim's death, she is never reunited with her two living children. The poisoned fruits of her power are loneliness and guilt, ostracism and an early death. Her zealous attempts to do her duty reap penalties of nightmarish ferocity. The transgressions of Cephas and Silas have only minor repercussions; Deborah is another portrait in that literary pantheon of woman-turned-monster because she has failed to relinquish autonomy.

Deborah's fate shows that when a woman becomes powerful, even in carrying out her socially and biblically prescribed role, she brings ruin on herself and her family, for, ironically, Deborah has given her wholehearted effort to living in accord with orthodox Old Testament beliefs. According to the doctrines she accepts, she must act as "the vicar of God upon earth for the child" (240), and this belief, of course, causes her to direct Barney to marry even after the quarrel, disown the pregnant Rebecca, and chastise Ephraim for failing to study the Bible. With complete devotion she enacts the role prescribed for women in patriarchal law: the teachings themselves and her entrapment in orthodoxy are responsible for the ruin of the family. Since the gospel Deborah lives by is male, biblical, and patriarchal, Freeman's text implies that great destructiveness develops in a woman who carries out patriarchal injunctions, as, of course, generations of women have. Freeman's underlying critique thus also implies that women must devise their own styles, modes, and institutions for the exercise of a constructive power of their own.

Pembroke's narrator recognizes prevailing, repressive attitudes without advocating them and paganism without condemning it. She associates repressive attitudes with male characters, while Deborah's fate underscores the destructiveness of the orthodoxy of Freeman's time. In this sense *Pembroke* can be seen, as it traditionally has been, as a critique of the Calvinism that lingered in New England. But by identifying these attitudes as patriarchal rather than as universal or human, Freeman significantly undercuts their force. Her narrator presents them as one particular, though sadly limited, perspective on reality. Through the narrative strategy of clearly identifying the traditional moral perspective as one possible view and locating it in particular characters, Freeman diminishes its power to influence her readers. In effect she denaturalizes the dominant ideology, revealing its sources and its implications while emphasizing its status as ideology. Simultaneously, the narrative voice of the novel proclaims a more egalitarian view by presenting female sexuality in positive, female terms and by analyzing attitudes that make it the source and symbol of human evil. Further repudiating conventional systems of belief, Freeman refuses to condemn Rose Berry's amorality and rejects marriage, an institution she portrays as handmaiden to patriarchal ethics. With striking clarity she asserts that marriage diminishes women by demanding the sacrifice of their strength and independence. As New England local-color writing faded before the modernist transformation, Freeman articulated women's values, the patriarchal beliefs that defeat women, and the abyss lying between. In its critique and in the attitude it espouses, *Pembroke* is an extraordinary, even revolutionary, work.

Freeman's life, her strong commitment to her own creativity that diminished in midlife and finally gave way before the pull of traditional femininity, reflects an intense struggle between the two modes of being she portrays. Symbolically exploring the poles of her conflict, her novel displays an inadequate match between existing social forms and women's more protean desires: marriage stifles, and sex and power destroy. Morever, the achieving woman, of whom Deborah is the miserable image, is most monstrous, most unloved, and most wholly defeated. In *Pembroke* no more than in Freeman's own life is fruitful reconciliation possible. Implicitly her text pleads for new forms and structures in which to clothe human desires.

Notes

1. Mary E. Wilkins Freeman, *Pembroke* (Chicago: Academy Press, 1978). I have chosen this edition since it is currently the most readily available. All subsequent references are to this edition and are included within the text. Because Freeman chose to use her married name despite the fact that much of her writing, including this novel, was done before her marriage, I have referred to her as Freeman, rather than Wilkins, throughout.

2. Victoria Aarons, in "A Community of Women: Surviving Marriage in the Wilderness" (*Rendezvous* 21 [Spring 1986]: 3–11), analyzes and compares these stories. For valuable discussions of reading and paradigms, see Annette Kolodny, "Dancing through the Minefield: Some Observations on the Theory, Practice, and Politics of a Feminist Literary Criticism," *Feminist Studies* 6 (Spring 1980): 1–25; Annette Kolodny, "A Map for Rereading: Or, Gender and the interpretation of Literary Texts," *New Literary History* 11 (Spring 1980): 451–65; and Nina Baym, "Melodramas of Beset Manhood: How Theories of American Literature Exclude Women Authors," *American Quarterly* 33 (Summer 1981): 123–39.

3. To date the only biography of Freeman is Edward Foster, *Mary E. Wilkins Freeman* (New York: Hendricks House, 1956). My account of her life is drawn from this work.

4. Unpublished story described in Foster, 143.

5. Quoted in Foster, 142. For specific discussions of women's languages of sexuality, see Ellen Moers, *Literary Women: The Great Writers* (New York: Doubleday, 1977), 382–91; Alicia Ostriker, "Body Language: Images of the Body in Women's Poetry," in *The State of Language,* ed. Leonard Michaels and Christopher Ricks (Berkeley: University of California Press, 1980), 246–63; and Terence Diggory, "Armored Women, Naked Men: Dickinson, Whitman, and Their Succesors," in *Shakespeare's Sisters: Feminist Essays on Women Poets,* ed. Sandra Gilbert and Susan Gubar (Bloomington: Indiana University Press, 1979), 135–50.

6. Edith Wharton, *Ethan Frome* (New York: Charles Scribner's Sons, 1911), 49–50.

7. Susanṇa Rowson, *Charlotte Temple* (Philadelphia: Peter Stewart, 1801), is a popular version, set chiefly in America, of the classic story of an innocent young girl's seduction, abandonment, and death.

8. For an interesting discussion of women's values in Freeman, as well as her modernity, see Josephine Donovan, *New England Local Color Literature: A Woman's Tradition* (New York: Ungar, 1983), especially 119–38.

The Liberating Will:
Freedom of Choice in the
Fiction of Mary Wilkins Freeman

MELISSA MCFARLAND PENNELL

Reflecting upon his first visit to New England, William Dean Howells recalled its people as those who "surround themselves with a subtle ether of disapprobation, in which at the first sign of unworthiness in you, they helplessly suffer you to gasp and perish; they have good hearts, and they would probably come to your succour out of humanity, if they knew how, but they do not know how."[1] As an outsider, Howells captured in this reminiscence the aura of rigid social decorum and fixed personal expectations that dominated the mentality of late nineteenth-century rural New England. He also suggested the emotional barrenness that accompanied this state of mind, a dryness he felt came not from choice but from habit. Conscious of a New England code of conduct and belief that brought into existence the very isolation and emptiness Howells observed, and that strangled individual expression while it endorsed an extreme individualism, Mary Wilkins Freeman explored in her fiction the tensions in and results of this paradox, especially as it related to the experience of women.

Freeman portrays characters who are trapped by the circumstances of life, but as Susan Allen Toth observes, she "puts much more emphasis on the positive drive toward fulfillment that motivates her strong characters, a fulfillment of what they believe to be their own true selves."[2] Freeman's understanding and her perceptive analysis of this type of character emerge from her own experience of life in New England during a period of flux and economic upheaval. Her ability to see "New Englandly" the plight of her characters results from two interrelated aspects of her own background: the presence of a residual Calvinism that shaped moral and social outlooks and the existence of a rigid social code that defined and limited her own and her family's social place and mobility. As a child she learned that all humankind was united by a bond of sinfulness and dependency on divine grace, but she also absorbed the notion that one was to be dependent on or indebted to no one.

This essay was written specifically for this volume and is published here for the first time with the permission of the author.

The New England attitude toward self-sufficiency and independence placed a twofold burden on the genteel poor, who not only faced a life of physical want but saw that life as a divine judgment against themselves. Freeman herself understood the pressure and toll of this burden since it affected her own youth and early adulthood. Her parents, Warren Wilkins and Eleanor Lothrop, were both descended from prominent Massachusetts families, and while they lived in Randolph, Massachusetts, their place in the social hierarchy was fixed regardless of financial conditions. Upon moving to Brattleboro, Vermont, however, the Wilkinses experienced both financial and social decline in a town where their names carried little influence and their economic situation even less. After her parents died, Mary Wilkins returned to Randolph to live, but the experience of being pushed to the margins of the social world gave her an insight into struggles that would beset the characters in her fiction.

While she draws upon the idiom familiar to her from her Calvinist upbringing, Freeman never simply reiterates Calvinist views but evaluates and transforms them as she deals with the choices women make in their lives. The issue of the will, as much Freeman scholarship notes, is central to her work, but she does not simply view the question of the will as an issue of individual submission to or conformity with a larger will outside the self (in orthodox terms, the will of God); rather, she focuses upon the freedom to choose, to allow the individual will (or self) to find its genuine expression. Those women in her fiction who exert their wills are often placed at the margins of communities, but this marginality gives them a degree of freedom to reject social codes and expectations. Through this process of revaluation and rejection, these characters come to new definitions of self, definitions with which they can live. Freeman further critiques the "cult of domesticity" in many of her stories and novels; unlike her New England predecessors, she rejects the notion that the domestic sphere by itself offers a solution to women's problem with identity. In fact, for some of Freeman's characters the expectations that form around the domestic sphere and from within the community of women are as destructive to the individual as those which arise in the male-dominated institutions of commerce and religion. Only when a character achieves a genuine "freedom of the will" (freedom of choice) does he or she find wholeness and identity.

In her early collections of short stories, *A Humble Romance* and *A New England Nun,* Freeman often considers the situations of young women who are trapped within the social structures and codes that dictate a path of life for them whether they are inclined to follow it or not. For some, this conventional path, which usually implies courtship and marriage, can be accepted with modifications. In "A Conquest of Humility" Freeman draws upon her Calvinist heritage and its rhetorical forms to examine the process of change within the individual and the means by which the code can be modified. The story is set in a typical New England village, and "like many New England towns, this was almost overshadowed by the ramifications of a few family trees."[3] The townspeople are proud and judgmental, expecting everyone to live up to the values of the code and ridiculing those who do not. There is little compassion in this environment, as people work to maintain divisions and animosities rather than to heal them—thereby heightening the irony, since the story revolves around marriage and the expectations accompanying it. Delia Caldwell's mother learns that her daughter's wedding is canceled with all the guests sitting in the best room; her first thought is not for Delia but of "all them Thayers and Caldwells. They'll just crow" (419). Social consciousness shaped by fear of failure interferes with Mrs. Caldwell's ability to respond to her daughter's need, forcing Delia to be her own source of comfort. This same consciousness affects the larger women's community as well, since its members have a "strong local conservatism" but bear only a superficial sympathy for one another, a false sentiment that repels Delia. When a cousin attempted "to draw [Delia] toward herself" in a show of false sympathy, Delia "released herself and gave her a slight push backward" (421). After the canceled wedding, the women take back their gifts, which were not signs of hope and good wishes for a young couple beginning a new life but material goods whose monetary value is a reflection of prosperity and status. These items cannot be wasted on one who will not be married and will therefore lack the proper domestic establishment in which to display them. Only Flora Strong, Delia's friend, asks her, "[W]hat made you send this back? . . . Oh Delia, I made it for you!" (425). This one handmade "tidy" is the only emblem of a genuine relationship within the circle of women, the only genuine expression of feeling.

Unwilling to retire from the world because of her rejection at the hand of Lawrence Thayer, Delia feels the "fine and exquisite stabs which [she] had to take from her own relations and those of her former bridegroom" (428). She is, however, as tough and resolute as her New England ancestors, and she stands "like a young pine-tree, as if she had all the necessary elements of support in her own self" (417). Listening to the explanation of Lawrence's failure to appear, Delia exclaims, "I've stayed in this hot little room long enough" (420), and throws open the door, indicating her refusal to be trapped and frustrated by the social expectations and gossip of the village. She reacts rationally to Lawrence's behavior and meets her fate directly, for "all the strength in Delia Caldwell's nature was now concentrated. It could accomplish great things but it might grind little ones to pieces" (423) as Delia hardens her heart to shield her vulnerability.

At first Delia does not lower herself to the level of village gossip by criticizing Lawrence, but gradually her feelings of resentment and wounded pride get the better of her. Hearing that he has been rejected by his new lover, she envisions him "in the midst of all that covert ridicule and obloquy, that galling sympathy, that agony of jealousy and betrayed trust. They distorted his face like flames; she saw him writhe through their liquid wavering" (429). In this vision Delia tries her former suitor in the furnace of public opinion, yet the trial by fire does not produce a redeemed or purified image of him since for Delia public opinion does not really matter. She still feels toward him a "fiercer coldness" because she does not see the inner nature that unites them.

While Delia continues to ignore Lawrence, his mother, Mrs. Thayer, asks her to permit him to apologize publicly, to make his public "confession of sin." Delia refuses, but on the anniversary of her wedding day, her family and Lawrence's gather at the Caldwell house with a hopeful Lawrence among them. In his apology and proposal, he makes his confession, which is not, as Alice Brand has suggested, "his public and official castration"[4] but is instead his profession of humanness and his assumption of an independent manhood that elevates him above the other residents of the town. While he speaks, Delia "heard what he said and heard her own thoughts with a strange double consciousness. . . . This revelation of Lawrence's inner self, which smote others with a sense of strangeness, thrilled her with the recognition of love" (435). She sees the true virtue of his nature: that he can be independent and wishes her to be as well. Their love and their acceptance of individual natures set them apart from the community, but their willingness to move toward the margins of this community rather than be engulfed by the rules of the social code liberates them to a fuller self-realization.

While "The Conquest of Humility" resolves with a conventional, if modified, union at its close, Freeman moves away from this expected resolution in other stories and offers more radical possibilities. In "Louisa" Freeman presents another young woman whose life will not follow an expected social path. Louisa faces a twofold crisis in this story: as the sole economic support of her family she must find some means to sustain them, but those means must allow her to maintain her own self-definition and perception of self-worth. Revealing the grim picture of rural poverty that forms Louisa's burden, Freeman writes, "The Brittons had been and were in sore straits. All they had in the world was this little house with the acre of land. Louisa's meager school money bought their food and clothing since her father had died. Now it was almost starvation for them."[5] Living on porridge and garden greens, the family teeters on the brink of final collapse, as physical energies are drained by the lack of sustenance. More severe than the physical debilitation, however, is the emotional deterioration of family life. Because of the tension generated by the code and by the competition for suitors, the mother-daughter bond between Mrs. Britton and Louisa all but dissolves when Louisa fails to meet her mother's expectations. When she loses her position in the local school, Louisa turns to other avenues to gain income, but Mrs. Britton challenges her daughter, exclaiming, "I don't see what kind of ideas you've got in your head" (384), as Louisa attempts to farm their small acre. Mrs. Britton's concern is not that Louisa is incapable but that she is "plantin' potaters out there jest like a man, for all the neighbors to see" (385). Horrified by her daughter's blatant disregard for the well-defined sex roles of rural society, Mrs. Britton complains and nags, wearing down Lou-isa's stamina. She encourages the visits of Jonathan Nye, a man who em-bodies all the values and restrictions of the code. In her assumption that Louisa's personal needs can be sacrificed for economic security, Mrs. Britton courts Jonathan for her daughter and allows her own dreams for the future to obscure her daughter's needs and nature.

Within this realm of economic and emotional poverty, Louisa Britton endeavors to sustain the life of both body and spirit. Her appearance, with hands "all brown and grimy with garden-mould," and her "coarse shoes" (384) are emblematic of her life of manual labor, but her inner life is one of dreams and hopes that enable her to endure her hardship. She tries to please her mother with little things, such as her gift of herring, but Mrs. Britton refuses any communion with her daughter as long as Louisa rejects Jonathan Nye. More than willing to sacrifice her social status in acts of honest labor, she cannot compromise her inner being by accepting a man she does not love.

No matter what effort Louisa makes, the environment, including her senile grandfather who uproots her crops, conspires against her. To Mrs. Britton the idea of debt is even more horrible than the fact of poverty, so instead of going to the bank Louisa makes an appeal to her estranged uncle, Solomon Mears. She believes he will help the family because of her "unsophis-ticated sense of justice" (403), whereas Solomon agrees to help because he is "an orthodox believer; he recognized the claims of the poor, but he gave alms as a soldier might yield up his sword" (404). He makes Louisa feel the sting of assistance; pointing to a huge pile of supplies, he tells her to leave what she cannot carry. Louisa "took up the bag of meal and the basket of eggs and carried them out to the gate; then she returned, got the flour and ham, and went with them to a point beyond. . . . In that way she traversed the seven miles home" (404). She taxes her physical strength and endurance to its limits, but her sacrifice enables her to preserve her family and her sense of self. Her trip home is "like a pilgrimage and the Mecca at the end of the burning, desert-like road was her own maiden independence" (404–5). At home, she is greeted with a "harsh tenderness" and the news that she may again have the town school. Mrs. Britton has learned that Jonathan Nye was willing to have Louisa but did not want her family "hitched to him" (406). Indirectly admitting her error, Mrs. Britton prepares a substantial meal that marks a new communion between mother and daughter. Louisa's rejection of marriage to Nye and her willingness to endure familial reproach for her actions suggest the lengths to which a woman must go to preserve her own freedom of will. As Susan Allen Toth observes, "Freeman has a surprisingly modern and complex sense of the constant mutual adjustment necessary between individual and community, between private fulfillment and social duties,"[6] but does not endorse in her female characters a negation of the self in the attempt to meet social or familial obligations.

While Louisa Britton's disregard for sex roles defined by the code suggests the increased strain of self-definition, the strict adherence to female rituals and behaviors can bring another form of independence. In "A New England Nun" Freeman creates the portrait of Louisa Ellis and presents one of the most challenging stories of her early collections, for Louisa's life defies conventional expectations and has posed problems for many readers in the resolution it offers. Living alone for years while awaiting the return of her fiancé, Louisa Ellis has gradually become the center of her own world, retreating from the larger world around her but finding increased fulfillment within herself.[7] Louisa's daily tea is "set forth with as much grace as if she had been a veritable guest unto her own self," and her house is filled with mementos that have meaning for her.[8] Her world is governed by the rituals of domesticity, and she takes pleasure in those rituals, even the sewing of a seam for the "simple mild pleasure" of it. Louisa has not been drawn into the American mentality shaped by the values of production and consumption; she is content to find personal pleasures in the "margin" of life she has chosen. Within her house Louisa keeps a caged bird, which many readers have interpreted as a metaphor for Louisa's own existence. Yet this interpretation overlooks a significant element that forms an undercurrent in much of Freeman's fiction focusing on women. The important distinction between the two is that the bird is caged whether it will or no, whereas Louisa makes the choices that shape her life; she exercises her will in finding the life that is right for her, even if it means following an unconventional path.

When Joe Daggett, the absent fiancé, returns, Louisa must confront the possibility of change in her life and the surrender of the control she has so long enjoyed. As Joe enters the house, both Louisa and the bird "flutter" out of nervousness, a reaction on the part of the bird to the intrusion, a reaction on the part of Louisa to the prospect of change and of male dominance.[9] During her period of forbearance, Louisa has chosen a path "so narrow that there was no room for anyone at her side" (7). When Joe appears, so does the tension in the story, a tension David Hirsch describes as an "understated conflict between order and disorder."[10] Joe feels uncomfortable, "afraid to stir lest he should put a clumsy foot or hand through the fairy web" (6) of delicacy that makes up Louisa's world. She confirms his discomfort with her own; she restores the books he handles and, when he leaves, sweeps up his tracks, effectively erasing his presence in her life. As Hirsch suggests, Joe represents a "constant threat of potential chaos," a disruption of the ritual patterns Louisa observes. The "peculiar features of her happy solitude which she would probably be obliged to relinquish altogether" (9) include her home and the signs of individuality and independence that have allowed her to endure. Her attachment to them reflects her attachment to self-direction, to an independence she is sure cannot exist in a marriage to Joe Daggett. Her fears extend to the anticipation of being obliged to entertain company and to exchange visits, part of that blend of business and social life which Edna Pontellier so profoundly rejects in Kate Chopin's *The Awakening* because it denies her personal volition. Louisa does not love Joe, and she does not wish to abandon that which is meaningful to her. Able to find fulfillment apart from the expectations dictated by social convention, she finds in her own will no desire to submit to these conventions now.

As she gives Joe his freedom and regains her own, Louisa gains far more than the "negative freedom" that Edward Foster identifies.[11] While the life she has chosen is unconventional and challenges the standard acceptable resolution, Freeman asserts the validity of the choice, as Louisa "gazed ahead through the long reach of future days strung together like pearls in a rosary, every one like the others, and all smooth and flawless and innocent, and her heart went up in thankfulness" (17). While spinsterhood at times appears a problematic state in Freeman's fiction, she does not present it as "a social anomaly to be avoided at all costs" nor is it "a prison . . . a frustrated existence."[12] Louisa Ellis is content to live at the margin of the social sphere if that marginal existence allows her to be the woman she wishes to be. In fact, it is the very expectation that all women should desire marriage as a means of attaining fulfillment that Freeman wishes to challenge in a number of her early stories and in later novels, including *Pembroke* and *The Shoulders of Atlas*.

In her short fiction Freeman develops issues of independence and the emergence of the will as a part of self-definition, and in her novels she continues to develop these issues in greater depth and detail. *Pembroke* addresses the problem of the will and the hardness of the New England way. In her own comments on this novel, Freeman explains that "*Pembroke* was originally intended as a study of the human will in several New England characters, in different phases of disease and abnormal development, and to prove, especially in the most marked case, the truth that its cure depended entirely upon the capacity of the individual for a love which could rise above all considerations of the self."[13] While these comments at first suggest that the free expression of will is a problem to be overcome, the key words in this statement are *disease* and *abnormal;* Freeman addresses the problem that arises when healthy self-expression has been thwarted by the social code and by economic conditions so that individuals are forced to assume and defend positions harmful to themselves and the people around them. This study of the human will begins when Barney Thayer breaks his engagement with Charlotte Barnard after a political argument with her irascible father, Cephas. Though the focus is on Barney and his inability to retreat from the unhappy position into which his will has forced him, the novel explores the similar positions of many characters.

Pembroke is much like the town Freeman presents in "Conquest of Humility," in which a few families make up the center of town life. The separation of roles for women and men follows the strict outlines of the code which dictates that women's work is the domestic sphere, while men's is the public sphere. For the men, however, the economic decline of the region has limited the possibilities for their activity and contributed to the disease of will they experience, for they believe the public and commercial sphere is the one in which they must achieve. Both Cephas Barnard, with the experimental diets and philosophies he inflicts upon his family, and Silas Berry, with his Yankee thrift that has degenerated to a life of greed that embarrasses his family, are examples of the diseased will exerted to excess. Caleb Thayer, one of the more sensitive village men, whose will is so repressed that he can neither act nor react, watches his family disintegrate because he can take no action to modify his wife's behavior.

The men in Freeman's novel are not the only characters who suffer from problems of twisted wills. Deborah Thayer, the Calvinistic matriarch of Pembroke, destroys her own family through her inability to accept her own feelings and those of others. She conforms constantly to the letter of the law and to the demands of the code, but her rigidity allows neither her own development nor that of her children. She believes she can guard her family against the danger of damnation by making them conform to her expectations, and, lacking compassion and understanding, she feels she can control her children's destinies by subduing their individual wills. Her domestic world is equally rigid; it is "a village story how Deborah Thayer cleaned all the windows in the house one afternoon when her first child had died in the morning" (99). These actions bring her little peace, but Deborah feels she is called to them by a will greater than her own. Unable to reach out to her daughter in a sympathetic and loving way, she drives Rebecca to seek love outside her home. When Deborah learns of Rebecca's pregnancy, she forces her out of the house and sweeps her tracks from the doorstep. In a final act of effacement, she places Rebecca's unfinished wedding dress in a chest in the garret, burying the last remnant of her daughter as a sign she has disowned her. Deborah not only has suffered at the hands of her deformed will but has inflicted suffering and deformity upon her children. Rebecca never develops the self-esteem that would allow her to make independent decisions, so she is pushed into a relationship that only brings her greater pain.

In contrast to Deborah Thayer, Freeman creates the character of Sarah Barnard, a woman who has a healthy sense of self-esteem and who wants her children to have the same. She does not feel a need to dominate those around her and can tolerate their differences. Even though she has suffered privately and publicly from some of Cephas Barnard's strange ideas, Sarah calmly says, "It's just his way" (63) when others appear ready to attack him. And when she observes the tasteless dinners her husband eats on his vegetarian diet, she makes an apple pie with a larded crust and feels "not the slightest exaltation, only honest pleasure when she saw, without seeming to, Cephas cut off a goodly wedge" (140). As Cephas becomes reanimated in the course of the novel, Sarah finds her own fulfillment.

The love and tolerance Sarah has for her husband extend to her relationship with her daughter, Charlotte, as well, and the two share the only healthy mother-daughter relationship in the novel. Sarah not only functions as an emotional shelter for her daughter, she has also passed down to her the important skills of the domestic sphere as means of self-expression. Charlotte is the only woman of the younger generation in the novel who is fully trained in the feminine arts yet not imprisoned by them. The mother-daughter relationship waivers only when Sarah must mediate between Cephas and Charlotte over the issue of Barney's care during his attack of rheumatism. Though Sarah strives for harmony within her family circle, she allows Charlotte to make her own choice of action, to express her own will, rather than forcing her to conform to her father's wishes.

Within this village of conflicting and struggling wills, Freeman once again raises the issue of marriage as a means of addressing both individual choice and freedom from the code. While each case resolves in a conventional union, these unions, like that in "A Conquest of Humility," grow out of a modification of community expectations and restrictions in order to redefine the relationships.

Sylvia Crane, a marginal figure in the community, living alone in the old family home, has been "courted" by Richard Alger for 18 years. Though she defends Richard before her sisters, she herself is not immune to the pressure of the code. To keep up appearances, she has made changes according to fashion in her home, hiding the truth that she can barely afford to live there. She has struggled to maintain her economic independence because she connects it with her personal independence; her need for independence, however, is constantly balanced against her need for approval. Sylvia feels she must live up to the code, up to the "village fashion," which is "as absolute in its way as court etiquette" (210).

Unable to maintain her household any longer, Sylvia is forced to retreat to the poorhouse, to accept "the peace of defeat" that makes possible her surrender to economic circumstances. The shock Richard Alger feels as he witnesses her journey forces him into action, and he brings Sylvia back to her house. Admitting his love and his need, he appears a new man, and while she listens, Sylvia experiences a regeneration as well, for her face "flushed and lit up like an old flower revived in a new spring" (222). Like Delia and Lawrence in "A Conquest of Humility," Sylvia and Richard are able to express themselves in a union made on their own terms, and not on those of the village.

The conflict between Charlotte Barnard and Barney Thayer, too, resolves in their union, and this union also bears the signs of modification. In the opening of the novel they are a conventional young couple planning marriage and a home together until their relationship is threatened by a quarrel between Barney and Cephas Barnard. Charlotte has an advantage in this situation, however, because she has grown up in the care of a mother who has set a pattern for self-esteem and healthy development. Though Charlotte makes her own demands on Barney in order to be reunited with him, she can serve as a mediator between Barney and those members of the community who attack him, much as her mother has done for Cephas. She confronts Deborah Thayer in a scene that reveals Charlotte's strength of character and independence of mind as she defends Barney against unfair accusations. And when Barney falls ill, Charlotte defies her father, who voices the code, and goes to care for Barney. Because she makes her own choice in this matter, she can honestly say, "I am not afraid, if I know I am doing what is right" (251). Her loyalty allows Barney to find his true nature and express his true will.

While Charlotte has attained a wider vision that allows her to act independently, Barney must struggle with his own immature and limited sensibility. After his argument with Cephas, Barney cannot see that "his misery might not be final" (49). Charlotte attempts to describe his problem in terms of will: "he can't get outside himself enough to break it"; he must suffer rejection before he can achieve the true expression of his feelings. When Barney realizes that Charlotte risks her own reputation and her future to care for him, he overcomes his pride and admits his love for her. He appears at the Barnard house "with that noble bearing which comes from humility itself when it has fairly triumphed" (254). Like Lawrence Thayer and Richard Alger, Barney Thayer finds true freedom of will when he overcomes his fear of censure and makes a public choice that reflects his inner feelings. The journey to self-realization and fulfillment is not easy, but the characters who are able to throw off the weight of the code and of public opinion are the only ones who enjoy freedom and happiness.

This desire for freedom and happiness remains at the center of human experience for many Freeman characters, and in the conclusion to *The Shoulders of Atlas* Freeman expresses both the pain and the hope they feel: "They witnessed happiness with perfect sympathy. It cast upon them rosy reflections. And yet every one bore, unseen or seen, the burden of his or her world upon straining shoulders. The grand, pathetic tragedy inseparable from life, which Atlas symbolized, moved [among them] . . . and yet love would in the end sanctify it for them all."[14]

In this neglected novel, published more than a decade after *Pembroke,* Freeman demonstrates a maturity in vision and style that creates a more complex work of fiction. In *Pembroke* Freeman uses the idiom of her Calvinist background to label the problems her characters face, and frequently this language draws attention to itself rather than to the characters and their experiences. In *The Shoulders of Atlas* she returns to the issues of freedom of the will and the burden of conscience, addressing them through parent-child and male-female relationships, but she is more subtle in approach, less obvious in language and situation. She also addresses more complex psychological motives and problems and, though she does not offer satisfactory resolutions to them all, reveals her own expanded sensibility.

As in *Pembroke,* a young woman faces the opportunity to marry, but her mother figure questions whether it is the right step, whether it is the means to fulfillment for the young woman she has come to care for as a daughter.

The relationship between Sylvia Whitman, an older New England house-wife, and Rose Fletcher, the young woman who comes to stay with the Whitmans, is central in the novel, and in it both women go through a process of growth and awakening. Sylvia's marriage is governed by the code and by social expectations that restrict gender roles and force a separation of spheres for husband and wife. These severely defined roles contribute to the emotional (and in the Whitman marriage, physical) barrenness of marriages that become states of coexistence rather than interaction because spouses have nothing in common but their living quarters. In the process of offering Rose alternatives to marriage as a means of fulfillment, Sylvia sees her own marriage in a new light and begins to believe that she and Henry have something between them worth sharing.

The opening chapters of the novel present Henry and Sylvia Whitman as characteristic of New England couples. Henry, like many of the men in Pembroke, has come to a point in his working life where there is "nothing else in store for him until he was turned out because of old age. Then the future looked like a lurid sunset of misery" (1). Though he has worked hard all his life, Henry has not found success in the public sphere, but he "came from a race who were impatient of debt, and who regarded with proud disdain all gratuitous benefits from their fellow-men" (2). Reserved in his expression of emotion, he has a "stunted thirst for beauty"; however, his experiences in life and his upbringing have kept him from allowing his inner nature to develop fully. Needing someone to whom he can "pour out his heart," he admits that Sylvia "was no satisfaction at such a time," as she, in her own fear of emotional vulnerability, "took refuge in Scripture quotations" (5).

Like Henry, Sylvia is "worn with her own work" as she has fulfilled domestic duties in her household, and she too has been shaped by her Calvinist New England upbringing, which has taught her to stifle her natural responses to life. Their areas of interest seldom overlap, and except at mealtime, Henry and Sylvia spend little time conversing. Even after they come into money and a large house through an inheritance, they are not comfortable in their moments together and often find that their views of life, which they had assumed to be identical, are in fact quite different. When Henry suggests that they enjoy fires in the fireplace because "it would look kind of pretty," Sylvia responds snappishly, "I was brought up to think a fire was for warmth, not for looks" (39), articulating that old New England fear of the beautiful. Each has in her or his own way absorbed the values of the New England code, and even when life brings an unexpected chance to break out from under the code's burden, neither seems able to do so.

The one thing upon which they do agree is their affection for Horace Allen, the boarder whose presence in their household fills the void left by their lack of children. He is an attractive and marriageable young man, and he serves as a link between the Whitmans' experiences and two of the subplots that emerge in the novel. One of these subplots focuses on the attempt and failure of Eliza Farrel to buy the love of a child because she does not seem to trust the goodness of her own nature, and the other focuses on the situation of Lucy Ayres, who feels driven to find a marriage partner. In each of these subplots Freeman offers elements of social critique that apply beyond the boundaries of village life in New England, and their inclusion in the novel reflects the greater range of female character she is willing to consider. Though at first these subplots seem disconnected from the main plot and neither is completely resolved or explained by the end of the novel, they form an important backdrop to Sylvia Whitman's concerns for and relationship with Rose.

Freeman introduces to the Whitman household the character of Rose Fletcher, the young woman for whom Eliza Farrel has sacrificed her life. In doing so Freeman places Sylvia in the position that Eliza had longed to assume. Through the development of the relationship between Sylvia and Rose, which soon becomes a mother-daughter bond, Freeman examines a mother's possessiveness and desire to influence a daughter's choices. It is the mother figure who encourages the daughter to break with social expectations. Sylvia articulates a critical view of marriage and of the reasons so many women marry, and Freeman makes the most of this paradoxical situation in which a mother wishes to encourage independence on the one hand, but submission to her own will on the other.

The relationship between the two women has a rocky start, as Sylvia, shielding her emotional vulnerability, at first maintains a formal distance but within a short time lets down her emotional barriers and, in helping Rose dress, feels "the same sensations that she might have experienced in dressing her own baby for the first time" (95). This experience brings about a change in Sylvia as "a maternal instinct which dominated her had awakened suddenly in the older woman's heart" (109), an instinct she had suppressed throughout her marriage for fear of the heartbreak that emotional ties to children might bring her. This emotional awakening in Sylvia engenders in her protective feelings toward Rose, feelings that Sylvia admits run to jealousy toward anyone else who might win Rose's attention.

Though Rose appears to be a product of the social code in terms of her habits and dress, she possesses a strong independent streak that periodically becomes evident. Rose's identity exists for her apart from her marriage potential, and she apparently lacks the superficial sexual responsiveness that motivates Lucy Ayres, for Rose "had charmed the young men whom she had seen, and had not thought about them when once they were out of sight. Her pulses did not quicken easily" (160). In Rose's character Freeman presents a portrait of a modern woman who can make positive choices because she is at the mercy of neither her own emotions nor the will of others.

Because she does not yet know her well, Sylvia is afraid Rose will look for love and affirmation from any man who pays her attention, and to prevent this, Sylvia attempts to provide everything she thinks Rose might long for, including jewelry and even a horse and carriage if Rose wishes. She also attempts to dissuade Rose from thoughts of marriage by discussing the subject with her. Sylvia indicates that "it doesn't do for a girl to get too anxious to get married" (201) and then goes on to explain that even though she was fortunate in marrying Henry, "every silly girl thinks she has found just that man, but it's only once in a thousand times she does" (202). She further asserts, "Folks can't tell girls everything, but marriage is an awful risk, an awful risk" (204). Sylvia states to Henry and to Rose that any young woman who has the financial means to support herself and a comfortable home has no need to marry, to accept the path of life laid down by the code. Henry tries to soften Sylvia's statement by asking whether their own marriage has not been happy, but Sylvia says that is different. When she learns of the engagement between Rose and Horace, Sylvia finally acquiesces, since she does think highly of Horace; still, her critique of marriage, like the choices made by characters in other Freeman works, undercuts the prevailing critical opinion of Freeman as a writer who saw marriage as the only way for women to find meaning and identity in their lives.

The novel closes on the occasion of Rose and Horace's wedding, an occasion that should be one of happiness and celebration, especially since Rose's choice of Horace has been her own and since she goes into marriage as an expression of her own free will. At the wedding, however, Sylvia must make a public confession, one that offers Freeman a chance to reintroduce the question of will and conscience before the marriage ceremony can be completed. Sylvia admits to having found a note from Abrahama White leaving all her estate to her niece, Rose Fletcher; Sylvia believes that she and Henry have been usurpers, and she must make this public confession to free her conscience. This burden of the "illegitimate" inheritance provides a tangible source of guilt for Sylvia; however, Freeman uses it in a symbolic way to suggest that the real guilt rests with Sylvia's attempts to exert her own will over others, no matter how well intended, rather than allowing them to make their own choices. This act of unburdening recalls the scenes in "A Conquest of Humility" and *Pembroke* in which confessions are necessary for relationships to be healed, and with this act of letting go, Sylvia is able to return to a sense of right relationship with the people who mean the most to her—Henry, Rose, and Horace. The marriage ceremony finishes, but the moment brings change not only for Rose and Horace but for Sylvia and Henry as well, for "[i]t seemed to Henry that never, not even in his first wedded rapture, had he loved his wife as he loved her that night. He glanced at her, and she looked wonderful to him; in fact, there was in Sylvia's face that night an element of wonder" (293). In the resolution of this main plot Freeman attempts to bring into balance the vital need for freedom of will and the importance of human relationships. Although she does not provide an ideal formula for finding that balance, Freeman suggests its possibility, but only when characters are free to make choices for themselves and are not directed by the will of others or by that of society as a whole. At the close of *The Shoulders of Atlas,* Sylvia finally enjoys the relationship with Rose that Eliza Farrel had envisioned: a human bond that has grown out of free choice rather than constraint or obligation.

During her writing career, Mary Wilkins Freeman captured the essence of a rural New England sensibility in her fiction. Her aim, however, was not merely to record but to analyze and even redefine that sensibility when necessary to get at the heart of human experience, and more specifically women's experience as she perceived it. She exposed the oppressive nature of social expectations, of values held and upheld only because they were part of a long-accepted code or tradition, and examined the ways women and men became victims of the limitations and gender-based restrictions placed on them. As she studied the individuals who lived in this region, she focused on the importance of self-realization and the expression of individual personality in all its uniqueness. As Perry Westbrook notes in his discussion of Freeman's work, "To achieve release from convention and shallow conformity is the most difficult task the soul can undertake, requiring as much effort and struggle as a Puritan conversion."[15] Drawing on the familiar idiom from her own background, Freeman presents her characters as they experience opportunities for a new conversion, one that has the power to transfrom and liberate them in profound ways. Her vision offers hope for those characters, especially women, who display the inner strength to reject the code, even if that rejection can be accomplished only from the margins of the social order.

Notes

1. William Dean Howells, "My First Visit to New England," in *Literary Friends and Acquaintance* (New York: Harper and Brothers, 1900), 51.

2. Susan Allen Toth, "Defiant Light: A Positive View of Mary Wilkins Freeman," *New England Quarterly* 46 (March 1973): 90.

3. Mary E. Wilkins, "A Conquest of Humility," in *A Humble Romance, and Other Stories* (New York: Harper and Brothers, 1887), 427. Page numbers are given in the text.

4. Alice G. Brand, "Mary Wilkins Freeman: Misanthropy as Propaganda," *New England Quarterly* 50 (March 1977): 86–87.

5. Mary E. Wilkins, "Louisa," in *A New England Nun, and Other Stories* (New York: Harper and Brothers, 1891), 394. Page numbers are given in the text.

6. Toth, "Defiant Light," 83.

7. See the discussion of this pattern of fulfillment in Marjorie Pryse, "An Uncloistered 'New England Nun,' " *Studies in Short Fiction* 20 (Fall 1983): 289–90.

8. Mary E. Wilkins, "A New England Nun," in *A New England Nun, and Other Stories,* 2. Page numbers are given in the text.

9. See Pryse, "Uncloistered 'New England Nun,' " 290–91.

10. David H. Hirsch, "Subdued Meaning in 'A New England Nun,' " *Studies in Short Fiction* 2 (1964–65):127.

11. Edward Foster, *Mary E. Wilkins Freeman* (New York: Hendricks House, 1959), 105.

12. See Brand, "Misanthropy," 85, and Larzer Ziff, *The American 1890's: Life and Times of a Lost Generation* (New York: Viking Press, 1966), 293.

13. Mary E. Wilkins Freeman, *Pembroke,* ed. Perry Westbrook (New Haven, Conn.: College and University Press, 1971), 33. Page numbers are given in the text.

14. Mary E. Wilkins Freeman, *The Shoulders of Atlas* (New York: Harper and Brothers, 1908), 293. Page numbers are given in the text.

15. Perry Westbrook, *Mary Wilkins Freeman* (New York: Twayne, 1967), 80.

The Sharp-edged Humor
of Mary Wilkins Freeman:
The Jamesons—and Other Stories

SHIRLEY MARCHALONIS

To propose a humorous reading of Mary Wilkins Freeman's work certainly contradicts most published criticism. Yet her earliest important critic, William Dean Howells, and most contemporary reviewers, even as they gave her the "local color realist" label that has so limited reading of her work, saw a mixture of "humor and tenderness" or "humor and pathos," particularly in her stories.[1]

It was scholars like Fred Lewis Pattee and Perry D. Westbrook who established Freeman as the "grim recorder of the last act of the Puritan drama in America," or, to quote a Pattee title, the "Terminal Moraine of New England Puritanism"—with *Puritanism* defined as a dark and bitter creed having no redeeming virtues.[2] Sadly, much of the criticism that followed built on these established perceptions. According to Perry D. Westbrook, "one need read very few pages of Mary Wilkins to realize that to her . . . life is moral struggle within the soul of two wills opposing each other, one driving the individual on to destruction, the other to salvation."[3]

But there is more to Freeman than the Howells label and the limited vision and direction of Pattee, Westbrook, and others perceived, and to read her work without these preconceptions, as her contemporaries did and now as more recent critics with wider viewpoints are beginning to do, brings unexpected discoveries and pleasures. Newer scholarship is in fact reaching out in a variety of ways and finding that Freeman's work is neither so restricted nor so repetitive as earlier scholars believed—finding that she is concerned with individualism, with integrity, autonomy, and self-definition, and that her "puritanism" is laced with wry humor.

In 1899 Freeman published a short novel called *The Jamesons*.[4] Since very little attention is paid to her novels, it is not surprising that little notice has been taken of this one, although it was a popular work. *The Jamesons* is a village novel, as her stories are village stories, and it is part of a tradition that includes not only the works of Sarah Orne Jewett and other American local-

This essay was written specifically for this volume and is published here for the first time with the permission of the author.

color writers but Elizabeth Gaskell's *Cranford* and Mary Russell Mitford's *Our Village*—two English works widely read in the United States; like these, *The Jamesons* fits into the group Sandra Zagarell has recently identified as the narrative of community.[5]

In 1891, several years before *The Jamesons,* Mary E. Wilkins had written to thank Joseph Knight for the copy of *Cranford* he had sent her.[6] "Yes, I already knew 'Cranford,' " she wrote, "but not in any such beautiful guise as this, and indeed I did not own it in any guise." Elizabeth Gaskell's *Cranford* was published in 1853 and had already won critical and popular approval. Sarah Orne Jewett's *Country of the Pointed Firs* appeared in 1896 and was followed three years later by Wilkins's *The Jamesons.*[7] All three novels, besides being village stories, are lighthearted, humorous, and written in a tone of affectionate goodwill. They present the mores of a closed village society in which small events are vitally large, and they focus on a group of people, chiefly women, within a nearly manless village. Gaskell makes this point in the opening lines of her text: "In the first place, Cranford is in possession of the Amazons; all the holders of houses, above a certain rent, are women. If a married couple come to settle in the town, somehow the gentleman disappears; he is either fairly frightened to death of being the only man in the Cranford evening parties, or he is accounted for by being with his regiment, his ship, or closely engaged in business all the week in the great neighboring town of Drumble. . . . In short, whatever does become of the gentlemen, they are not at Cranford" (1).

Gaskell and Jewett structured their stories in the same way. *Cranford's* narrator is a perceptive young woman with connections in the village, who visits at varying periods and chronicles the oddities and activities of her friends there. That plan makes the story somewhat episodic, but Gaskell uses the structure advantageously; there are ongoing subplots, and what happened between the narrator's visits can be summarized, usually by Miss Matty as she recounts news of the village and her own reactions, a process that allows Gaskell to advance the action and show Miss Matty's character at the same time. Other subplots can begin and end within the space of one visit. This description of narrator and structure also fits *Country of the Pointed Firs.* In that novel the relationship between the narrator and the village is similar; the narrator is the objective but affectionate chronicler of the village life and people, while Mrs. Todd reveals herself in her actions and in her tales of others.

Cranford may have directly influenced Jewett and Freeman, or both writers may simply have been working within a familiar genre; perhaps the directness of the influence is not important. Critics certainly compared both Jewett and Freeman with Gaskell, and both American writers had done something of the kind before: sketches of people and life held together by their village location, as in Jewett's *Deephaven* (1877) and Freeman's *People of Our Neighborhood* (1898). A search for sources and influences would push back even farther, to Mary Russell Mitford's *Our Village* (1824), enormously popular in both England and America.[8] There are differences; Mitford's book is a kind of anatomy of a farming village, with much emphasis on nature and the changing seasons, and the village she portrays is not manless. But her introductory paragraph could apply to any of these works: "[A] little village far in the country . . . a little world of our own, close-packed and insulated like ants in an ant-hill, or bees in a hive, or sheep in a fold, or nuns in a convent, or sailors in a ship; where we know everyone, are known to everyone, interested in everyone, and authorized to hope that everyone feels an interest in us" (3). Mitford, in her turn, cites Jane Austen's novels and Gilbert White's *History of Selbourne* as her models of good reading.[9]

The similiarities among *Our Village, Cranford, Country of the Pointed Firs,* and *The Jamesons* make it worthwhile to examine at least the last three, however briefly, as examples of the same kind of work. Such an examination discovers in Mary Wilkins Freeman's writing a side of her talent that is frequently, if not consistently, overlooked.

What is common to this kind of story is, first, the village setting, realistically portrayed. These small worlds are governed by codes—mores, customs, usage: patterns of behavior, not consciously learned but known to all, that regulate attitudes and actions. If the worlds are small, they are nevertheless full of variety and are vital to the people who live in them, and the writers present the details of daily life in the microcosm pleasantly but unromantically.

The second likeness is the tone: affection, warmth, humor—qualities attributed to Gaskell and Jewett but not often associated with Freeman. Much of the humor lies in the importance of seemingly small events within the depicted world. The social hierarchy the ladies of Cranford uphold, for example, presents them with earthshaking questions: when widowed Lady Glenmire marries the doctor, several social levels beneath her, what is her place in society? It is a situation that brings disorder into an orderly microcosm.

Like the others, *The Jamesons* tells the story of the interaction of an outsider with a country village. Its tone, too, is affectionate and gently humorous, and it is a tale of small events that loom large within a small world. But if *The Jamesons,* like *Country of the Pointed Firs,* may be an American *Cranford,* Freeman is neither Jewett nor Gaskell, and she gives the theme her own characteristic knife-edge.

One difference is that the first-person narrator is part of the village. Mrs. Sophia Lane is a widow, not rich but financially comfortable, living in her own house, which she shares with her sister-in-law and her niece. The outsider is Mrs. Jameson, who brings her city sophistication to "widen the spheres" of the country people among whom she will spend the summer.

In *Cranford* the top of the social hierarchy is the Honorable Mrs. Jamieson, who occupies that position because her husband was the younger son of a baron, and whose pronouncements on matters social are the last word. She is not like her American namesake, since Gaskell describes her as being "fat and inert," or "apathetic," but she can be roused on matters of precedence, and she remains the village arbiter. When the ladies want to defy her—specifically, to call on the former Lady Glenmire, who has become Mrs. Hoggins—they wonder, "Would they [the Hogginses] be visited? Would Mrs. Jamieson let us?" (208). Unalike as the two ladies are in character (the American is explosively and aggressively energetic), the similarity of names and the position of arbiter, or would-be arbiter, suggest that the *Cranford* lady may have been a model in reverse for Freeman's character.

Mrs. Jameson, her three children, and her mother board for the summer in Linnville, a village whose inhabitants, in the words of the narrator and in contrast to the people of neighboring towns, "plumed ourselves upon our reputation of not taking boarders for love or money" (2). Why Caroline Liscom, with plenty of money, is opening her home to strangers is the subject of speculation as the story begins. The narrator and the reader first meet the incomer when a false alarm summons firemen and watchers to the Liscom house. Though the false alarm was accidentally caused by her son, Mrs. Jameson does not apologize, and ignores the cold fury with which her land-lady surveys the water-soaked ruin of her once-immaculate kitchen. As Mrs. Lane is leaving the house, she hears a voice call, "My good woman," an address she cannot think is meant for her. When her attention is finally caught she goes to Mrs. Jameson, who commands her to find them another place to board. Mrs. Lane, astonished, says she knows of none:

> "My good woman," said [Mrs. Jameson], "you look very neat and tidy your-self, and I don't doubt are a good plain cook; I am willing to try your house if it is not surrounded by trees and there is no standing water near; I do not object to running water."
>
> In the midst of this speech the elder daughter had said in a frightened way, "Oh, mamma!" but her mother had paid no attention. As for myself, I was angry. The memory of my two years at Wardville Young Ladies Seminary in my youth and my frugally independent life as wife and widow was strong upon me. I had read and improved my mind. I was a prominent member of the Ladies Sewing Society of our village; I wrote papers which were read at the meetings; I felt, in reality, not one whit below Mrs. H. Boardman Jameson, and moreover, large sleeves were the fashion, and my sleeves were every bit as large as hers, though she had just come from the city. That added to my conviction of my own importance. "Madam," said I, "I do not take boarders. I have never taken boarders, and I never shall take boarders." Then I turned and went out of the room, and downstairs, with, it seemed to me, much dignity. (22–23)

So it goes on. At the village picnic, traditionally an event that allows the women to display their finest cooking skills, Mrs. Jameson arrives and, with "a brisk air which rather took our breaths away, it was so indicative of urgent and very pressing business" (38), pulls other women's offerings out of their boxes, destroying some delicious cookies in the process; comments, "These are enough to poison the whole village" (39); sets out her own health food, "thick, hard-looking biscuits" (41); and calls, "Ladies, attention!" before she delivers a lecture on her own version of nutrition.

She reads Browning to the Ladies Sewing Circle, whose members do not want to hear him, preferring to exchange news, gossip, and opinions, and she continues to read while the supper spoils in the kitchen. In short, as the village women realize, Mrs. Jameson is determined to improve them, and there is no polite way of penetrating her armor of complacency and her complete belief in her own infallibility.

The stage is set at this point for what could be an ugly tale of anger, hatred, and all the supposed dark New England suppressed passions or the neurotic behavior some of Freeman's critics have expected from her characters. In fact, it does not take long for the villagers to find Mrs. Jameson absurd. In the beginning they tolerated her actions out of shock: "We were all quiet, peaceful people who dreaded altercation; it made our hearts beat too fast. Taking it all together, we felt very much as if some great, overgrown bird of another species had gotten into our village nest, and we were in the midst of an awful commotion of wings and beak. Still we agreed that Mrs. Jameson had probably meant well" (43–44).

Gradually, as she reveals herself, their attitude changes. When a farmer complains that her children have picked his squash and potato blossoms, everyone hears her grandly assure him that "if, when you come to dig your squashes, you find less than usual, and when you come to pick your potatoes the bushes are not in as good condition as they usually are, you may come to me and I will make it right with you" (46). Realizing that she is completely out of her depth in his world, the farmer is no longer angry and laughs, and the villagers discover that Mrs. Jameson's overbearing ways, her complacency, and her complete absence of sensitivity toward others do not have to change their lives. She becomes a source of fascination: she is the most interesting and amusing thing that has happened to the village in years. By the time she moves to a farm where she can plant her crops in August and make shoes of thick cloth for her hens to keep them from scratching, the townspeople wait delightedly to see whether this imposing woman will really get the better of nature.

She returns to the village for a second summer: " 'I consider that my own sphere has been considerably widened this winter,' said Mrs. Jameson, and Louisa and I regarded her with something like terror. Flora Clark said, when she heard that remark of Mrs. Jameson's, that she felt, for her part, as if a kicking horse had got out of the pasture, and there was no knowing where he would stop" (116). This summer Mrs. Jameson has determined to reform dress, advocating a bicycling costume for daily wear; a few other women follow her lead. The always-suitably-dressed narrator notes that "Mrs. Jameson was very stout, and the short skirt was not, to our way of thinking, becoming" (117); she and her sister-in-law imagine other women in the same dress: "Some of our good, motherly, village faces, with their expressions of homely dignity and Christian decorousness, looking at us from under that jaunty English walking-hat, in lieu of their sober bonnets, presented themselves to our imaginations, and filled us with amusement and consternation" (118–19).

More important, Mrs. Jameson plans to beautify the village. Jonas Martin, hired by Mrs. Jameson as her gardener, probably best represents the attitude all the villagers eventually share. He quickly learns not to reason with her but to let her go and enjoy the results. Instructed by Mrs. Jameson, who ignores the village wisdom that vines bring spiders and are bad for expensive paint, he digs up vines from the woods and plants them wherever she thinks they are needed: "The calm insolence of benevolence with which Mrs. Jameson did this was inimitable. People actually did not know whether to be furious or amused by this liberty taken with their property. . . . If they did expostulate, Mrs. Jameson only directed Jonas where to put the next vine, and assured the bewildered owner of the premises that he would in time thank her" (122–23). She extends her efforts beyond individual houses to the countryside:

> When, thinking that corn-cockles and ox-eyed daisies would be a charming combination at the sides of the country road, she caused them to be sowed, and thereby introduced them into Jonas Green's wheatfield, he expostulated in forcible terms, and threatened a suit for damages; and when she caused a small grove of promising young hemlocks to be removed from Eben Betts' woodland and set out on the sandy lot in which the schoolhouse stands, without leave or license, it was generally conceded that she had exceeded her privileges as a public benefactress. . . . Mr. H. Boardman Jameson had to pay a goodly sum to Eben Betts to hush the matter up; and the trees soon withered, and were cut up for firewood for the schoolhouse. (124–25)

Through all this, Jonas the gardener is enjoying everything. A man who had had a "steady, hard grind of existence," he now has "a quizzical cock to his right eyebrow, and a comically confidential quirk to his mouth, which were in themselves enough to provoke a laugh" (123). Mrs. Jameson has revitalized him. And Jonas represents the village in his way as the narrator does in hers.

For it is not so much Mrs. Jameson's activities that create the comedy as it is the village attitude. Though they watch warily, the villagers do not really feel threatened, and they have no intention of changing their lives, but they give Mrs. Jameson her head and watch with incredulity, steadily growing amusement, kindness, and tolerance this new source of interest and humor. Part of the fun is ironic: the difference between the way the village perceives her and the way she perceives herself in relation to them. That the villagers watch her with amusement and grow to anticipate her next performance never occurs to her, and she misinterprets the good manners with which she and her acts are received. In fact, her city sophistication is far surpassed by the village people in their politeness, their kindness, and their willingness to accept this "overgrown bird" who has taken up residence in their orderly nest. But in one way she is right; she has indeed "widened the sphere," although not in the way she planned or recognizes.

Individuals get angry, but generally their anger is overcome by laughter. And Mrs. Jameson's commanding self-image is undercut by her wisp of a husband; by her unpretentious and somewhat vulgar mother, who visits all over the village and talks incessantly and honestly; and by the affection the village people quickly learn to feel for her children. The only person who can neither tolerate nor forgive is Mrs. Liscom, her first landlady. The romance between the Jameson daughter and the Liscom son provides a subplot, since the watching villagers know that both mothers will be violently opposed to a marriage: Mrs. Jameson because she considers a country boy, no matter how handsome, good, and prosperous, as beneath her family, and Mrs. Liscom because Harriet Jameson has been so inadequately brought up that she cannot create a comfortable home for Mrs. Liscom's cherished son. Mrs. Jameson, guided by her interpretation of a Browning poem, gives in, but Mrs. Liscom remains adamant. By the time the situation is resolved, Mrs. Jameson has been, certainly not reformed, but accepted as she is, with all her foibles, into village life, thus providing the classic ending for comedy.

The Jamesons dismayed some critics and delighted others but was immediately popular with the public. According to Brent L. Kendrick,

> The first large edition published in May 1899 was exhausted by advance orders, and by June eight thousand copies had been printed. Most of the reviewers agreed with the public. They delighted in the humorous, tender, and shrewd sayings: "The note throughout is a joyous one, a welcome change from some of her recent books." They also praised the descriptive powers and vivid character portrayal; "Mrs. Jameson is not a caricature: such reformers exist on this side as well as on the other side of the Atlantic, and on the whole in real life they afford quite as much amusement and exasperation."[10]

That Freeman could write a novel that must be classified as comedy suggests critics should look for this quality in other places. Her letters, for example, reveal a gentle, straight-faced humor that is often ironic and frequently rests on the perception of absurdities. And the brisk, no-nonsense, attractive unmarried aunt who upset the other contributors to the multiauthored novel *The Whole Family,* and especially Howells, because she at age 40 is not the stereotypical "old maid," is the strongest and most amusing character in the novel.[11] Throughout Freeman's work, including those early stories described by Pattee and others as grim, there is often a core of humor—perhaps irony, perhaps the absurd, but humor nonetheless. Characters are placed, or, rather, have placed themselves, in situations that are, quite simply, funny. Or, to put it another way, the opposing forces ("wills") have created a conflict that is both trivial and vital. The result is neither simple nor single.

The core situations, or the conflicts, of most of Freeman's short stories and a few of her novels depend on this mixture of comedy with grimness, perversity, or near tragedy.[12] In "A Conflict Ended" Marcus Woodman sits on the church steps every Sunday morning because 10 years earlier he objected to a ministerial candidate and swore he would never step inside the meetinghouse if the man were called to the pastorate. His grudge against the minister has long since faded, but he has made his vow; he suffers silently as his amused neighbors go into church. His face shows the inner self; he has "a mild forehead, a gently curving mouth, and a terrible chin, with a look of strength in it that might have abashed mountains" (338). Esther, the woman he was to marry, describes the problem to her apprentice and admits the situation is ridiculous: "That makes it the hardest of anything, according to my mind—when you know that everybody's laughing, and you could hardly help laughing yourself, though you feel 'most ready to die" (341). When, strengthened by Esther's decision to marry him—and, if necessary, share the steps—he at last enters the church, the watching neighbors do not laugh: "They had felt the pathos in the comedy" (348).

The two old women in "A Mistaken Charity" who are taken from their subsistence living and put into a comparatively luxurious home by the kindness of their neighbors are anything but grateful: "nothing could transform these two unpolished old women into two nice old ladies" (308). They are both angry and unhappy, for in spite of their infirmities they had controlled their limited world, where "all that they cared for they had in tolerable abundance" (303). With daring that intoxicates them, they escape from the home and "as jubilant as two children" (309) come back to their beloved status of poverty with autonomy.

Sarah Dunn, the protagonist of "The Lombardy Poplar," lived most of her life as a twin until her sister died. A cousin who has the same name, looks like Sarah, and has inherited the dead sister's clothes is now her closest relative and companion: "Name, appearance, dress, all were identical" (451). Near Sarah's house is a single Lombardy poplar, strikingly different from nearby trees. Sarah's admiration for the tree leads to a disagreement with her cousin, who calls it an "eyesore":

Then [Sarah] gazed at the tree again and her whole face changed indescribably. She seemed like another person. The tree seemed to cast a shadow of likeness over her. She appeared straighter, taller; all her lines of meek yielding, or scarcely even anything so strong as yielding, of utter passiveness, vanished. She looked stiff and uncompromising. Her mouth was firm, her chin high, her eyes steady, and more than all, there was over her an expression of individuality which had not been there before. "That's why I like the popple," said she, in an incisive voice. "That's just why. I'm sick of things and folks that are just like everything and everybody else. I'm sick of trees that are just trees. I like one that ain't." (455)

The disagreement becomes a quarrel, but Sarah Dunn does not care. The separation from the voice that criticized her "small assertion of her own individuality" (458) and the kinship but difference she sees between her own Lombardy and a nearby silver poplar are steps to self-realization. She does something; the next Sunday,

> a shimmer of red silk and a toss of pink flowers were seen at the Dunn gate, and Sarah Dunn, clad in a gown of dark-red silk and a bonnet tufted with pink roses, holding aloft a red parasol, passed down the street to meeting. No Dunn had ever worn, within the memory of man, any colors save purple and black and faded green or drab, never any but purple or green or black flowers in her bonnet. . . . Even the old minister hesitated a second in his discourse, and recovered himself with a hem of embarrassment when Sarah entered the meeting-house. (460)

Absurd though she may look to the congregation and to the reader, Sarah is totally confident. As she walks out of meeting with her amazed and black-clad cousin, "[t]here seemed no likeness whatever between the two women. . . . Sarah was a Dunn apart" (461). Her cousin accepts a cheerful invitation to dinner, and Sarah goes home in deep satisfaction, with a friendly nod to the poplar tree as she enters her house.

"The Givers," one of Freeman's lesser-known stories but one of her most characteristic, further illustrates her ability to balance humor with other elements.[13] Aunt Sophia and her niece, Flora, are preparing for the young girl's wedding. They are financially secure, with their own house and enough to live on, but by no means rich; Herbert, the young man Flora loves, is hardworking and ambitious, but he must support his widowed mother, whose illness caused them to lose their farm. In spite of obstacles, the young couple decides, with Aunt Sophia's help, to marry anyway. As the story opens, cousins arrive with wedding gifts: a silver afternoon teakettle, cut-glass finger bowls, and embroidered doilies on which the bowls can sit—all expensive gifts, and all useless. Flora manages to sound grateful, but her aunt is tight-lipped. When the girl leaves, Aunt Sophia, questioned by her cousin, tells what she has done about gifts and givers.

She begins her narrative with the preceding Christmas, when kind relatives had sent Flora a "sort of a dewdab to wear in her hair! Pretty enough, looked as if it cost considerable—a pink rose with spangles, and a feather shootin' out of it; but Lord! if Flora had come out in that thing anywhere she'd go in Brookville she'd scared the natives" (25). Other pres-

ents were an embroidered silk shawl and, the target of Aunt Sophia's incredulous scorn, red and white carved ivory chessmen and a table chessboard. Her
demand to know "what's them little dolls and horses for?" is followed by a
swift interchange:

> " 'Chess?' says I.
> " 'A game,' says Flora.
> " 'A game?' says I.
> " 'To play,' says Flora.
> " 'Do you know how to play it, Flora?' says I.
> " 'No,' says she.
> " 'Does Herbert?'
> " 'No.'
> " 'Well,' says I, and I spoke right out, 'of all the things to give anybody
> that needs things!' (26–27)

To make matters worse, the price tag is still on the chess set, and Sophia
discovers in utter disbelief that it cost forty dollars. Furthermore, she learns
from Herbert that his rich Uncle Hiram sent him a silver ashtray and, for
another Christmas, a silver cigarette case; his mother received a silver card
case and a cut-glass wine set. Herbert does not smoke, and his mother has
neither calling cards nor wine.

Telling no one, Sophia bundles the gifts and herself into a neighbor's
sleigh and sets off to return them, keeping only what she defines as "presents,
because the folks that give 'em had studied up what Flora wanted, and give
to her instead of themselves" (34). She flatly tells each giver why she is
returning the gifts. Most of them see her logic and eventually replace the
extravagant and showy presents with useful articles. Her final call is to rich
Uncle Hiram, who laughs at her but also sees her point and instead of silver
cigarette cases gives his nephew enough money to buy land and start a small
business.

Originally published in *Harper's* as "The Revolt of Sophia Lane," the
story has an obvious affinity with Freeman's famous "The Revolt of
'Mother' " and with the lesser-known "Gentian."[14] Here and in other stories
the protagonists violate the codes of their world, motivated by love for
someone else, by personal need, or by conviction; because the world, the
codes, and the people are not in themselves of conventional heroic stature,
readers often miss the back-to-the-wall courage in the action, just as they
miss the comedy.

Freeman's humor is Yankee: subtle, straight-faced, tongue-in-cheek,
dry. Her comedy is certainly not hilarity, farce, wit, or any of the other
obvious subdefinitions, nor is it the formal structure of comedy. Though it
does expose human folly, the exposure is not for purposes of satire; satirists
need a commitment, and Freeman remains detached. Rather, it is a wry

comic perception of humanity, an ungenial Chaucerian vision of human beings in all their many-sided reality: tragic, funny, irritating, silly, generous, loving, hating, pitiful, strong, weak, but always unpredictable. It says "Lord, what fools these mortals be" in amused compassion, not contempt. Perhaps this long-ignored ability to present many-sided human beings and to bring about a resolution that is not particularly tidy contributes to what Elizabeth Meese calls "undecidability," so that the reader is left with a complex response that the author has caused to happen.[15]

Most definitions of comedy agree that its appeal is to the intellect, and that perception of incongruity, the forced joining of things that do not belong together, is the trigger that creates the shock of the unexpected. Above all, the comic writer is detached, keeping an emotional distance between herself and her characters. In Freeman's work there is the obvious incongruity between individual behavior and the conventions of the protagonist's society; there is the more subtle discordance within the mind of the character who is so often hoist with his own petard; there is the smallness of the scale contrasted with the internal importance of the protagonist's act. Many Freeman characters balance on a thin line of their own rationality, ready at any moment to fall to either side.

These stories present a meeting point of responses—a sharp edge from which the characters could drop into tragedy or comedy, or, better, into a kaleidoscope of reactions as they are saved from silliness by their integrity. The absurdities are complicated by the fact that it takes courage for the protagonist to assume and maintain an incongruous position. Marcus Woodman trapped by his will is tragic, but Marcus Woodman sitting outside the church every Sunday morning is the stuff of comedy. If Marcus Woodman is silly, he is also courageous in maintaining his position as his friends enter the church Sunday after Sunday, with amused glances in his direction; he is even braver when he breaks his vow after all those years and walks into church with his wife. If Sarah Dunn's defining herself by a tree and presenting herself in garishly unsuitable clothing is laughable, both the joy the act gives her and the need of a human being to claim her own identity are not.

Aunt Sophia's outspoken direction of gift-givers is delightful, and so are the startled responses of her neighbors, who have followed a convention without thinking about it. But while Aunt Sophia may be unconsciously humorous when she speaks out to her neighbors, the courage it takes to break through her social codes almost breaks her. At the end of "The Givers," the guests rewrap their gifts, asking questions about what Flora needs as they depart:

> Sophia untied the horse, which had been fastened to a ring beside the door; still the guests did not move to get into the sleigh. A curious air of constraint was over them. Sophia also looked constrained and troubled. Her poor faithful face peering from the folds of her gray wool hood was defiant and firm, but

still anxious. She looked at Mrs. Cutting, and the two women's eyes met; there was a certain wistfulness in Sophia's.

"I think a good deal of Flora," said she, and there was a hint of apology in her tone. (49)

Her guests understand—or her world understands. Sophia has taken a risk, challenging the codes and endangering her relationships with the people with whom she must live, but her mixture of common sense, honesty, courage, and love succeeds.

Not every Freeman story works this way, and not every story has the same kind of humor; Freeman ranges widely within her little worlds—one could almost say she has traveled much in Concord. If there is humor, for example, in "Old Woman Magoun," whose protagonist allows her dearly loved grand-daughter to die rather than be degraded, it is very dark humor indeed. Generally her tales have to do with characters who live in a small, organized world with its own rules and who, driven by legitimate (at least to them) motives, oppose or challenge the codes. The local-color label, with its implication of truth limited by geography, has hidden the fact that not only small New England villages have codes and conventions: all groups do.[16] All individuals within groups must determine how they will deal with the codes; Susan Allen Toth points to "the constant mutual adjustment necessary between individual and community."[17] To those outside, the problem, lacking immediacy and direct connection, may seem small. The conflicts for Freeman's people are both trivial and vital; the world is small, but the emotion is not.

Like *The Jamesons*, Freeman's short stories create a variety of awarenesses. Mrs. Jameson is silly, overbearing, and obnoxious, but there are things in her to admire. When she organizes the village centennial, the villagers are exasperated, amused, aware of her mistakes, but, in the end, proud. The flawed, human result of her work is something they would not have had without her. With both intellect and emotions involved, sensitive readers do not go away from this story with a single response. The story will not let them.

Despite neglect, Freeman's work has never been entirely lost, and her reputation and appeal continue to grow. She is too vital to remain in the neat category in which earlier critics placed her, and her vitality comes from her wide, detached perception of humanity in all its colors. From portrayals of self-realization or of individuals dealing with their world's codes to wry humor to sensitive perceptions of human relationships to nature (as in *Six Trees* and *Understudies*), Freeman offers a variety of readings—the mark of a fine artist.

Notes

1. In "Puritanism in American Fiction" (in *Literature and Life* [New York: Harper's, 1902], 279), William Dean Howells mentions the difficulty outsiders have in seeing Free-

man's (and New England's) humor. His young visitor to the area "had been too little sensible of the humor which forms the relief of these stories, as it forms the relief of these bare, duteous, conscientious, deeply individualized lives portrayed in them." Nearly all the contemporary critics included humor as an element of Freeman's work.

2. Fred Lewis Pattee, introduction to the 1920 edition of *A New England Nun, and Other Stories* (New York: Harper's, 1920), vii; "On the Terminal Moraine of New England Puritanism," in *Side-Lights on American Literature* (New York: Century, 1922), 175–209. Early in his career Pattee praised Freeman for her contributions to the short story form; his later criticism seems to condemn her content. Since Pattee had much influence on the shaping of the American literature canon, his attitude toward Freeman may be a factor in her virtual disappearance from the literary scene.

3. Perry D. Westbrook, *Mary Wilkins Freeman* (New York: Twayne, 1967), 116–17.

4. *The Jamesons* (New York: Doubleday and McClure, 1899; Philadelphia: Curtis, 1899). Originally serialized in the *Ladies' Home Journal,* this was one of the few Freeman novels not published by Harper's.

5. Sandra Zagarell, "Narrative of Community: The Identification of a Genre," *Signs* 13 (Spring 1988): 498–527.

6. Letter to Joseph Knight (28 December 1891), in *The Infant Sphinx: Collected Letters of Mary E. Wilkins Freeman,* Ed. Brent L. Kendrick (Metuchen, N.J.: Scarecrow Press, 1985), 133; Elizabeth Gaskell, *Cranford* (London: Oxford University Press, 1965). *Cranford* was originally published as a serial in *Household Words,* 1851–53, and in book form in 1853. All citations are to the Oxford edition.

7. Sarah Orne Jewett, *Country of the Pointed Firs* (Boston: Houghton Mifflin, 1896).

8. Mary Russell Mitford, *Our Village* (London: G. and W. B. Whittaker, 1824–32). At least six different editions of her work were published in the United States between 1830 and 1898.

9. Mitford goes on, "Nothing is so tiresome as to be whirled half over Europe at the chariot wheels of a hero, to go to sleep at Vienna, and awaken at Madrid; it produces a real fatigue, a weariness of spirit." Critics compared Jewett with Gaskell and Mitford, and Freeman with Gaskell and Jewett, although the latter comparison was usually based on their "local color writers" status. Freeman insisted she did not read any writers who might influence her.

10. *The Infant Sphinx,* 200–201. Kendrick quotes reviews from *Literary News* 20 (June 1899): 168 and *Spectator* 83 (14 October 1899): 536.

11. See the introduction by Alfred Bendixen to *The Whole Family* (New York: Ungar, 1986), xi–li, and see "*The Whole Family* and Its Troubles," *New York Times,* 24 October 1908, 590.

12. Unless otherwise noted, the stories discussed here are collected in *Short Fiction of Sarah Orne Jewett and Mary Wilkins Freeman,* ed. Barbara H. Solomon (New York: New American Library, 1979). All citations are to this text.

13. In *The Givers* (New York: Harper's, 1904), 3–50. All citations are to this text.

14. "The Revolt of Sophia Lane," *Harper's Monthly* 108 (December 1903): 20–34.

15. Elizabeth Meese, *Crossing the Double-Cross: The Practice of Feminist Criticism* (Chapel Hill: University of North Carolina Press, 1986), chap. 2, "Signs of Undecidability," 19–38.

16. There is a useful analogy here: folklorists define "group" as more than one person with at least one thing in common; as soon as a group exists, it begins to generate its own folklore, which, in the broadest sense, includes or generates mores and customs.

17. Susan Allen Toth, "Defiant Light: A Positive View of Mary Wilkins Freeman," *New England Quarterly* 46 (March 1973): 83.

Index

♦